The Great
Saharan
Mouse-Hunt

When a gang of likeable eccentrics somehow happen to get talking about the Sahara Desert very astonishing activities can follow. This enchanting and amusing book records them and explains why fourteen apparently sane sophisticates embark upon ruining their cars in soft sand; get themselves fly-bitten and filthy, stunk out by camels, lost, cross, thirsty and happy.

Leader of the 'expedition' is Liv Pomeroy, a member of the U.S. Information Service in Benghazi, with his English wife Miggs, his American sister Catherine and her husband Alan Collins, who is a literary agent before whom his publisher genuflects. And then, of course, although it is difficult to know quite why, there is Randolph Churchill, who dominates the book and the scene until his pâté de foie runs out. He is accompanied by his son Winston, who nobly stays the rigours of the course. There is, too, Dr. Hank Setzer, in search of mammals for Washington, and six unlikely British soldiers, commanded by their Scots lieutenant, all in search of desert experience. This they achieve.

The pampered Americans learn to eat hard-tack and beans for breakfast and the soldiers are exposed to pancakes with maple syrup and Randolph gets his pâté. While Lieutenant Gibb solemnly navigates for the erratic convoy, Hank disappears into space in search of mice, Catherine paints her toe-nails and Winston dismantles his truck. But everywhere this assorted caravan went, from the Tibesti ranges to the oases of the plains, they were welcomed with hospitality and amazement both by the French officers at the posts and the Arabs of the open spaces. And they want, one day, to go back.

The Great Saharan Mouse-Hunt is the dottily happy account of a dotty adventure by a lot of dotty people, and already a few sensible people think we are dotty to publish it. We differ, and are more than confident that a great many readers will appreciate the reason why.

MIGGS POMEROY
& CATHERINE COLLINS
(*or vice-versa*)

The Great
Saharan
Mouse-Hunt

HUTCHINSON OF LONDON

HUTCHINSON & CO. (*Publishers*) LTD
178–202 Great Portland Street, London, W.1

London Melbourne Sydney
Auckland Bombay Toronto
Johannesburg New York

First published 1962

*This book has been set in Bembo type face. It has
been printed in Great Britain by The Anchor Press,
Ltd., in Tiptree, Essex, on Antique Wove paper.*

To our husbands
without whose unfailing
impatience and churlish behaviour
this book would never have been written

Camera work

On 13th March 1961 a group of six cars started from the North African coastal city of Benghazi for a trip across the Sahara Desert to one of the most inaccessible mountain ranges in the world—the Tibesti.

The party consisted of fourteen people. Liv Pomeroy, with the U.S. Information Service in Benghazi, was the leader of the expedition; he took his wife. Alan and Catherine Collins, his brother-in-law and sister, came from New York to go on the trip, and Randolph Churchill and his son Winston from England. Dr. Henry Setzer was collecting mammals for the National Museum in Washington. The British Army stationed in Benghazi sent six soldiers under the command of Lieutenant Francis Gibb of the Royal Scots Regiment. Three of the cars belonged to the Army, three were privately owned by the civilians.

WE ARE DUE to leave for a six- to eight-week trek into the Sahara tomorrow and everyone suspects everyone else of being disorganized. The Collinses' trunks, shipped out of New York a month ago, arrived only yesterday, having met up with a change of Italian shipping schedules which delayed their being trans-shipped from Naples, a storm in the harbour which delayed their being off-loaded at Benghazi, and Ramadan (the ninth month of the Mohammedan year, a month of fast by day and feast by night) which delayed their clearing Customs. Catherine is not desertworthy without her trunks. She has only a couple of cocktail dresses and a little sports number with her. Hank Setzer's things are packed with the Collinses' and he and Catherine spent yesterday sorting and repacking. Aside from twenty pairs of socks, Hank has brought scientific equipment, such as mouse-traps, scalpels, ammunition and cotton batting. A bottle of formaldehyde has broken, and Catherine, sniffing worriedly at her underwear, prefers Arpege. In the meantime Liv has been called to Tripoli by the deities who run headquarters there. I have seized this opportunity to give him a last-minute shopping list four pages long. The Army's yellow-fever shots have not arrived nor their permits to enter Chad. Only the Churchills are in order.

This morning I go to help the Churchills with their list of supplies, in case they have forgotten something or need help with their shopping. At 9.30 a.m. Randolph is in a shirt without trousers or shoes. He shows me his neat packages of clothes and equipment, and insists that Winston put out a camp-bed so that I can be zipped up in one of their new mummy-style sleeping-bags. He is proud of his cooler—his Magical Box, as he calls it—which he says will be kept perpetually full of ice to chill his pâté de foie gras. Ice in mid-Sahara is a novel idea, but Randolph, if anyone can, surely will manage it. Over breakfast, which Winston ate but Randolph drank, we discuss supplies and Winston decides that all he needs is deodorant. Father explodes that he's been seeing too much television, but Winston and I go shopping and buy two jars. We also buy ten kilos of charcoal for camp-fires.

'We shall,' Randolph says, 'sit around a jolly camp-fire and talk.' As he is a great conversationalist, we shall more likely sit around a camp-fire and listen. The first contretemps has reared its ugly head. Randolph insists that the 'other ranks' will have their own little cook-fire elsewhere. When Catherine and I protest at both the unfriendliness and inefficiency of this system Randolph's voice rises two full octaves of irritated authority.

'Don't you women go mucking up the British Army,' he cries. 'We've got a jolly good army and we don't want any American women interfering with it.'

The tense moment passes as Randolph cajoles us. 'The soldiers won't understand our jokes, you know, and we shan't enjoy their language. Let them have their own camp-fire. Every now and then we'll send them jolly little presents and converse.'

Suspicions are solidified. Everyone knows that everyone else is disorganized. At our house there is a marshalling of children and pets to be left with various kind friends. Catherine is sorting the four pages of shopping which Liv did in Tripoli, My arm, broken a month ago while watching a polo game, is still in a cast. It was broken out-guessing a rearing horse, but everyone thinks it was gamesmanship. X-rays are not satisfactory and I will have to wear the cast for another two weeks. A pest! There is so much to be done and I am getting very lopsided. The halls are stacked with packing-cases; the children, multiplied by hordes of friends, run in and out pilfering casually from cases of chocolate or biscuits and scattering anything left in their path. The men are busy checking the cars, spare parts, sand-tracks and jerry-cans. Threading their way through the halls at meal-times, they complain loudly that there is no room in the cars for all of the stuff we are bringing. Catherine reluctantly eliminates a case of fruit juice and one of minute rice. Everyone is to regret this bit of austerity. Winston is tinkering with the Churchill Land Rover, installing a radio.

'The boy can take one of these cars apart,' his father says proudly. He ambles between cases occasionally picking up something he feels he might need. 'Just get yourself another,' he says grandly, and then, putting his arm about one of us, he coaxes, 'Come into a quieter room, dear child, and let us have a little conversation,' or, 'I must read you the jolliest little poem by Hillaire Belloc, marvellous chap.' He reads from *The Modern Traveller*. Amusing, and we think a delightful parallel to our trip. He reads beautifully. Altogether a gifted man who should have been spanked more frequently in childhood.

We cannot possibly get off tomorrow and have set Monday the thirteenth. Randolph is wild. 'We limeys,' he thunders, 'are steady on parade; but you bloody Americans . . .' He says (a) he is going back to England to watch his tulips grow, and (b) he is starting out ahead of us. His affairs are in order. His Land Rover is tickety-boo! He roars off, singing loudly, 'When the roll is called up yonder I'll be there!'

| 12TH MARCH | RANDOLPH AND WINSTON did in fact take off at dawn for Agedabia, where they have promised to wait for us. Agedabia is the jumping-off place for the desert. We'll see our last petrol-pump and our last road there. The packing-up is going forward and the extra day has given us time for detail. Alan has acquired viper and scorpion serum from the Pasteur Institute in Paris. This is supposed to be kept on ice, which despite Randolph's 'Magical Box' we are not so naive as to think possible. None of our French is up to differentiating between vipers, which we all feel would be better given international names. Something to take up with the U.N. We've heard some shocking snake-bite stories, and Catherine, who is not a nature-lover, is getting nervy. She says she doesn't mind dying of snake-bite so much as she does meeting with the snake. Everyone agrees that snakes and scorpions are nocturnal creatures who quarter the desert at night in search of diet. Also when cold they like to cuddle up in the toe of a shoe or sneak into a sleeping-bag. At one of the many farewell parties Tony Hamilton Browne, Mobil Oil of Canada representative in Benghazi and with the Long Range Desert Group during the war, tells of returning to his sleeping-bag after a late-night reconnaissance to be bitten in the rump by a viper.

The L.R.D.G. had a medical man along and within one minute the viper was dead, the poison extracted and the proper serum injected. Catherine has made up her mind not to get up in the night. There are various types of vipers in the Libyan Sahara, and viper and cobra in the Tibesti Mountains. The viper's poison attacks the nervous system and the victim has exactly one minute in which to get the proper anti-toxin. Liv has taken our serum along to the Seventh Day Adventist Hospital for sorting and instructions with very confusing results. He is told that American hospitals in the area have been advised to destroy all serum on hand as more people have died of toxic reaction to snake serum than have died of untreated snake-bite. There are many varieties of snakes and vipers, and if the victim has not recognized the species by which he has been bitten it is unlikely the doctor will be able to diagnose. A snake streaks at you, and if you are Catherine or me you screech and pass out. By the time you have been revived all you can say is that it was ten feet long, had green and orange spots and looked like Khrushchev. You are immediately treated for a horned-viper bite and as the snake was really a garter snake you die from the serum. As to scorpions, we are advised that few people die of scorpion-bite and that the serum is more dangerous than the bite. So some doctors now recommend waiting to see if the patient survives without the serum. A tricky bit of curiosity, we think. At a later date the French in Chad told us that the bite of a horned viper will kill you if the serum is not administered immediately in small doses every few minutes in a ring around the bite. However, Liv has brought home a batch of hypo needles and some extra-powerful vitamins for Randolph. His way of not eating his meals is worrying and we don't want him breaking out with scurvy, or whatever people get when they don't eat (aside from good figures). Mahmud Abeidi, Liv's Libyan assistant at the information centre, has taken Alan to call on His Excellency Hussein Masek, Governor of Cyrenaica. It seems unlikely that this expedition will ever get off without Mahmud. He has met planes, shepherded arrivals with all of their weird paraphernalia through Customs, manœuvred special permits where they are needed and dragged his friends back from their Ramadan holidays to open banks and offices for us. What is more, he will hold down Liv's office while we are gone, seeing to it that America's friends do not backslide into being someone else's friends. Today the Governor gave Alan a beautiful document to all his local authorities, the Mudirs and Mutaserif, asking that they help us and make us welcome to their diocese. Personally I think that anyone who can write Arabic is by nature an artist. With schools in every town and most oases, a vast population of artists is on its way. Literally translated for us, this lovely flowing script reads:

NAZARAT OF INTERIOR

The Nazir's Office
March 11th, 1961

To whom it may concern
Departing this week, group of Mr. and Mrs. Alan C. Collins from the United States of America, Dr. Henry W. Setzer of the National Museum, Smithsonian Institute, Mr. R. S. Churchill and his son Winston. R. Churchill is the son of ex-Britain Prime Minister and the well-known journalist. Mr. and Mrs. Robert L. Pomeroy the Director of the American Cultural Centre in Benghazi, Lt. Francis Gibb and six others from the British Army.

The group with their six cars are leaving this week for touring through Gialo and Cofra from there to Chad. The purpose of the trip is visiting, studying and adventure.

It is requested from the departments concerned that to give all the assistance needed by the above mentioned and also any facilities which they may require during their trip to the Sahara.

(Signed) Mahmoud Abu Shraida,
Nazir of Interior.
(The Nazara Stamp)

13TH MARCH

SOMEHOW WE GET packed up and loaded. The take-off looks more like a gymkhana than a well-mannered expedition. The daisies in front of our house are trampled for ever into the dust by milling friends and well-wishers, children careering about on bikes, bouncing on pogo-sticks and skipping-ropes, curious Arabs, dogs and goats. Yorick, our pointer, has to be forcibly

15

ejected from one car. Piglet the dachshund looks desolate. Julia, our seven-year-old, clings to me and sobs, though she is considerably cheered with a goodbye present. Eugene, who is ten, unable to resist the audience, stunts by on his bike. Colonel O'Lone, commanding officer of the British garrison in Benghazi, who is sending a small detachment with us, can only, we think, look with pleasure on his three vehicles, every jerry-can and case of food and every soldier neatly in place. It must be a relief to him that the rest of us, rushing from house to car with last-minute remembered bundles, hugging children and restraining dogs, are not part of his garrison. In the end Liv forgets to say goodbye to the children. Late at night, by the headlights of the car, he writes to them, a letter still being mailable from Agedabia.

The hard-surface coastal road streaks like an arrow from Benghazi to Agedabia. We scarcely know what we will find at the rendezvous with the Churchills. And if we had guessed at either place or condition we would have been wrong. Ahead of us, first a dot on the horizon and then looming as a road block, is a Land Rover mounted with a great six-foot flag; white, emblazoned with a blue U.N. In the middle of the road, at a formica-topped card-table, sits Randolph with refreshments laid out. Winston stands beside him with a gun at the alert. They both wear white tin helmets on which have been painted blue bands and large U.N.s.

'Stopping all cars,' Randolph shouts as the five of us brake up. 'I've been sent up from the Congo to investigate. The U.N. is worried about conditions in North Africa. Come, come, identify yourselves.'

Assisting the Churchills in their manœuvre are two amiable Dutchmen whom they had found at a near-by oil rig and impressed into amusing—Randolph—duty. Everyone is pleasantly intoxicated and we are all in a mood to join them. A party of Libyans, travelling their humdrum way from Tripoli to Benghazi, ogle as they squeeze by, their expressions setting us all into a gale of laughter. At six o'clock Colonel O'Lone sends us a good-luck message over our radio. We reply, 'Thanks, we need it.' We do.

Everyone who heard of our expedition wanted to know where we were going and why. The first question was a matter of maps, not always accurate, and routes, sometimes never before travelled. The why had as many answers as there were members of the expedition. Liv wrote in one of those many letters which batted back and forth between Libya, England and the United States during the two years of planning and preparing for the trip:

In this day of great scientific achievement every considered action that man undertakes ought to have a purpose. This expedition will have none at all. We travel for adventure, for pleasure and to satisfy our insatiable curiosity about a little-known part of the world. Neither profit, science, politics nor serious work of any sort will be remotely considered. There is nothing to be gained and every chance that we shall all be lost. The Royal Scots will be allowed the illusion that they are testing a new type of vehicle—the long-wheelbase Land Rover—the operational characteristics of which are already well known to everyone else in the country. The Libyan members of the party will be allowed to examine their far-flung frontiers and mark them with neat white lines extending them in any direction they see fit. (Buseiri Shelhi, Chamberlain of the Household of H.M. King Idris, and Raoulf ben Amer, a doctor, were unfortunately unable at the last minute to come.) Scientific specimens may be taken provided they are properly prepared and eaten on the spot.

Altogether fourteen of us started out from Benghazi. Colonel O'Lone, commanding the British Army garrison in Benghazi, detached a young officer of the Royal Scots Regiment and six men, whom he placed under the direct command of my husband, Livingston Pomeroy. Liv's experience with the O.S.S. during the war promised that he would be able to get us out of any undue predicament he happened to get us into. Colonel O'Lone's reasons for sending these men were to test out the Land Rovers of which Liv wrote, and to give the men desert experience. Our officer, Second Lieutenant Francis Gibb, is from Perthshire. He is twenty-one, six foot, a broad-shouldered Scot, a keen but carefree soldier. He will navigate the expedition. Four of his men are fellow Scots with accents that mystify the rest of us. None of them is over twenty-three. Frank White from Midlothian is short, chunky and tough. He once said he was a weight-lifter before joining up, but never seems to be around when there are heavy boxes to lift. Frank is sandy and jovial.

He is also a shocking tease and you can't tell when to take him seriously. He and Archie Aitken are assistant and sometimes chief cooks, according to whether the meals are 'compo' (British Army ration) or those unpopular little gourmet meals which Catherine and I concoct. Archie is from Edinburgh, with a lean Spanish look to him. Catherine and I think him rather gallant. Whoever is cooking, he and Frank between them brew the best steaming black tea the world has ever known. They make it in a wholesale biscuit tin and life would be bleak indeed without it. Charlie Pollock is our first-aid man, at least the Army gave him a two-week course in first aid and supplied him with a formidable box of medicines. Charlie is from Lanarkshire; fair and neatly built, he has a boyish look and wants to teach when his army service is up. He has a literary turn of mind and, as we discovered, speaks French. John Ferguson is dark but gentle looking, in contrast to the only other dark Scot, Archie, who looks more the dagger-totin' kind. John would always be kind. He is from Ayrshire, a cabinet-maker whose gifted hands help Taffy with the machinery or Hank Setzer with his 'Wee Beasties'. Craftsman Taffy Jones, sometimes called Crafty, is from Denbighshire in Wales, a superb mechanic and fitter. Most of the men grew beards and Taffy's was the curly saintly sort. I thought he looked like a man of God, but Catherine said not to be too sure. His accent was even more difficult than the Scots to understand, so we were never to know whether he was godly or otherwise. Jack Thompson, the radio operator, is a Yorkshireman. He is tall and thin and sad looking, and can coax voices out of the ether under the most forbidding circumstances. With ear-phones glued to his head, his hair perpendicular in the wind, he can, and does, like that other but chubbier Yorkshireman, Sam Small, soar away, leaving the rest of us earthbound. As the military group were detailed to take part in the expedition, they couldn't be said to have personal reasons for going, but not one of them, I think, would have given up the chance for as many days' leave.

Randolph Churchill was one of the charter members of our expedition, for he had asked to be counted in a good year before we got down to serious preparations. There is a saying that he who drinks from the Nile must always return to Egypt, so perhaps whoever gets an eyeful of Sahara sand is also for ever drawn back to the desert. Randolph had his first taste of the Libyan sands during the war when he took part in one of the most ambitious and daring British raids behind the Axis lines. The time was 1942, the goal to mine ships anchored in Benghazi harbour. The raid was carried out by the famous Long Range Desert Group which had proved its worth in many seemingly impossible runs across hundreds of miles of trackless desert to strike the Axis far behind its lines. The operation was a well-planned and smoothly carried-out fiasco. The British got their truck past the German and Italian road blocks and into the city of Benghazi, where Randolph had charge of camouflaging and guarding it while the sappers made their way into the port area with rubber boats and demolitions. But the long bumpy ride across the desert had proved too much for their boats, which were so damaged by chafing in the back of the truck that they could no longer be inflated.

Now the old war-horse has come back to the desert, perhaps to see whether he can still stand up to it, perhaps for sentimental reasons, or to show it to his son Winston; but more than anything, I think, he has come back to taste the tranquillity and quiet strength of this, his 'vast desaart'. Randolph is a big man with a round head and brooding eyes. For a man who says that he likes things straight and simple, he seems to have made a very interesting job of his own personality. He says that he prefers his flower garden in Suffolk to any of these outlandish places, and yet the mere mention of a distant horizon is enough to set him packing his bags. Like some allegorical beast, he combines the dragon and the teddy bear; unable to turn his back on a challenge, he is as brave and heedless as the first when confronted, or sweet as the second when he thinks that no one is looking. Winston, who is twenty, is the youthful figure of a one-day sizable man. He has that pink-and-white British complexion, with big eyebrows which give him an authoritative air.

Alan and Catherine have nothing but curiosity to excuse their presence on this expedition, except perhaps that Alan has some claim to having dreamed it up in the beginning. In the winter of 1954, the Collinses took a trip by car across North Africa from Tangier to Cairo. Of all the countries which they visited Libya was the most primitive. The roads still showed signs of tanks and bombs, and the hotel beds were no smoother, but the country fascinated them. They had good precedent for this. The Phoenicians, the Greeks and the Romans colonized much of North Africa, but they built their most beautiful cities in Libya, and of Libya they told their tallest tales. Where else were the Gardens of the Hesperides? 'The silent, dull forgetful' waters of the River Lethe? Here Herakles and Ulysses adventured, and Perseus scattered Gorgon's blood to make the desert flower with vipers. So, charmed by Libya, and haunted by their one slight brush with the desert, the Collinses came back to visit after Liv and I were posted here. Together we talked and concocted, and later from a distance we have written and cajoled one another into forming this expedition.

Alan is a New York literary agent—one of that strange breed as unknown to the reading public as they are well known to writers and publishers. He is tall, balding, with an aquiline nose and a quick and ready smile. The fact is that his sense of humour really dominates his sound business judgment. If it didn't he would never have headed for any oasis more distant than the Plaza bar, or Sardi's. The difference between him and Catherine is that Alan knows why we are going into the desert—for pleasure, curiosity and relaxation; mental if not physical. Catherine's reasons are more of a practical nature. She secretly hopes that we may find the fabulous lost oasis of Zurzura—that apocryphal paradise which is only revealed to desert travellers in the last stages of thirst and madness—or a new source of the Nile; or the valley of diamonds which Sinbad visited aboard his pet roc. Obviously Catherine is practical from the word go.

Despite Liv's plea that the expedition should have no purpose, Alan invited the Smithsonian to send a man along if they felt that it would be of interest. And so Dr. Henry Setzer, Associate Curator of African Mammals for the National Museum, joined our party. Hank had been in Libya six years earlier, making a collection of small mammals from the Fezzan and some coastal areas of Tripolitania and Cyrenaica. He had never been to the southern oases of Cyrenaica, and, as far as he knew, no American museums had any collection from the Tibesti. Of the five Americans on the trip Hank is perhaps the most American looking of us all. This is no doubt due to the fact that his hair is crew-cut and that he wears trousers instead of shorts. Though Hank wears glasses, he can with the naked eye identify an ant's tracks at fifty paces. He is the only one of us who has had any real desert experience.

As to ourselves, we had a dozen reasons for involving our-selves in this expedition. After four years in Libya, living on the edge of the desert, we have made only a few brief trips into its fringe. We are due to be re-posted, and before we go we are keen to see what this Sahara really is. City Libyans think we are mad. On their vacations they go to Paris. And then Liv has discovered that there are these Tibesti Mountains in the south of the Sahara. They cover an area as large as England, with mountains the size of the Alps. They must be very barren, for the entire population numbers less than a medium-sized American town. He thinks he would like to set up a kingdom down there if nobody objects, and he has told Alan that he can be Prime Minister; he feels he is in a strong position to do this with a ready-made army of British troops under his command. The Tibesti Mountains, to-gether with the Hoggar and Tassili to the west and the Ennedi to the south-east, are thought by some archaeologists to be the birthplace of the Egyptian and Mediterranean civilizations. Cer-tainly the people of the southern Sahara left a wealth of fine rock-paintings and carvings as evidence that they were a people gifted in the spiritual as well as in the material. Now so arid, theirs was then a land of great herds and great hunters, and in it thrived many animals now extinct or retreated these thousand years or so to more sustaining country. And here lived men who could paint and carve and who had the eye and the heart to do so. The Tebu who live in the Tibesti today may not be descendants of these artists, but in their way they are as completely the product of the Tibesti as were the rock artists of six thousand years ago. We have a theory that in these people we may see a reflection cast on time of our own descendants of six thousand years from now.

Liv also wants to see just how bad the track is from the Mediterranean to the interior of Africa, as he believes that one day the central plains of the continent can be connected, through the desert, by a great north–south highway. This would bring back to life the caravan routes which once carried the wealth of Africa to Europe.

Liv is tall, thin and wiry. I think that St. Francis might have looked like him and even been like him, but Liv doesn't fancy being likened to a saint. Nor is he. He is both quick and impatient and quite horribly absentminded. He often forgets to come home for dinner, and nearly always forgets things like cocktail parties. On the other hand he has an amazing tolerance for children and animals and is kind and forbearing just when I wish he wouldn't be. Like many tall men, he has married a little wife. I can remember as a child in England being teased at school and told that I would grow up a midget. Those horrid girls were wrong; I am all of five feet two. Catherine says that it is very bad for the ego of a tall woman to travel with a small one. She says that our twelve men are always quick to tote and carry for me or string up my laundry line, but that they all think she is a fine strapping figure of a woman and can take care of herself. The truth of the matter is that no one seems anxious to tote for anyone in this group. If anything we are travelling with men who might adopt as their own the saying of Randolph's little daughter, 'Papa likes to see women work.'

That is us, all fourteen. We have six cars, three of which belong to the Army and three are privately owned. They are all Land Rovers. We will drive south from Agedabia on the Libyan coast, crossing the eastern side of the Libyan Sahara to Kufra. From Kufra we will bear still further east to Uweinat, almost on the border of the Sudan. From Uweinat we will bear south-west and enter the Republic of Chad at Tekro, or thereabouts. From Kufra on, all available maps are vague.

Alonzo Pond and Paul Nesbitt, authors of a small and superb work on desert survival, tell of a group of men dropped in the desert and observed from the air. As they made their way from A to B, they were sometimes as much as two hundred miles off the trail, though they were following a map and the trail could be clearly seen from the air.

From Tekro, a desert outpost, we will make our way to Faya-Largeau, Zouar, Bardai, exploring the Tibesti and then through the Kourizo Pass northward into Libya again, to Sebha and back to Agedabia. These are our plans. We are on our way and Randolph is sitting in the middle of the highway passing the time of day. We join him in a toast to the success of our expedition, gather him, Winston and the two Dutch oil men whom Randolph has invited for dinner, and find a camp-site in a eucalyptus grove near Agedabia.

Randolph claims the right to cook the first dinner. As we have brought along a cold roast of beef, potato salad, tomatoes, bread-and-butter and a Bel Paese cheese, we think it will not be too strenuous for him, and having laid out our provender Catherine and I drape ourselves about the grove and wait. Randolph calls first for his table, his two chairs and some light refreshment. Then he sits down and orders Winston to open the pâté de foie gras and to put on the lobster bisque from Fortnum and Mason. The pâté is delicious, but when we try to find a Dutchman to feed they have both disappeared. Randolph has objected to their hovering helpfully about the women, who were only too obviously delighted with their good looks and charming manners. 'Leave the women alone,' he'd shouted. 'Bugger off'—and they had.

The moment came when 'the women' have to undrape themselves from the grove and rescue the bisque which Randolph shrieks is being ruined. It is a superb soup, but Randolph pouts that the 'white ladies' have ruined it and refuses to eat. I don't think he intended to eat, anyway. However, he has endeared himself to me by presenting me with his hot-water bottle which has a velveteen cover decorated with his initials. 'For your poor little arm,' he says. I have forgiven him the banished Dutchmen.

We must never again allow camp to be so chaotic. We have had a hard time finding pots and pans and toothbrushes and pyjamas. But finally the beds are set up, teeth brushed, and the last sleeping-bag is zipped up with a sound that screeches in the silence and sets Catherine giggling. Her air mattress has been over-inflated and bounces her off on to the ground, where she flounders helplessly in her cocoon until Alan and Hank come to the rescue. Being near a town we post a guard. Once in the night Randolph's voice challenges the guard with a booming 'Who goes there!' And in the dawn Alan's bronchial cough is answered from beyond the grove by a donkey's bray.

THE STARS WERE bright and the night cold and we awaken in the morning to find ourselves covered with pools of icy dew. Boiling tea brings the blood back to our hearts and we attack our 'compo', sausages and hash hotted up over the primus, with appetite. Little boys from nearby Agedabia gather round to watch and Hank gives one of them the first discard of his twenty pairs of socks. Randolph complains that I had promised to look after him and where the hell are the bacon and eggs. So I carefully cook him two eggs which Winston eats, because the tea is gone and Randolph says he cannot stomach eggs without tea. It is a test and proves what I feared: he has no appetite. I even try to give him a vitamin pill, but Winston is right in saying he won't take those either. Catherine says he's going to develop a divine figure, and how do you lose your appetite?

We have packed up with last night's chaos fresh in our minds. Five cars have to carry twenty-five jerry-cans of petrol each, three each of fresh water, one of oil. Also distributed among the vehicles is a jerry-can of distilled water for the batteries and two of white petrol for the primus stove. The primus will work, if it has to, on regular petrol, but the lead in it would eventually clog the stove causing a poor flame, and in time no flame at all. Finding white petrol in Benghazi took a good half-day in itself. Each car has twelve cases of 'compo', various cases of our civilian food supply, spare parts, tools, sleeping and camping equipment, personal effects, and, always at the ready, sand tracks. We carry our sand tracks (chopped-off pieces of World War II airplane landing-strips) tied to the bumpers in front. Put under sand-bogged wheels these give enough purchase to get the car moving again. We are also experimenting with strips of heavy canvas, a lighter and more portable sand track. The sixth car, a small open Land Rover, is mounted with the wireless. There is barely room for that, two men and their bags. Last night we had to unpack everything to find the stove and a can opener. We think we put ourselves together rather neatly today. We stop off to take pictures and fill up at the last petrol-pump we will see in five thousand kilometres. A curiosity, not a worry. Liv has arranged for petrol dumps to be sent ahead at Kufra, Faya-Largeau, Zouar and Sebha. If these are where we expect them to be there will be no problem. If they are not we will have to build huts and colonize whichever oasis has let us down.

Catherine has bought herself a barrakan, a blanket fourteen feet long. The Bedouin use these as robe by day, sleeping-bag by night, and sometimes as a prayer-mat or a floor-covering when guests are invited into the tent. Catherine's is a brilliant red, bordered with orange and blue. She says she was cold last night despite woollen pyjamas and a down-filled sleeping-bag.

At last we turn away from the coast on a bumpy track through scrub and sage brush. The sand is rubbly and red. After a few kilometres we have trouble with the radio vehicle. Everyone climbs under it except Alan who photographs the workers and advisers in action, and the Churchills who with flag flying disappear southwards. The radio car is definitely ramshackle. It has a canvas pannier on either side, a cockeyed antenna, a couple of much-travelled suitcases, a case of Coca-Cola and a handsome but ponderous radio. Four of the other Land Rovers, long wheel-based, are sleek and new; their chassis are neat with canvas covers lashed in place. Our vehicle is two years old and has seen a good deal of the world. It has a box-like station-wagon body with windows and doors through which all of our possessions can be seen like the displays in a pawnshop window. A blue tea-kettle is nested on top of a sheepskin and a mountain of camera equipment is wedged between a carton of chocolate bars and a suitcase, the lid of which is labelled hopefully, 'This Way Up'. Everything hops up and down frantically when we cross rough ground.

The little radio car takes an hour of skilled attention and then staggers a few more kilometres before breaking down again. At the third break we start talking of sending it back. It is late in the day and we will make camp. After supper the radio car and one army vehicle will go back to Agedabia. From there the radio car, with Jack Thompson driving, will return to Benghazi alone. Francis Gibb and John Ferguson in the army vehicle will catch us up on the track five kilometres south of Gialo, our first oasis. It's a hard decision, but obviously this car can never survive the trip.

During one of the delays today Hank Setzer opened up some mole-rat mounds. One rat poked his flat head out as he busily shovelled earth to stop up the hole Hank had made. The sand is crossed and criss-crossed with car tracks made by supply trucks running down to the various oil rigs. The Michelin map shows a neat, thin red line from Agedabia to Kufra indicating a 'piste', or trail. Sometimes it doesn't exist at all, sometimes it's a mass of tyre tracks, as much as twenty kilometres in width. We've made our camp under a low scarp but even in its protection, and with tarpaulins rigged, we can't get out of the wind. We're below sea level here, and the sand is littered with clam-shells and bits of petrified wood. While we make camp Hank and Liv set out a string of fifty mouse-traps in some nearby clumps of grass and stunted palms. Somewhere along the line we have picked up Randolph and Winston again and they have delved into the lovely Fortnum and Mason surprise box and produced petit pois à la Française which are *ravissantes*. Randolph has been having little generalship meetings with Liv and Francis ('Just a word with you, dear boy') about the track, about travel procedure, about sending the little car back. He talks late into the night, and late into the night we all hear the little car being towed and whirled about in the desert bowl below our camp in a vain attempt to get it started. In the end it has to be towed most of the way to Agedabia. Poor Francis, John and Jack, no sleep for them.

| 15TH MARCH |

DEW AGAIN, COLD and saturating. Alan's cough is bad and arthritis, with which he has been troubled a good deal in the past, has stiffened up his right leg. He is worrying for fear he will prove a second 'little car' and hold us all up. Liv says we'll put up a tent at Gialo tonight and see if we can't beat this incredible dampness.

I scramble eggs for breakfast which everyone pronounces

26

delicious except Randolph. 'My dear girl,' he says despairingly, 'you've obviously never read Escoffier. It is essential to beat the eggs well first, then add the seasoning. Don't just *throw* a hunk of butter into a frying-pan full of unbeaten eggs.'

While the eggs are cooking Hank is busy with the bagful of pretty little sand-coloured Jerbels, desert mice, that his and Liv's trapping expedition of the night before has yielded. They found hyena and jackal-tracks which they followed to a camel-carcass. Hank says hyena-tracks are easy to identify as the front feet are so much larger than the rear. He is a fountain of information and talks quietly as he works, measuring body, tail, feet and ears, entering every measurement in a ledger. Then both skin and skulls are labelled and tagged. Hank skins his catch with the speed of a good laundress rolling, tucking and putting away socks. The skins are stuffed with cotton and pinned to a tray which is stored in his seven-layered locker-trunk. The skulls, like so many miniature head-hunter trophies, are hung out to dry in the back of Alan's Land Rover.

Catherine asks anxiously if they will smell, but Hank tells her that there is no bacterial action in the desert and that they will be completely without odour.

We are without our navigator today as he is of course on his way back to Agedabia while we are on the south track racing towards Gialo. Liv is navigating by intuition, having done this leg of the journey before. The hummocks and land formations are gone now as are the sage and gorse. Here the world seems to be a platter rather than a globe. Nothing—a complete disc of nothingness. We feel the ancients were not so wrong, the edge of the earth is in sight and at the speed we are going we shall pop over it in no time. And again we think that this is Dali land. We would not be surprised to see a clock, a limp telephone and a lone eyeball appear before us on this pale blond canvas we are crossing. The Churchills' car continues to career off in maverick fashion seeking new routes to the south. When they have given us sufficient lead they stop, and get out the card-table and chairs. Randolph passes the time of day with his philosophy while Winston scouts the terrain or naps under the car.

Late in the day Randolph decides to play at being lost. He flags down Alan and Hank who are riding together and calls for a little conference. The other cars, all unaware, disappear over the horizon.

'We have over-shot Gialo. We must instigate rescue procedure,' he says firmly.

Hank, who is an old desert hand, says: 'Well, yes, but let's just follow Pomeroy. We're not in any danger.'

Alan, who has had no desert experience but has a built-in bump of direction, agrees with both of them. 'We're lost, but let's get on with it. We just waste time sitting around here. Give me a drink, Randolph, and let's catch up with Liv. If he doesn't discover his mistake we can always tell him.'

But Randolph will not be out-generalled. 'Goody!' he says. 'We will have a little drink. Get the table,' he orders Winston, 'and get me the binoculars.' Hank and Alan grin and Alan wonders wistfully if any of his three sons could ever be counted on to give him the cheerful service that Winston gives his father, and decides not. Of Alan's sons, Philip is married and not at hand. Duff, who is Winston's age, when home from college, is always just on his way out of the house, and Pom, aged nine, is at the 'in-just-a-minute' stage, which precedes the on-the-way-out stage.

Rescue procedure by daylight consists of sitting still and waiting until someone misses you. Every car is supposed to check on the car behind it every fifteen minutes. A vanishing car is allowed a little time for privacy. If within a reasonable lapse of time it does not reappear a halt is called, and one car is sent back to investigate. Basically, the same procedure goes by night except that the members of the lost car are supposed to find high ground if any is available (and it is amazing how even the flattest-seeming desert has its depressions and swells). The Lost proceed to this spot, both the better to see and to be seen. Each car carries an orange distress flag which should be run up on the bamboo pole which is lashed to the top of each cab. The three civilian cars also carry five-foot box-kites. When one is flown a spotlight can be trained on it and so help the searchers to locate a lost or distressed car. Finally, each vehicle carried a Very pistol, supplied by the Scots; the main body to fire their rockets at twenty minutes after the hour throughout the night and to keep a look-out; the Lost to fire their guns on the hour, and of course keep a look-out too. Our rescue procedure also gives us instructions on how to behave and what precautions to take when lost in the desert. Liv had been thorough.

Numbers have been painted on the doors of all the cars excepting Randolph's. He does not want to mar his for future sale. However, the spectacular flagstaff identifies the Churchill car readily. Our car is No. 1, the Collinses' 2 and the army cars are 4 and 5. When the flag car and No. 2 are missed a halt is called. Liv spies out the land from the top of our cab. The missing cars are not in sight. While we wait he spots a peregrine falcon circling high in the sky. To pass the time he tosses his hat out and we watch the great bird plummet down to investigate. Perhaps it hopes that the hat is a juicy small bird. Within a foot of the ground the peregrine wheels off, and Liv retrieves his hat and gives us our orders. One car will remain and he will go back to look for the stray sheep. And so are Randolph and Co. rescued, but fierce in denial that it is they who have strayed. Another little conference is held and Randolph declares that he is beetling off westward on his own. Liv shrugs. For the moment it is all right. We are in known desert. The oasis is not far off, although invisible, and there's the tall rig of a seismic camp somewhere in front of us. In another day when we have left such things behind we must travel close together. Separation in that desert can end the adventure once and for all.

Randolph has a homing instinct. Without a brush or clump to guide himself with he has found Gialo which he has entered, conversing with the school-teacher and drinking tea with the Mudir. He has also found the seismic camp where he has delighted the men and outraged the manager. He has invited ten men to dine with us tomorrow night and instructed them to bring ice and four loaves of toast, hot and crisp, to serve with his pâté. He has also found his way to our own camp on the Gialo–Kufra track. The tent is pitched and the bed-rolls are out. Liv and Hank have gone to the oasis to set traps. Randolph and Winston give us the news and race off for an evening with the geologists. On our own we have a quiet supper, and as darkness falls we assume the Churchills to be dining at the rig, and pack away the kitchen. Late in the night the flag car roars into camp and we are berated for not having hot soup ready in language Randolph's Nanny never taught him. So the kitchen is unpacked, and Winston and I cook up a second supper. We have a difficult passenger in this great creature with his commanding presence, his brilliant wit and rough manners. It has reached the point where we relish the peaceful moments when he is sleeping and yet we all recognize his sweetness and find that he can be amusing and companionable. In the midst of the bruha-ha tonight he takes me aside in one of his 'may-I-have-a-tiny-word-with-you' confidences, walks into the darkness and tells me that he'd been touched by my concern for his health, and that he is enjoying the trip and already feels better.

'But pills,' he says, 'what an impossible, American idea. I never take pills.'

FRANCIS DID NOT turn up in the evening as we had hoped he would. We heard a motor in the night and fired off a Very pistol at eleven o'clock. Liv ran up the kite and we spotlighted it. When Francis and John Ferguson turned up this morning they said that they had gone south on the track forty miles, passing us within a few miles without seeing a sign of us. This flat-seeming camp-site is in fact in a depression. We had not seen the flare they shot off at eight o'clock and they had not seen ours. When Catherine and I went for an early morning ride both camp and its high-flying kite disappeared within three kilometres.

| 16TH MARCH |

Francis reports that far from getting rid of the radio, which none of us really wanted on the trip, Colonel O'Lone has promised to arrange with the R.A.F. to fly it down to Kufra to us. Francis and Liv are gloomy at the prospect for we will have to fit this extra five hundred pounds and a man into our already overloaded cars.

Alan has decided to leave the expedition. Despite the tent he cannot bend his knee now, and in the night he coughed more than he slept. He and Liv are going to the rig to pay their respects and see when the next supply plane is coming down. They will fill up on drinking-water, tighten up some bolts, drill holes in the roof of Alan's car for the spotlight which has not yet been mounted, and radio Benghazi our revised schedule since we have been delayed so much.

Catherine dispiritedly sorts through the Collinses' suitcase, making up a bundle of things for Alan to take back. She keeps his heavy equipment. He won't need it in Benghazi or Rome or Tunis where he may go to visit friends, but if he recovers he may fly down to Chad to rejoin the expedition. He is a methodical man and at the same time a dreamer. Realistic as his action is, she knows how hard it is to give up the dream.

In the afternoon Catherine and I are invited to the oil camp to bathe. The bathroom is a trailer equipped with showers and basins. Other trailers are mess, kitchen and workshop, and in the circle about are the sleeping-tents with double roofs, mosquito-netting and real beds. In the bath trailer we open all of the windows, letting a cool breeze in and privacy out. There are gallons of hot water and piles of white towels. We bathe and perfume ourselves and wash our hair and clothes, taking a bag of fresh laundry back to camp to hang on a line strung from No. 2 car. We pay marked unattention to the soldiers' giggles. They will just have to get used to females in camp.

The oil people have offered hospitality to Alan and Randolph, who says that since pâté and caviar are finished he may as well go home. A supply plane is due at the rig Monday and will fly them back to Benhgazi. Winston will keep the Churchill Land Rover and come along with us.

'He's a good boy,' says Randolph. 'He's steady on parade. But I spent sixty pounds on tulips this year. It would be a waste not to see them come up. Besides, my little spaniel is in whelp. Very irresponsible of me to go away from home for six weeks.'

Only five of the oil men come for dinner. Randolph has countermanded the other invitations saying firmly, 'Five is enough and bring your own plates and forks.'

At least he did not put off bearded André whom we all love. André has taken care of the men and their problems, invited the women to bathe and conversed fearlessly with Randolph. We don't know what they conversed about, for Randolph set up his two camp-chairs in the desert well away from camp and the two big men sat there, on the shore of a mirage of blue water, a bottle of Scotch and one of Drambuie on the sand beside them.

Even from a distance it was apparent that André was no mere listener. André is a Frenchman, from the Pyrenees. He told us that he commanded a battery of horse artillery during the last war and was taken prisoner on horseback. We think it must have been a singular honour.

The last of Randolph's pâté is delectable served with the crisp toast which our guests have brought us. For dinner we have green turtle soup, also from Fortnum and Mason. It is flavoured with sherry and we tell Randolph that he is a great gourmet, with which he readily agrees. We also have tamales, hot chili beans, beet salad and whisky. André holds a lantern for the women to do the dishes and Randolph complains that American women demand too much attention and that Frenchmen give them too much. An Englishman, now, knows how to treat women! Catherine thinks she has earned the Victoria Cross for not throwing the dish-water at him.

Late in the night our guests climb into their Rover, packing in Alan and Randolph and their gear. Randolph has kissed both of us and promised me a spaniel pup. Catherine watches the lights of the car as it draws away. Nothing diminishes in the desert, but suddenly disappears. When that has happened she walks weeping in its wake with Liv to comfort her.

| 17TH MARCH | THIS MORNING WE set off for Kufra, an oasis seven hundred and fifty miles from Benghazi. We really feel now |

that we are on our way deep into the desert. We stop first at the seismic camp to pick up Catherine's passport and the carnet for her car. Perhaps both she and Alan had a psychological block about remembering them yesterday. Catherine says that she found Alan sitting up glumly in bed, his leg propped on a pillow, a whisky glass, a bottle of aspirin, and two inches of cigarette ash beside him on a box clearly marked 'Dynamite'.

Now the desert is hard and as smooth as a race-track. In car No. 2 Catherine drives for a while. She does not like desert formation. Accustomed to driving in New York traffic, she says the lack of a road-bed, signs and jostling humanity confuse her.

In this expanse of nothing, where five solitary cars are racing along, she is for the first time in her life afraid of running into someone. Her fears are not entirely unfounded, for every now and then one car will break formation to chase off after a migrating bird or to follow the trail some animal has left in the sand. There is no telling, she decides, who is going to turn unexpectedly across your bow. Hank says that she is doing fine, and tells her when to shift gears, and she thinks crossly that her son and husband do that same thing but that at least she can talk back to them. There is a haze of green on the desert. Hank says that it lasts about six weeks and shows how, with irrigation, the desert could be made to blossom.

The air is brilliant, the temperature comfortably warm. We see mirages—lagoons and bays and waving grasses. The cars ahead are reflected in each mirage they cross, and we are surprised not to see them send up a fountain of spray. Yet when we approach the spot the body of water has gone, replaced further on by an inland sea, complete with islands and lonely blue headlands.

Francis has given Catherine and me a lesson on the use of a sextant, and navigation in general. He thinks it highly doubtful that Catherine has understood anything. She is very much in the dark ages about the wonders of the world. She is satisfied with a simple concept of the moon going around the earth and the two of them whirling around the sun. Stars, planets, nebulas and galaxies delight her to look at. She does not even want to contemplate the fact that they do their whirling on schedule in a sort of infinite orchestration of time and space. She listens for a while and then wanders away looking bemused. I too am quite fuddled about it, but don't want Francis to suspect. He has charts and tables, and after much complicated adding and subtracting and reference to at least three different volumes, he finishes his demonstration by drawing two perpendicular lines on the map saying, 'Here we are!' His pencil rests somewhere in the middle of the Mediterranean, so he starts all over again.

As Liv explained it to me, navigation in the desert is much like navigation at sea, though the horizon does not rock about and one can use a theodolite rather than a sextant. With a theodolite you have an almost perfect and fixed horizon; an advantage, as you can shoot late at night. Actually we have a bubble sextant. This is not as accurate as a theodolite but has the advantage of always giving the navigator a perfect excuse for being ten to twenty miles off. We have no altimeter, and if in the desert you don't know your altitude the best navigator can be thrown off. I never did hear mention of altitude, and scented in our navigation an aura of incantation and crystal ball. Unfortunately in this day and age navigators seem to be trained to follow a formula without being expected to understand why, so when one thing goes wrong, as it is bound to now and then, we may well find that according to our navigator we are behind the Iron Curtain. Still, Catherine and I are impressed with the arithmetic involved, let alone the interpretation of it.

There are many landmarks and cairns throughout the desert, at times too many. If you are not careful it is easy to mistake one set of them for another which may be ten miles to one side and headed in quite a different direction. It is as though our road and route signs at home were unmarked posts and there was nothing to say where they were leading. In the desert it is important to start out with the best available map without ever quite trusting it. As Alonzo Pond, co-author of *Desert Survival*, says, maps of the Sahara have been known to be as much as two hundred miles off the mark, sometimes record non-existent sites or alternatively do not show a clearly visible trail. Hank has brought along some aerial maps, and Alan has unearthed French maps which are more detailed than any that have been done up to this time. Francis marks these, carefully keeping an accurate record of mileage and direction of travel. He is for ever to be seen sitting on the top of his speeding car, his torso bare to the sun, his hair on end and a map flapping in the wind. Already his maps are much spliced and taped up, and the dry air has made them brittle. But he has a good tan.

We were, and continue to be, against taking guides. In the Sahara they have the reputation of being able to let the sand run through their fingers, sniff and tell you where you are. It is a dangerous fallacy, and often means that they are lost themselves and trying to stall off your impatient questions, or seeing if they can get a tiny hint from Allah as to where on his earth they may be. We suspect that all this filibustering really tells them is that it is indeed sand. Many desert guides go by dead reckoning, camel-time, and are hopelessly confused in a car by the speed with which the familiar landmarks whizz by. They are also sometimes short-sighted, which means that from the car they have not even seen the landmark. Apart from this, they have to eat and drink and take up space, and it may turn out in the end that all they had in mind was a free ride to wherever you happened to be going. In ancient days, when a caravan was lost, they say it was customary to murder the guide before all died of thirst. This sobering thought tended to keep the boys on their feet and wide awake. But of recent years desert travellers have become lax and, like maids and butlers, guides are not what they used to be. However, if the worst comes to the worst, we can always revert to tradition and murder Francis.

We are not lost today, but Francis admits to being somewhat surprised at sighting an oil rig. We pull up to a British Petroleum camp, which has been drilling for oil in one of the most southern concession areas of Libya.

Someone once said that the junk of one generation was the treasure of the next. He was probably referring to antiques, but it might just as well have been said of deserts. A generation ago the Sahara was considered worthless, except as a route between one oasis or market and another. The Europeans, the Arabs, the Berbers, Tuaregs and Rifs fought over it for this reason, and not because they placed any value on the desert itself. Mussolini com-plained bitterly about Italy's 'collection of deserts', but the pre-diction has again come true, and the 'junk' of yesterday has suddenly become one of the great treasure-houses of the world.

Less than twenty years ago the oil of just one of the recent discoveries in the Libyan Desert might have changed the history of the world. If either side had had the use of it in 1941, the course of the war would have been far different, and, going back a step further, would Mussolini have entered the war if he had known the potential economic and political power that such a tremen-dous source of oil could have assured him? But of course the game of historical 'ifs' is an endless one. Although her resources may never match those of Venezuela or the Persian Gulf countries, the Sahara has already proved itself the greatest source of oil west of the Suez Canal, and in the world of finance and international politics 'West of Suez' is a far more interesting direction than that chosen by Kipling.

Nobody seems to be about at this British Petroleum camp. We look at our watches and guess that everyone must be having lunch. But we have caused a stir and soon Mr. Gibson, the camp manager, emerges from a trailer, and, with true desert hospitality, invites all twelve of us into an air-conditioned mess for a little snack of antipasto, baked noodles, steak and potatoes and unlimited beer and wine. Most of the men are French, and have those delightful heavy lids and expressive tragic eyebrows which seem to be handed out to that nation. The mess has the spirit, if not the decor, of a little *bistro*. The walls are plastered with pin-up girls which the men of our party like, and Catherine and I are told not to study so darn' closely. Mr. Gibson tells us that their well was a 'duster', a dry hole, and that the camp will shortly move a hundred miles to the east across the sand sea. We have had a lovely welcome, and are glad that he is not yet so far away.

A sand sea is a vast area where the sand is soft and blowing. Ridges of dunes, usually running north-east to south-west, cut the horizon like white-crested waves. The wind whips them on inch by inch, continually changing their contour, even as a hurricane lashes and changes the sea. Those so unwise as to cross these areas bog bumper-deep. Even the mammoth equipment of an oil company has a tough job crossing a sand sea. The B.P. camp will move to the gravel plain just south of it, very close to where the World War II bomber, *Lady-Be-Good*, lies. Her nine men finished their first and last bombing mission in that dead and hopeless land.

The *Lady-Be-Good* was discovered two years ago by a British oil-exploration crew. They came upon the plane, its tail snapped off, but otherwise in good condition, having apparently made a successful belly-landing on rough ground; at first they thought it must have crashed recently—there was no rust, no decay of any sort. The coffee in the thermos was drinkable. The clock on the panel worked. The Englishmen reported it to the American military people at Wheelus Base in Tripoli, who pieced the story together.

On 14th April 1943, in the middle of a sandstorm, the *Lady-Be-Good* took off from its base at Solluch, near Benghazi, to make a bombing raid on Naples. Of the twenty-five planes which took off, only eleven reached their target. Going north to Naples, the *Lady-Be-Good* made excellent time with a strong tail wind. When they turned for home the crew did not know that the wind had also turned, with the suddenness and strength which seems to be a peculiarity of that area. Again they had a tail wind, but this time, when they estimated their position, they figured on a head wind. They were therefore much further south than they thought. It was night, and they must have looked for the dimmed lights of their home base at Solluch. They could never have seen them, for they had long since left the Mediterranean and the North African coast behind—they had overshot Solluch and were flying over a land as featureless as the sea itself. They were four hundred miles into the desert when they began to sputter through their last tank of petrol and decided to bail out, as they thought, into the sea. Instead they rolled over on to the hard sand and the *Lady-Be-Good*, their only hope of salvation with her radio and coffee and shade, went on alone for eight miles.

The bodies of all but one of the crew have now been found. They left a pitiful trail of hope. Parachutes cut arrow-shaped to show the direction they travelled, mask-shaped to protect them from the sun, a pair of boots, a dwindling diary. They were walking north, and covered nearly eighty miles without food and water. When they reached the great waves of the sand sea, the hope that over each crest they would see the Mediterranean must have kept them going until the life and the hope were finished.

Driving with Liv in the afternoon, Catherine takes the wheel again to give him some much-needed sleep. I am still too one-armed to drive on this rough stuff. The five cars are strung out in the desert in a rough spearhead, sometimes as much as a mile apart, but each in sight of at least one other car. A Land Rover in the distance looks like a tin can, and sometimes we race to overtake what proves to be in fact a tin can, cast out by some other explorer or by Leclerc's army twenty-odd years ago. Mistaking a hill for a cloud-shadow, Catherine fails to contour in time and hits it with an impact that sets the entire load about their ears and breaks the speedometer and mileage-gauge. Liv refrains from saying some of the many things he could, she reports, but the look he gives her is adequate; a mileage-gauge is vital in the desert, for keeping track of where you are and how far you should go before you start worrying about where you first went astray. Liv rearranges the load, takes the wheel and says mildly that sleep is polished off for him in any case. They talk as they drive along, and Liv says that he will build a house in this great peace. It will be completely surrounded by a million square miles of beige lawn which he will never have to cut. He may have to fence it in, of course, to keep people from putting footprints all over. In No. 2 Hank is telling me about his family: his wife who is a school-teacher, his three little girls at home in Maryland and his Devon bulls and his Minks. Mink, it seems, are temperamental and delicate. I was fascinated to hear that the male has a bony penis. Hank says that his prize stud was deprived of breeding power (and I imagine his good nature) when this member broke off and got lost somewhere about the run. The Devon bulls, I was relieved to hear, are sturdier. According to Hank, museum work is sometimes tedious. Schoolchildren are given to writing innumerable letters asking for such things as 'all information about rodents'. And a schoolchild must always be answered. For Hank, field work holds the greatest charm. He has been to all three Libyan provinces. This year he expects to spend a total of six months out of the United States. He will go to Aden later, and to Ethiopia, where he will join a team working on a medical-research grant. They will study the spread of various diseases by parasites. Almost all of our men are growing beards, and Hank's is the bushy type that makes him look like the thieving prospector in an old-time Western movie. He is hard-working, kind and helpful, and knows more about the desert than any of us.

In No. 5 car Frank and Charlie are telling Francis about women. Two years older than their officer, who is twenty-one, they claim to have learned from experience. Frank says that he joined the Army to get away from a shrewish wife and has learned to keep strictly unserious with the dames—'Just don't let them get a toe-hold,' he patronizes, 'and you'll be all right.'

Charlie agrees sagely. They are pulling Francis's leg badly for neither of them has been married. Charlie, really getting into the spirit of the thing, says: 'The best thing that ever happened to me was my divorce. Women! All they want is everything they see and some poor bloke sweatin' away to provide it. Take my advice, surr, and keep that young leddy of yours at a distance.'

Francis grumbles disconsolately and pops up through the hatch on to the roof of the car to scan his fleet. Despite Frank's and Charlie's jaundiced view on women he hopes for a letter from 'that young leddy' on the R.A.F. plane which is scheduled to fly our wireless and operator to Kufra.

In the late afternoon the desert commences to boil up in little hummocks topped with a weird hairy growth. Hank, who has eyes like a hawk, spots some infinitesimal tracks and holds up the convoy to examine them. Neither he nor anybody else can identify them.

'A verra sma' abominable sand-man,' John Ferguson suggests wisely. John is a cabinet-maker by trade, doing his National Service with the Army, but by choice he would be back in Scotland, stalking deer or fishing for salmon. He is a real country-man, but to me he looks more like a poet of ancient Greece, who should be wearing a toga and sandals instead of sneakers and khaki shorts. He has a lilting speaking voice, and I feel sure he can sing. His beard is not bushy, like Hank's, but Lincolnesque.

We come to a clump of palms. This is either Bir Harasch or Bir Buzaregh—we argue about it but there is no one to ask. Bir means 'well' in Arabic, and if we need it we could dig for water. Hank and Liv set out traps. They use oatmeal for bait, chewing the dry stuff until it wads and will stick to the trap. Like cows they munch as they walk and there is no conversation. Hank marks each trap with a fluff of cotton so that it will be easy to find in the morning.

At camp, Frank and Archie get the tea going and Catherine and I consult about food. Winston has music coming over the radio of his car. His table is set up, furnished with a large white plastic bowl and soap-dish and a gallon jerry-can of water. He is bathing. The men are variously setting out beds, sorting equipment or changing the oil in the cars. Archie digs a garbage dump under the dining-room table where we could throw eggshells, if we had eggs, and debris. Francis takes time out from his charts to protest. He tells us that it is insanitary, improper and un-military.

From the stove where Frank squats, looking as though he were praying to the tea, we hear him mutter, 'Wimmen arr unmilitary, I told ye so, Mister Gibb.'

But we win this little battle. 'No inhabitants, no flies!' I say, 'and we don't want to have to walk a sanitary distance every time we scrape a plate.'

It is dark. Winston has rigged a small lantern for his bath, but the large lantern is broken and we have set the big flashlight on the table. Francis keeps borrowing it to read by as his own flash is not so powerful, and we fumble blindly for pots and pans. The pots are in a canvas bag, the dishes and 'eating irons' (as the Army calls its cutlery), mugs and such in a carton. Everything is covered with layers of dust. We have brought an enormous amount of food to supplement the 'compo' ration which, although adequate for twelve men for forty-five days, would be dull fare if unrelieved. We have tins of ham and tongue, tuna and sardines, tamales and pancake mixes, fruits, sweets and biscuits. We have one carton devoted to seasonings: oil, vinegar and wine, lemon concentrate and extracts with which to disguise anything too boring or, as may be, high. We hope to be able to buy eggs and tomatoes at the oases, and to shoot gazelle. In addition to the three-burner primus we have a charcoal grill. We did not bring enough fruit and juices and vegetables and as the weather gets warmer we crave these. Dried fruits, raisins, figs and dates would have been easy to bring and a welcome relief from those incredibly weighty army productions, mixed-fruit pudding and jam roly-poly. We have brought enough whisky for an occasional tot, but had to draw the line at beer. One can apiece a day would have added twenty-three cases to our heavy load.

When the last dish has been sand-washed, the last lantern put out, we retire, each to his chosen spot, for a wash-up. These men certainly are unaccustomed to travelling with women. We decide that in future we will have something to say about the way in which the cars are squared off for camp. It is necessary to use a car as a washroom as you need a fender on which to put wash-bowl, toothbrush, mug, mirror and all of those jars of cream. Tonight there does not seem to be an unprotected side to any car. To the east Hank is already in bed, to the west Winston is rearranging his sleeping-bag, the north and south are teeming with men and in the centre Francis is taking a fix on the stars. Disgusted, Catherine and I do a contortionist job of undressing behind a blanket rigged over a car door. I have striped pyjamas which offer a good camouflage. Catherine has made the mistake of bringing white wool. Walking away from the camp to search out a convenient clump she looks fluorescent.

What do we all think at night when the last weary bone is laid to rest, the last zipper pulled up against the already penetrating cold? Even great thoughts cannot last long. The stars, as big as apples, hang out of the sky. With a ceiling over one's head one may fight for sleep, toss and turn; here one fights to keep it off. The day is done, with whatever problems or hardships or heartaches to some. Does your body ache, it is resting now. Your spirit is free as it has never been before. The stars in this immense solitude unroll all of history, and you are present at the Creation. A flash of thought that you would like to contemplate, but already you are asleep.

18TH MARCH

HANK'S TRAPS HAVE yielded another jerbel and a lovely pale jerboa, the desert rat which is built like a miniature kangaroo. They are both covered with fleas which Hank stores away in a plastic bag for the benefit of medical research. The Army, he says, has a very good flea man, and the Navy an excellent tick man (or was it the other way round?). They are both friends of his and he will collect for them.

We find weird palm-fronds and decorate the breakfast table, thinking nostalgically of Randolph, who had complained at the lack of flowers on that first breakfast table. He does not like things to be ordinary, and pinning us with his brooding eyes he'd say: 'This is the age of the common man and the commoner woman. You should put flowers on the table.'

Yesterday there were clouds in the sky, flocks and herds and ecstasies of clouds casting their shadow on land and mirage alike. Today the sky domes up from the horizon, pale to a clear bright blue. We set out through scrub-covered dunes, more hostile than the hard open desert, closed in by a pretence of life that gives neither food nor water. Occasionally a bird—how do they live? —a wagtail, as nosy as a town sparrow, will come into camp; a falcon will dive if you fling up a hat for it to investigate, or a swallow will skim between the cars. We forge through tall grasses, knobbled like bulrushes and as high as the cars. Until we emerge five miles on we have no idea where the others are. We find them waiting ahead so that Liv, who is official scenarist, can *faire le Kodak*, as Randolph called it, of an old Long Range Desert Group vehicle axle-deep in sand. Later the country opens into rolling dunes, miles of quilted golden velvet. We are up and down; now we see one another, now we don't. Each driver thinks he knows a better route. And suddenly we are among the crested dunes. These dunes are so soft that they must be taken at full speed to reach the top. Then it needs skill and quick reaction to choose the precise moment to stop (without using brakes, which dig you in) in order to avoid flying over the far side which is steep, almost concave. Francis, in the lead, stops on the brink of a sharp crest. The rest of us leave our cars at the base of the dune and scramble up to peer over, and tell him how lucky he is. They say you can ski your car down some dunes if you manage to turn head-on in time, but taken at an angle you will surely turn over.

We're bogging in the sand continuously now. I am keeping a book on each vehicle, somewhat to everyone's annoyance. I am doing it to see whose tyres are best. So far our sand tyres are winning, though the newer Land Rovers have more powerful engines which help carry their heavy loads at a high enough speed to get through the soft sand. While the army cars do not have sand tyres they do have a wide-tread tyre. The Collinses' car was originally intended for the British Petroleum people to use in towns and on hard-surfaced roads, and according to Hank its tyres are fit only for bicycles. Despite this, Hank manages well with them. He is a deft driver and when he senses a soft spot he steps on the gas and goes like fury, regardless of obstacles or direction. Once on hard ground again he will coast the car to a stop and cheerfully walk back a killing distance to help any bogged vehicle he may have sailed by so hard-heartedly. Fortunately this hard and soft sand alternate, or we would spend six weeks in one spot instead of covering five thousand miles.

Now we are going along a stretch chewed up by the Free French forces of General Leclerc, whose epic march north from Lake Chad to join the Allies on the coast was one of the most memorable achievements of desert warfare. Our cars rock like little boats in a heavy sea. Our loads are no help, and sometimes when we bog we find that we have dug in clear to the springs. Each car has a slightly different load, and each of us suspects the others of running around empty, for each knows that he is carrying five times more than he bargained for. Every morning at take-off you can be sure to hear, 'Just look at these springs. I don't know how far . . .' and you can be just as sure that no one but the owner will bother to look. The rest are all too busy mourning their own load.

The Army have heavy tarpaulins and a tent on top of their normal load and of course they have more men to carry. The Collins-Setzer car has all of those traps as well as a growing horde of pebbles, petrified wood and other oddities, for Catherine is the scavenger type. We all think the Churchill car remarkably carefree, but Winston claims to be almost anchored to the earth. Besides he has that great ice-chest (the Magical Box) in which the ice from the oil rig has already turned to water. We think that we are probably in worse state than anyone, as our car is older. Designed to carry a quarter of a ton, our Rover is carrying two thousand three hundred pounds. The breakdown (treacherous word!) is as follows:

29 jerry-cans of petrol	1276 lb.
3 jerry-cans of water	120 lb.
10 cases of army rations	330 lb.
10 cases of other rations	200 lb.
Personal kit, spare parts, tools, etc.	150 lb.
Two persons	250 lb.
Total:	2326 lb.

Everyone has his own formula for not getting stuck and his pet theory of how to get out when he does get stuck. Put her into four-wheel drive, low ratio, and leave it there . . . stay in two-wheel drive . . . keep in high ratio . . . don't shift too soon

. . . shift the moment she drops below forty miles an hour . . . don't shift at all. It doesn't seem to matter what you do. When the sand is soft enough a great invisible hand reaches out and holds you back; and a disembodied voice whispers, 'Stay a while, brother, and dig and push; there's no real hurry, is there?' So all the theories go out of the window, and you go with them. You dig a little sand away from each wheel, and where you have dug someone comes along and says, 'What kind of a job is that?' for in fact the sand has all run back in. So you dig more and deeper, and you put down the canvas sand mats and the sections of airplane runway and everyone available pushes and shouts advice to the driver, who isn't paying any attention, and you pray a little or a lot depending on how hot it is and how long you've been stuck. You watch spellbound as the car gains a little speed and then reels drunkenly just before it sinks hopelessly into the next soft patch, and you wonder how many desert drivers die of heart failure, and whether it is possible to get so badly stuck that you never will get out. Then, suddenly, the soft sand is behind and all five cars are ski-ing along. You are never, never going to get stuck again. After such an experience those who did not get stuck give the others a short lecture on how, with a little experience and skill, etc. . . . These talks are most appreciated when the lecturer illustrates his point by disappearing axle-deep into a dune. As Frank says, we have pushed enough miles to last us the rest of our lives and we're not a week on the way.

Liv discovered that it is possible to push out of some soft spots if, before the car has stopped, you fling open your door and push along the ground with one leg, scooter-fashion. He says that it has the double effect of taking your weight off the car as well as forcing it a little forward, and that it gives a sense of power over the infernal machine. Frank and Archie shout with laughter as they sweep past on harder ground. I suppose we do look like some weird lopsided beetle with Liv's lanky leg pedalling frantically on one side of the car and my shorter member gyrating from the other.

Yes, everyone has his own formula. One we heard of was tried by a driller stationed in the desert near Gialo. He was driving along from one camp to another when he bogged and couldn't budge his car with any of the usual tricks. A wily old desert hand, he put his car in gear, set the hand throttle, and while the wheels were spinning he jumped out and pushed as hard as he could, counting on the first slow movement to give him plenty of time to hop back in. The car churned slowly and then suddenly hit a hard patch and lurched forward, dumping the man on his face. Before he could pick himself up it had taken off across the desert at a neat pace, leaving the oil man puffing and panting in hopeless pursuit. He had to walk back to camp and never did see the car again, which may one day build up a sort of Flying Dutchman legend—a Land Rover sailing across the desert under a curse. A lot of them are.

In the late afternoon we have come to the edge of a sea, or lake perhaps, of soft sand. We have drawn up to look it over and decide how to proceed. We judge it to be about fifteen miles across, though distances are deceptive in the desert and it may be more. On the far side is a coast of black sandstone hills through which we must navigate to find the gateway to Kufra. Hank says gloomily that if we bog we will be pushing the cars the whole way across. It is decided that we must go like hell and not stop with any of this brotherly-love or helping-hand business or we will all bog. Stopping to help has in many instances got all five cars into trouble where only one had bogged to begin with. We think that if we can get moving at all we can probably keep moving, but once stopped in this crustless stuff we will be in. So we take flying leaps off the scarp and throttle down, prayers in our hearts, and skim without a single mishap to the mountains on the far side. These are pyramids of black sandstone geometrically as precise as though they came off a drawing-board. As we approach we see that there are rivers of sand running between and winding among them, sometimes ending in sand lagoons and fjords locked in by the towering mountains. Liv says that he can imagine a spy from the moon returning to his own people and reporting:

'They live in crowded green belts fighting the vegetation and bacteria for an existence while they have millions of miles of beautiful country like ours that they neglect.'

Having seen this place we think that the Russians didn't photograph the moon at all, they photographed the Sahara.

We explore the hills, each thinking that he has found the

best route, and soon we are scattered and can neither see nor hear one another. But like needles drawn by a magnet we come out of the hills on to a rough plain, everyone accounted for. The cars ahead disappear in clouds of dust and when the dust has settled the car that was there is gone, making the drivers in the rear weirdly uncomfortable. The sand is turning red. El Hawaria, a flat-topped mountain known as the gateway to Kufra, is looming in the distance and the sun is setting. We must find a campsite, but we need protection from the wind which is blowing fiercely, so we push on until twilight when we come down a long escarpment to the base of a cliff.

We are all in wonderful spirits with our early nights under this magnificent sky, and everybody seems to be getting along well. Winston, somewhat lordly to start with, has taken up dishwashing, digging and toting with the rest of us. We still think he is too clean, but this is something we are never to cure him of. Frank is all bristly bonhomie. He says that the stars have softened him, and Charlie says that the desert reminds him of the streets of Glasgow on a Sunday. I think that we have all come to a sort of least common denominator. It is extraordinary; whatever your temperament, your past, education or experience in life, here one and all are equally bemused—we are all penetrated by a hitherto unheard-of element, star-dust.

This is not to say that we are going around in a daze of sweetness and light. The heat and trials of desert travel tend to trigger tempers, but there is not one of us who does not awaken in the dawn full of philosophy and pleasure. Frank and Archie are perhaps the worst teases of the party; they are bouncing and voluble and always ready for a laugh. There is a story that they dressed up their barracks for a general inspection once, with ribboned curtains, little rugs and crocheted antimacassars, and then stood at very dead-pan attention. The inspecting officer seems to have had his own sense of humour. 'So this is the little home awa' fra home!' he bellowed, strutting about; and told them they would take K.P. as there was dust on top of the wardrobe.

Frank and Archie man the stove and the army rations, and are great hands at stirring whatever concoction is on the flame. I tell them hopefully that some things are not supposed to have the texture of porridge and explain the principle of what the cook-books call 'folding' as opposed to stirring. Soldiers, I am afraid, prefer one texture and one taste to their food—no surprises. Taffy is quiet, and has not been needed to doctor the machinery since the ill-fated radio car was sent back to Agedabia. We feel that he is biding his time with philosophy. Charlie looks in vain for a patient. His large box of medical supplies has a great deal of competition. We all have our pet pills and remedies —cures for itching and insomnia, dysentery and dyspepsia; we have morphia ampoules, antibiotics and band-aids. Hank keeps a spoon permanently by his side and takes nips of some soothing preparation whenever we have too many beans or roly-poly pudding on the menu. Catherine was the only one to think of eye-wash and has fortunately a huge bottle. She has even brought along a box of temporary fillings for teeth. It is obviously a case of too many doctors, and Charlie is going to have a hard time. He is looking quite beatnik these days. We have all gone to seed somewhat, but Charlie is more convincing about it. Give him a Hyde Park soap-box and he could surely concoct some burning message and collect a crowd. Perhaps he is given to soap-boxing anyway, for when we asked him how he came to be chosen for the trip and why he wanted to come he said that his platoon officer wanted him out of the way! For his part, Charlie wants to be an instructor in mountaineering one day, and says that he has an affinity for silent places—deserts and glaciers. He is something of a student but says that his language studies at Glasgow University were considerably hampered by his investigations into female students and their habits, and a census of the better pubs of Glasgow.

Everyone has peeled down to shorts, bare feet and sunburn. The army vehicles always have a half-nude man on top, coming up through the opening of their cab roofs like human conning-towers. They have a head start on sun-tan. It is very unfair, as Catherine and I must stay in cabs and clothes. I have changed to shorts, however, and Catherine has sheared off the legs of her expensive New York slacks. The edges are frayed and one leg is longer than the other. I have also broken the zipper on my trousers and they are decorated with safety-pins. Liv has lost his dark glasses. He says he knows exactly where they are and the next expedition to go to Kufra can be told to pick them up. Besides, he knew that he was going to lose them so has brought an extra pair. Francis has broken his watch, Winston's plastic plate and mug have melted and Catherine has lost her underpanties. We are disintegrating, but happily.

We are within less than a day's run from Kufra, and Francis says we must all be up at dawn. Besides, we can photograph the Gate of Kufra with the sun on it. This plan is wrecked by four bottles of whisky. We are normally an abstemious lot, often forgetting our evening tot entirely. But Francis says that tonight we must listen on Winston's radio for the outcome of the England-Scotland rugger match, and celebrate or mourn as the case may be. We mourn. We are sad not only for the Scottish rugger team, but for the way the finer things of Scottish life are bandied about all over the world: like Hindus in kilts, Americans brewing Instant porridge and fierce Arabs of the Libyan Army armed with bagpipes playing 'Over the Sea to Skye'.

'Now there's a bonny song!' Frank says, and

'Speed bonnie boat like a bird on the wing . . .' the Scots chime in. It is a lovely song, and the boys have fine voices. John runs to mournful Scottish airs, Frank to jazzier stuff. Taffy will not sing us Welsh songs as he is too bashful to sing alone. Catherine and Hank can't carry a tune, but are not bashful. Charlie says he can only sing when he's drunk and when he's drunk he can't remember the words. Late into the night we gather around the dying embers of the bottle, American vieing with Briton in the taller telling of already tall tales. We finally put away our mugs and weave bedwards. Archie asks Catherine which is her sleeping bag, and makes it a sweeping bow before he is led away by John and Frank. A casualty to conviviality we hear him bellow in the night that we are surrounded by Russians.

'Go to bed,' Francis snaps in his most military tone. 'Go to bed, Corporal Aitken. That's an order.' It occurs to me then that an officer is like a mother, and I could tell him that it is a losing game. Archie's voice echoes against the cliff.

'There are Russians out there—forty million of them,' he yells and he rushes to the attack.

'Gallant fellow,' Catherine murmurs from her cot.

There is laughter and shouting and we hear the clonk of bone meeting bone, a few scrabbling sounds and silence. We take it that Archie has obeyed the order.

<table>
<tr><td>19TH MARCH</td></tr>
</table>

FIRST MORNING WITHOUT dew. Dawn is, however, cold. We wear heavy coats and sheepskins until the sun is up, when from one moment to the next we peel from winter wear to as close to the nude as we can decently get. At dawn the hot tea is hovered over with delight. We are anxious to get on our way but Winston has disappeared along the cliff, no doubt to get rid of that green feeling. No one looks like a better-babies ad. No formation today. The sand is a brilliant orange streaked with crimson.

'Iron,' Charlie says. We're all becoming geologists and very authoritarian. Whenever we stop we begin hunting for oddities. In the normal course of things one or two of us might have been interested in rocks, but in the desert the pebble is king. Each of us has his own little hoard of bright treasure: green, red, orange striped with black, speckled and streaked, bubbly and sand-polished. Some specimens are quite large. Frank exclaims over one extraordinary melted-looking black stone that Catherine is holding. 'Och,' he says, with respect, 'that's no stone, that's a rock.' Catherine says that it is a statue which she will exhibit at the Museum of Modern Art in New York. Winston chides her with wanting to be the artist's agent. Liv wants to call it 'Hate With a Fly in Its Eye'. Hank agrees with Frank that it's no stone; he says it's a boulder and that the springs are not going to take much more. But he helps Catherine load it, telling her that it is sandstone, not basalt or lava, and that it will break to pieces before she gets it anywhere near New York.

Catherine says: 'Nonsense. I'll wrap it in Alan's long underwear and wedge it under your sleeping-bag. Besides it can't be sandstone. It looks like iron and I think it's petrified water.' A non-scientific person is very hard for a scientific person to talk to. Had Alan been there he could have explained to Hank that

Catherine never believes things she doesn't like unless they are told her firmly by a member of her own family.

Kufra is more than one oasis, it is a belt of oases covering approximately a thousand square miles. Catherine thinks that 'oblong miles' would be a more suitable description. We arrive at the first oasis, El Hawari, by noon. As we are so close to Kufra we have relaxed travel formation and done some independent exploring. Each of us now comes in to the oasis from a different direction. Hank and Catherine have followed a prehistoric lake shore where Hank tells the boys, 'We unfortunately found some rather good petrified wood. Most of it's in the car,' he adds grimly.

Generally an oasis appears first as a bluish haze on the horizon, clarifying to a thin green line of palms. As you approach the line of trees may lengthen in both directions, to the left and right, as far as you can see. You can usually drive on hard sand to within three or four miles of the trees, but from there on the surface is chopped up by the passage of people, flocks of goats and camels and occasional trucks. The crust of yellow gravel has been ground in, leaving sand as soft and fine as baby's powder. An oasis is always in a depression formed by some ancient river-bed or fold in the hills. As you pause a few miles away from the trees and look through binoculars there is often no landmark, no speck of white to indicate a house, no track-marker to show you the way in. If you make a bad guess you may be three or four hours fighting your way through soft sand under the palms without finding a living soul to wave a vague arm in the direction of the village. An English friend of ours once asked a prominent resident of one of these oases why the people did not make it easier for visitors to find their way in.

'It is not hard to get into our oasis,' the man replied. 'We just want to make it difficult for our friends to leave us.'

We have come upon Kufra suddenly from atop a plateau and the track into El Hawari is clear enough to follow. Four of us have gathered on the outskirts of the village. The Churchill car is missing. We are surrounded by men, children and flies. We shake hands all round and swat uselessly at the flies. These are tough flies and fearless. They thrive on blows and drink insecticide. We think they are the reincarnation of worthy Marines.

We all take pictures and Catherine makes an alarming hit with her Polaroid camera. She develops and distributes pictures trying vainly to keep some for herself, and starting a miniature war between those who have pictures and those who have not. The men and boys commence to push one another around, each in an attempt to be photographed alone. She ends by saying deceptively that she has no more film and retreats to her car, where she sits in stifling heat, the windows closed to keep the flies out, and writes in her diary about the beauties of the desert.

Liv converses with the headman in Arabic, Hank wheedles a little boy into accepting sweets in exchange for a home-made bird snare. I feel as though we have arrived at an island. We're a fleet of ships, and everyone has come to the harbour to see us sail in, to ask us where we're from and where we're going and what cargo we bring.

It is finally decided that Winston is what we, at any rate, regard as lost, and Francis takes Taffy and goes off to look for him. The rest of us proceed to El Giof, seat of government and chief of the Kufra oases. We hope to find some word from Benghazi at the police station. We are anxious to know whether we are free to get on with the trip, or whether a plane is in fact coming down which we will have to wait for. A radio and an operator are going to mean a lot of readjustment of our loads, and will add to our problems. Then there is the chance that Paul Barringer, from the American Embassy, and Colonel O'Lone will come for a visit. Catherine, of course, is hoping that Alan will be on the plane as well. We had also asked for another clutch-plate, as we are only carrying two spares, and oatmeal for Hank's traps—he is using all of our breakfast food.

From the oasis village of El Hawari we cross a desert plain before we climb the escarpment to Er Tag, the hill which mounts guard above El Giof. Here stands Leclerc's old headquarters, shell-marked and empty. General Leclerc was a famous tank commander of the French Army who was captured by the Germans at the time of the fall of France in 1940. He made an escape, and during the years of the German Occupation justified the hope and pride of his compatriots by his exploits in the Libyan Desert. In 1943 he led his Free French across some three thousand miles of trackless desert from Fort Lamy to join General Montgomery's Eighth Army in Tripoli. This was such an epic achievement as to be scarcely believable. *Operation Victory* by British Major-General Sir Francis de Guingand gives a first-hand account of Leclerc, who reported to Sir Francis on his arrival in Tripoli. He writes of the wonderful spirit which made it possible for this group of men, some French, some native soldiers, to make this remarkable trek. They had a motley collection of vehicles and were short of every comfort and of most necessities, food, clothes and medicines included. Describing the man de Guingand says:

I remember my first meeting with Leclerc. I was sitting in my caravan outside Tripoli when he arrived to report. At first I thought one of the characters of Wren's *Beau Geste* had come along to pay a call. His appearance personified the hardened French colonial soldier. He was thin and drawn, but intensely alert. His clothes had long since seen their day. Thin drill uniform with threadbare breeches, and old but shapely riding-boots. A French kepi completed the picture. He told me who he was and from whence he came. He said this just as you might say you had dropped over from the next village for tea. I took him along to the Army Commander, who shook hands and looked him up and down. Leclerc said, 'I place myself and my troops under your command.' Montgomery then said he accepted the offer, and told me to discuss with the French General details of his co-operation and matters affecting material and supplies. Later, Montgomery told me, 'I can make use of that chap.'

From what we have seen of this forbidding and desolate countryside we all think that General Montgomery's summing-up was probably one of the understatements of a war which was after all noted for its understatements.

Beyond Leclerc's old headquarters is the tomb of As-Senussi al Mahdi, father of the present king of Libya. Below in the oasis we see adobe houses; a few of them whitewashed, some in ruins; everywhere the date-palms tower and lean. Palms that have not been tended bush out from the ground, giving the place the appearance of a botanical garden. There are neither grass nor weeds, but patches of barley and wheat are fenced in and grown in rice-paddy fashion, with a handy well to draw water for the irrigation ditches. I wonder if we have lost our perspective, or is this green more brilliant than any we have ever seen?

The holy month of Ramadan is at its climax. The Mudir is away, and the police tell us that while someone seems to be trying to get a message through from Benghazi, it will not be received until the following day. We are invited to use the King's guest house, a pleasant whitewashed building in the centre of the village, but it is small and we are many. We decide to accept the hospitality of Mario de Mezis, a friend of Liv's in Benghazi, who has a date-processing factory here and has offered us the use of it. We will be able to drive our vehicles into the courtyard and close the gates against hordes of curious children; this will make unpacking and repacking easier. We go there now to wait for word from Francis and Winston.

At the date factory we find that Mario has other guests. Herr Janni, a German ornithologist, who speaks beautiful English, is in temporary-permanent residence. Signori Pandolfi, Bellini and Toia, Italian geologists, from the C.O.R.I. oil camp some hundred miles to the north-east, are there for the night. They seem happy to see us and are delightfully gallant. Catherine and I decide smugly that we're a rare commodity down here in the desert. They give us cold cokes, fresh bread and espressos. We sit around a table in the cool warehouse and talk.

Francis comes in at last, hot and glum, to report that Winston has burned out his clutch-plate. Taffy is already at work on it. We decide that we will presently go back to make camp at the work-site. In another day or so, when the repair is done and when the oil men have left the factory, we will return and join Herr Janni. But first we are going to the market, a twice-weekly affair which no one in Kufra wants to miss.

The flat and sandy expanse before the mosque and city hall is thick with people, camels, donkeys and flies. It is both brilliant and lively. But nothing we can see can possibly be so entertaining to us as we are apparently entertaining to the inhabitants of Kufra. Catherine and I have modestly put on slacks, and whether it is these trousers or our not-very-well-disguised shapes, or just that white women are a rarity here, we cause gales of laughter. One old crone, black and wrinkled, with pigtails protruding from the sides of her head and a silver ring in her nose, laughs so hard she

53

rocks, finally rolling in the dust. Later she chases after me and pats my hand, trying to stifle her giggles and spluttering 'Buono, buono.'

Italian is still spoken here, particularly by the older people. The Americans in our group speak Italian, and Liv and I also speak, we think, an impressive amount of Arabic. We have armed the others with a handful of useful phrases: *Ah-halan*, *marhaba*, and *keif halek* are all greetings. *Shukeran* means 'thank you'. *Kwais* means 'good', *mush kwais* 'no good', and *la* 'no'. *Min Fadlak* means 'please' and *Insh'allah* 'God willing'. But, most useful of all, and a phrase without which a Libyan could not talk at all, is *El Hamdullilah*—this means 'Praise be to God', and can be thrown in almost anywhere to keep things going should the conversation lag. At the market everyone tries out his new vocabulary, especially *la*, to the floods of children, who have learned from the flies how to pester. On a tide of giggles we hear the boys chant their own Scottish version of an Arab greeting. '*Ahlan-wa-sahlan* my name is M'Laughlan,' they intone, and we think there is a guttural similarity to the way both Scots and Arabs talk, as though the palate had been lobbed off.

We see many Tebu from the south, bringing wares from as far off as the Sudan; rhinoceros-hide whips, ostrich-feather fans, hammered knives sheathed in leather arm-bands, and a rich variety of dried foods, nuts and grains. We are especially interested in their faces. The Tebu and the few Tuareg we see are a black race, tall and finely boned; the Tuareg are famous for their blue eyes and the Tebu often have the aquiline features of American Indians. Though the tribes seem to be quite unrelated, in both of them the women are unveiled, while the men wind a scarf or the end of their turban across the bridge of the nose to cover the lower half of the face completely.

Kufra was originally inhabited by Tebu from the Tibesti, who a few hundred years ago were overrun by Arabs and converted from their pagan beliefs to Islam. Through the oasis went one of the main caravan routes between the Mediterranean and Central Africa. As late as 1913, the most profitable commodity traded was slaves. The slave trade is gone now, although it is said that slavery still exists nine hundred miles west among the Tuaregs in the Hoggar Mountains in and around Tamanrasset.

There is also some evidence of it in the Tibesti. Here the French, who have done everything to eradicate slavery, admit wryly that they are defeated when the slave, either born in slavery or bought in infancy, does not know he is a slave. However, the traffic is certainly dead. Caravans still ply, but they carry other wares today. Some of them have a disappointingly 'mail order' look to them too. We were told of one sheik who, leafing through a mail-order catalogue, was taken with three ready-made ladies' dresses displayed on attractive models. He sent in for them and was outraged when the dresses arrived without the girls.

Sleepy El Giof, with its scattering of mud huts, its quiet mosque, its long lagoon, surely harbours the ghosts of a thousand thousand tents. Here for almost a hundred years was the stronghold of the mighty Senussi when it was they who ruled the Sahara. Today the grandson of the Grand Senussi, Idris I, is King of Libya. His Majesty is building his new capital at Beida in the north, where his grandfather built his first Cyrenaican monastery, the Zawyia al Beida, or White Monastery. But Kufra, which played so dramatic a part in Senussi history, is all but forgotten.

The Grand Senussi was born in Algeria in 1787. Al-Sayyid Mahammad bin 'Ali al Sanusi al Khattabi al Idrisi al-Hasani was descended from Mohammed through his grandson al Hasan and was also descended from that Al Idris who, having rebelled against the Caliph Harun al-Rashid (of Arabian Nights fame), fled to Morocco where he founded a kingdom and where his son founded the city of Fez.

As-Senussi, as this man of many names was called, studied at Fez and as a young man wandered the desert from Morocco to Cairo, and finally to Mecca itself, preaching a reform of the faith. To go to the seat of any great religion and preach reform is surely work for none but a saint, and saint he seems to have been. At Mecca As-Senussi joined the Khaderite order of which he became head; and there, near Mecca, he founded his first monastery. As-Senussi was, as might be expected, looked upon with disfavour by the Ulema of Mecca, who considered him unorthodox, and finally succeeded in driving him from the city. From there he went to Cyrenaica to found the famous White Monastery. The story is told that when As-Senussi looked for a following to go as missionaries into the desert the local Marabout, or Holy Man, jealous of his influence, warned all men against having anything to do with this new and unorthodox order. The Grand Senussi, however, was one not to be easily stopped. A caravan of slaves had recently come from the south. As-Senussi bought the lot, freed them and put them through his school. When they were ready he sent them south to carry his teaching through the desert and to their own homes. The word commenced to spread that the world would find regeneration through the influence of a holy man who would bring others to lead temperate lives, to honour labour and self-restraint. Technically the Senussi are an order within the Mohammedan faith, whose tenets they follow with some additions and interpretations of their own. To the prohibition of alcohol is added that of tobacco and coffee, though drinking tea is not only allowed but encouraged. Nor is this an order of chastity or poverty. Much of the early following were drawn from wealthy and educated people. There was no prohibition against the wearing of fine clothes or the multiplicity of marriages. The present king was first married at Kufra at the age of seven, his wife being twenty-three. Marriages were many, divorces sometimes as soon as fifteen days after a marriage, and close family relationships no bar to marriage. Of course, in the matter of marriage the Senussi do not seem to differ in any way from other followers of Mohammed. Primarily the order teaches a pious life, permitting its following to interpret the Koran for themselves—which is in itself not customary. They encourage colonization and trade. In the early days this was especially important; wells were dug in the desert, oases cultivated, rest-houses built along caravan routes where merchants and missionaries were welcome. And so the Senussi movement grew, drawing followers from Morocco to the Sudan, from Constantinople to India, from Fez to Damascus.

Cyrenaica was at that time part of the Ottoman Empire. While As-Senussi's influence was a religious matter, it was increasing so rapidly that the Turks seem to have wondered where it might lead. They began to make difficulties for the Senussi and to dream up trouble for the people at Beida. As-Senussi was a man of religion, not war, and he decided to move his headquarters further south into the desert to Jaghbub. Here he founded an even greater religious school and collected an important library of Mohammedan literature. One of the modern mysteries of the desert is the whereabouts of this library today. It is said that during World War II the Italians decided that this famous library should be moved for safe keeping. The trucks carrying it away were lost and have never been heard of since. Perhaps some day travellers like ourselves will come upon them, waiting in the desert like the *Lady-Be-Good*, without a screw or bolt out of place, every precious scroll intact and no sign of drivers or crew or any indication of what might have happened to them. This desert is niggardly of yielding up its store of surprises.

When As-Senussi moved to Jaghbub it is said that he thought of the future of his following, and, calling his two sons before his entire Zawyia, he commanded them to climb the highest palm-tree of the oasis. He then ordered them in the name of Allah and his Prophet to leap to the ground. The younger of the two sons, Al Mahdi, leapt to the ground and was unharmed. The older boy refused. Therefore the younger, 'who feared not to commit himself to the will of God', was chosen as successor to his father, while the elder was to act as chief administrator. The Grand Senussi died in 1859 at Jaghbub, and As-Senussi al Mahdi, then fourteen years old, took up the mantle of holiness. As charming as this story is, the official geneology of the Senussi lists Al Mahdi as the elder son.

Al Mahdi was born in a cave near Massa in the country of the Bar-asa tribe, today a place of pilgrimage. It was he who brought the Senussi to Kufra—for the same reason that his father had moved from Beida to Jaghbub; for Al Mahdi, young though he was, seems to have followed closely in his father's footsteps, and the Turks were worried by the strength of his following. Al Mahdi brought law and order to the Bedouin, then still mar-vellously savage, and trade to the desert; and so in Kufra flourished the thousand thousand tents.

So far, the Senussi history had been one of resisting trouble, but at Kufra the Senussi had retreated as far as they could go. When the French commenced to move up from the Congo to-wards the western and southern borders of Wadai and to Lake Chad, then Senussi territory, Al Mahdi took up arms. Along the border heavily garrisoned monastery-forts sprang up to be used as trade posts and religious centres as well as for defence. But

Al Mahdi was old and not a soldier, and at one of these forts he finally died. The French were gaining on him, several of his Chad forts had been taken. A truly religious man who wanted nothing of war, this must have been a bitter end for him. He was brought to Er Tag for burial. The desert Bedouin believed him to be alive for many years, away on a secret journey.

At the time of the death of Al Mahdi, his son, the present king, was twelve years old. Mohammed al Idris studied at Jaghbub with his brother al-Rida, and later went to live in Egypt. In the meantime Ahmed A-Sherif, nephew of Al Mahdi, became leader of the Senussi, though he never called himself As-Senussi. During his rule the French took over Chad and the Senussi influence waned, though they remained at Kufra and continued to rule the desert oases and to have a large following in Egypt. In 1911 the Senussi joined the Turks to repel the Italians, a losing fight which they carried on in guerilla fashion long after the Turks had withdrawn. During World War I the Turks and the Germans persuaded the Sheik Ahmed to proclaim a Jihad, or holy war, against Egypt and so keep the British occupied on another front. Mohammed al Idris came from Egypt to try to dissuade his uncle from this venture, but Sheik Ahmed was already committed and did declare, and carry out briefly, a violent but abortive war in Egypt and the Sudan. When this failed the Sheik Ahmed retired to Turkey. In 1917 the Italians and the leader of the British recognized Idris as Senussi, and in 1919 Idris acknowledged Italian suzerainty under a treaty that gave him jurisdiction over the desert oases, including Jaghbub, Gialo and Kufra. In 1923, under Fascism, the Italians renounced the agreement, and Idris retired to Egypt. He had no desire to fight, for his interest, like that of his father and his grandfather, lay in a spiritual leadership. His brother Al Rida remained to carry on a diminishing guerilla warfare. By 1929 only Kufra was left to the Senussi.

During World War II, Idris, still living in exile in Cairo, rallied the tribes of Cyrenaica to the support of the British. His Cyrenaican Scouts served with the Eighth Army. In gratitude, the British assured the Senussi that Cyrenaica would never revert to Italian domination, and even before the end of the war Idris returned to his country as Emir of Cyrenaica. Less than six years later, after a jockeying for power between Italy, France, England

and Russia reminiscent of the nineteenth-century race for African territories, Libya gained her independence—the first of the new African nations.

Kufra's remoteness, the difficulty of reaching it, its history— coupling as it does religious fanaticism and desert power—have romance for any traveller who has heard of it. The first of these came to Kufra only eighty-three years ago. He was the German explorer Rholfs whose expedition was so ill-fated. He travelled with a large caravan, hostages were held in Benghazi against his safe return, and he carried with him gifts of great reputed value from the Emperor of Germany to the Senussi. The Rholfs expedition did reach Hawari but there, between treason within his ranks and the suspicion and resentment of the people of the oasis, calamity took over. Rholfs was imprisoned for a month and in constant danger of his life. He is said to have been rescued in the dark of night by a friendly sheik who got him safely back to Benghazi. There the sheik died and Rholfs came in for unfortunate suspicion of dark deeds. Why he should have harmed his benefactor is a mystery which only the oriental mind can fathom. I think in some lovely Machiavellian way this myth was fostered to discourage fellow arabs from rescuing embattled 'unfaithfuls'. The next European visitor to Kufra can't have enjoyed his trip much more for he was a French prisoner of war sent down by Ahmed A-Sherif and is said to have spent some time there. The next expedition of note was that of Rosita Forbes and Hassenein Bey in 1921. Miss Forbes, the first white woman to make this journey, still in 1921 a dangerous adventure, wrote a fascinating account in her book *The Secret of the Sahara: Kufara*. Her companion on this trip, Hassenein Bey, was an Egyptian explorer, an Oxford graduate and a man of some importance in the Islamic world. He had been secretary to the Italo-British Mission which arranged the treaty of 1916 with the Senussi. From the photograph of him reproduced in *The Secret of the Sahara* he was handsome in a lean saturnine way and from Miss Forbes's description was possessed of both wit and humour. They both would have needed that for this was no easy trip. They went by camel, which means that they walked much of the way, for in the desert the camel is used more as a pack-animal than for riding. Agedabia on the coast to Hawari, the first oasis in the Kufra group, which we have made in a week, took them more than a month. For this epic achievement Miss Forbes wore Arab dress and lived spartanly on tinned meat, rice, flour and dates. Forty years later she is still talked of here with a wonder and admiration that no car-borne creature can hope to equal. Hassanein Bey, who has been back several times, is now dead. Miss Forbes, married to a British colonel, lives on a remote island in a house that could only have been built by a great romantic. Still young in spirit and appearance, she has a garden-party look to her, and it is hard to visualize her trudging day after day over these burning sands. But she did it and she has continued through the years to find out the surprising and the adventurous.

Winston has chosen a reasonably good spot for his breakdown; a bit of hard desert with some convenient dunes near by. We square off the cars and make ourselves comfortable, for we will be here a good twenty-four hours. We are near the oases and children apparently will walk miles to see a circus such as ours. They form a ring around us and hunker down to watch. We will do guard duty tonight.

Francis bought ninety eggs at market today and a basket of tomatoes. Everyone wants his eggs done differently. It is cold and damp again tonight and the guard drapes himself in a groundsheet. When it is Winston's turn to do guard duty I watch from one sleepy eye as he lurches by, almost completely hidden by his father's greatcoat. It is as though the ghost of Randolph keeps watch upon us.

20TH MARCH

WE TRY MAKING pancakes on a tray but it melts and the cakes are shot with glittering bits of lead. Catherine has discovered sweet little footprints round her bed which Hank says are fox. She doesn't think the guard was very good, after all. Liv and I go off to explore and Catherine washes her hair in petrol, to save water, and then watches with disgust as the men all do an enormous quantity of laundry, disappear behind a tarpaulin with full jerry-cans of water and reappear with empties.

Some children have brought us a couple of scrawny chickens and Frank, in a pair of brilliant blue bathing-tights, is plucking them while he sunbathes. Charlie is washing his feet. The sun climbs high and hotly into place, and the men rig a shade between cars into which everybody crawls. Catherine is still reluctantly puttering about the kitchen-stove area, having embarked upon a batch of corn bread. But presently she too creeps into the shade and asks everybody please to put out their cigarettes on account of her hair, which reeks of petrol. Winston is sleeping with a book under his head. He is on a sort of reading-leave from Oxford and has a stack of books with him which he keeps with his boots in his father's icebox. Francis is reading something called *The Black Baroness* and he is not asleep. Hank has a board full of raw mice in front of him, and Archie is writing a long letter. Catherine thinks it must be to a sweetheart as in her experience mothers get postcards. Archie, who is sweet-natured and always helpful, looks more Latin than ever now with his black, pointed beard. We feel that he would be quick on the draw in the defence of a lady, and perhaps nippy at rolling the dice. It is characteristic of Archie that when he gets epically drunk, which has happened once or twice in his career, he is a crusader. After all, he did defend our little band the other night against forty million Russians, and once he seriously damaged a military hospital because he thought the patients needed cheering up. He sketches and draws cartoons, and has had work printed in newspapers at home in Scotland. He is keeping a route report and helps Francis with navigation, since he too has had a course on it.

Taffy's real name is Bryan Jones, a good name and a pity not to use it, but then to the rest of the world how can a Welshman not be called Taffy? Like the other boys Taffy says that the expedition is that chance in a lifetime that he never expected to come his way. I am beginning to think that scratch even the most solid citizen and you will find a vagabond at heart. Taffy grew up in a mining village. His father was a coal-miner until his health gave out and he went into office work. His mother belonged to the old school of religious, hard-working women who make the character of a nation. Certainly Taffy learned to work, though he says the Army has made him lazy. When he left school he apprenticed himself to a trade and for five years went to night school, finally getting his full technological and National Craftsmen's Certificate. Not a dreamer, you'd say, yet here he is worshipping the stars and the lure of the horizon with the rest of us. He is a quiet boy with a gentle way to him. Catherine and I have wondered before whether he is deeply religious, or just quietly a devil. He has that beautiful musical Welsh tongue in his head, and we cannot understand a word he says. Whatever his magic, by nightfall the new clutch-plate is in place and Winston's car is running smoothly. Taffy and John now have a fine look of coal miners to them, a jet-black nonchalance. We give them two full jerries of water.

In the morning we will move on to El Giof. Our Italian friends stop off to see us on their way back to their own camp. They have a radio mounted on their C.O.R.I. jeep, and we ask them to contact Benghazi. We have only one spare clutch-plate left and want another spare for insurance. Then, of course, there is always that oatmeal. The Italians have difficulty transmitting 'oatmeal' which doesn't translate readily. They entice us to visit their camp which they say has much better mice, and lovely little white foxes as well. They take off in a whirl of sand, first kissing the women's hands, which makes Francis scowl as he thinks that it is effete and he doesn't see why we should look so pleased, anyway.

The two scrawny chickens stretch amazingly well. We've stewed them up with this and that, and everyone is hungry and pleased. We have tea with our dinner, and go to bed early and to sleep quickly.

ONE WEEK FROM Benghazi. On our
| 21ST MARCH | way across the sands that separate Hawari from El Giof we meet a caravan: two turbaned men in billiant blue robes, with fifteen camels and a herd of nubian goats. Each of the camels carries a full load, each a couple of garbas, which are goatskins filled with water, and one has a brilliantly striped tent strapped to its back. With a little French, a little Arabic, and a few lines in the sand the drivers tell us that they have come from Faya where we will be

heading in a day or so. It has taken them forty-three days. While we think happily that it will take us only four or five, Catherine asks them when they are going back. She would like to leave us and go with them. We say, 'Yes, dear,' and lead her away thinking of things with which to distract her. Alan is always complaining that she is unrealistic about time and we think that he has something. He might just say unrealistic and let it go at that.

The Kufra date-processing factory is at the moment not processing dates. We drive our cars into the courtyard and commence to unpack. The men put their gear and cots into a large storeroom, already full of sorting-tables and stacks of collapsed cardboard boxes. Liv, Catherine, I and the kitchen share the second warehouse room with Herr Janni. He offers courteously to go away, but we will not hear of it.

'Why, we have been sleeping with all sorts of people,' I assure him. 'Catherine and I won't mind sleeping with you at all.'

Desert travellers never show a blush, but Herr Janni does rig a blanket in one corner of the great room and the area behind this blanket is as neat and immaculate as a monk's cell.

Not so the rest of the room. We have to reorganize for the next leg of our trip. We have learned something about desert travel and we think we now know how to fit a load together so that the one thing most needed, like the salt or the can-opener, is not under half a ton of stuff we won't need until we get to Zouar. The cars are completely emptied and the men are servicing them. Contents are stacked and strewn about our community bed-dining-room. In addition, Catherine and I have done an impressive quantity of laundry and this is strung across the courtyard and zig-zagging on plastic lines about the room. Water is plentiful here as there is a well in the yard. It only requires a bucket, a long rope and a strong man to wind the winch. Toilet facilities are one jump from the stone age: primitive, casual and hygienically negligible. However, the throne-like adobe outhouse has a certain charm in that rabbits are kept in it, and pigeons coo soothingly from its roof. It is fenced off from the rest of the courtyard with a garden gate. Catherine says that she found Archie leaning on the gate early one morning talking

63

to the rabbits. He opened the gate for her without batting an eye and went away whistling.

Herr Janni, we learn, is on vacation from his job in an American library in Berlin. He goes out all day with his binoculars to study bird migrations. He says that the daytime fliers drop like stones when the sun goes down and that today he has seen the first white stork on its way to South Africa. He also studies the meteorological conditions here and in the early morning, before the rest of us are awake, he goes out to whirl his hygrometer. During the war he was a member of Rommel's Afrika Korps, and since then has returned several times to Libya on scientific expeditions. He has accepted our swarming into his domain with philosophy and good spirit, and we have been happy in return to have him share our table. Every one of us has felt the impact of what Herr Janni is, surely of the last of the individuals; a man without a foundation, grant, scholarship or Fulbright, or other hand-out backing him, pioneering on a shoestring—bird-watching in the Sahara, not knowing any more than his brother birds do whether or how he is going to get out of the place. He is trying, with the help of an Arab friend, to make arrangements to hire a camel caravan to take him to the Sudan.

The long-awaited wireless message has been received. It is from the Royal Air Force Base at El Adem, whence the plane we are expecting will come, via Benghazi. It asks how many drums of aviation petrol are on hand at the Kufra airport and requests that we kindly see that all jerboa-holes on the runway are filled in.

Liv went out to count the drums and check on the rat-holes. The hangar, or what framework is left of it after numerous bombings and twenty years of nature's sand-blasting, contains five separate dumps of petrol and oil. None bore any markings, but presently an old man shuffled up from somewhere and pointed out the drums that belong to the R.A.F. He said that the rat-holes are few and small as it has been a bad year. There are only about thirty drums, but counting them took a good half-hour as the old man had his own system, which was to scramble over the top of the stack, thumping alternately with his elbow and palms, while he chanted out a sort of counting litany. Liv counted twenty-eight, while the old man came up with twenty-

Miggs Pomeroy looking cheerful

Camels with humps

We advance in mouse formation

six. The next time round, Liv got twenty-six and the old man twenty-five. In the next count Liv got twenty-nine, but by now the old man's antics were making him dizzy and he thinks he may have included the old boy in his count. They settled on twenty-five. Once back in the village, the old man told Liv that the count does not mean much as some of the drums are empty and some contain oil.

We still don't know who is coming on the R.A.F. plane. It should be in tomorrow and perhaps Alan will be on it. People who don't have arthritis hopefully expect it to be cured by a call on the doctor. Liv and I are praying for letters from the children; Francis is probably praying for something to happen to the wireless, whose extra five-hundred-pounds weight is giving him nightmares. Catherine is certainly praying for Alan to drop out of the skies, and perhaps Hank is praying for oatmeal.

For the first time in a week we sleep under a roof, and the more urban the individual the louder his complaint. We are old desert rats unaccustomed to walls and ceilings. We miss our stars and cannot sleep in these enclosures.

| 22ND MARCH |

THIS MORNING WE pay our respects and deliver the letter from the Governor to the Mutaserif, Mr. Bufarwa. The Chief of Police, Mr. Susi and the Kaimakaan, Sheik Mohammed Salih, who is head of the Zawiya—the school run by the Senussi—are also there to receive us. Mr. Susi and Mr. Bufarwa wear tarbooshes and the former has on a raincoat, although it has not been known to rain in Kufra in twenty years. The Sheik is handsome and jovial, his turban is white and his beard flowing. He wears a blue kafkan embroidered in gold, and he talks with evident pleasure of Rosita Forbes and Hassanein Bey whom he told us returned many times to Kufra. We are in a long reception-room with chairs along the sides and a desk at one end. A portrait of the King as a young man hangs on the wall, and in a handsome frame on the desk is a picture of an ashtray and a burning cigarette—advertising a well-known brand. Although there is no electricity in Kufra a solitary light bulb hangs from the ceiling. We realize as we sit down just how infrequent visitors are. The arm falls off Catherine's chair and a cloud of dust spurts up from Winston's.

Liv, as leader of the expedition and diplomat into the bargain, opens the conversation with a flowing exchange of formal salutation. He translates for us and we all ask questions. While we drink the ritual three glasses of tea, boiled with mint leaves and heavily sugared, we learn that olives, pomegranates and figs are raised here as well as dates. Wheat and millet are also grown and some flowering trees called susayas acacia. We find Kufra warm, but our hosts all laugh when we say that it is like summer. They think we should come back in summer and we would change our minds. We are offered sweets and biscuits. We think that Mr. Bufarwa has a very sweet tooth. The Sheik asks Winston after the health of his grandfather and says that of course he himself is a good deal younger, being only seventy. We take pictures and as we leave Liv translates that His Excellency 'hopes to God we will soon be on our way'. Adding firmly, 'And I hope so too,' Liv asks permission to take a moving picture of Their Excellencies, but we cannot convince them that it is permissible to move during the photographing. I try to speed the action but am left with my hand out and no one to shake it as our actors stand in frozen dignity.

By noon the R.A.F. plane has not appeared, and we know that they will not start out late in the day. We have decided to take this opportunity to visit Jebel Sherif. Hank will remain at Kufra to trap, and we will take only two cars; with Francis, Winston and John in one, Liv, Catherine and myself in the other. We will look for traces of the Long Range Desert Group/Italian skirmish at Jebel Sherif, about eighty miles south of Kufra. We had been impressed with Kennedy Shaw's account of it in his book *Long Range Desert Group*, and the incredible walk by Moore. We wanted to try to find the burnt-out British and Italian trucks.

According to Kennedy Shaw, 'T' patrol of L.R.D.G., on 31st January 1941, were coming north from the Chad when they were attacked in a valley among the rocks of Jebel Sherif by an Italian motorized patrol. Their officer, Clayton, had eleven cars and thirty-odd men, and the enemy five cars and forty-five men, with four 22 mm. Breda guns and three aircraft overhead working in close co-operation with their ground force. The Italians entered the valley from the north, and it was not very long before three British trucks were burning and a British officer and two Italian prisoners on his truck killed. Clayton was wounded and taken prisoner and the rest of the patrol withdrew south. Unknown to them, four of their men remained alive at Jebel Sherif, hiding among the rocks until the Italians turned north again for Kufra.

Now they were alone. As Kennedy Shaw says, the alternatives were not attractive: to make for Kufra and surrender to the Italians, or to follow the tracks of their own patrol southwards in the hope they would be picked up. They chose the latter. From Mr. Shaw's book, this* is the record of the next ten days:

So at dawn on February 1st this was the position. Moore—wounded in the foot. Easton—wounded in the throat. Tighe, Winchester. An Italian. A two-gallon tin of water with a bullet-hole through it near the top and containing about one and three-quarter gallons. No food. The clothes they wore; everything else had been burnt in the trucks. . . .

February 1st—Walking southwards following the tracks of the patrol. At some period during this day the Italian disappeared and was picked up by his own people.

February 2nd and 3rd—Walking. The night temperatures here at this time must have been near freezing and it was almost impossible to get any sleep and rest.

February 4th—Tighe beginning to tire; he was feeling the effects of an old operation. They found and ate some lentils thrown away after a meal on their way north.

February 5th—Tighe could not keep up so he was left with his share of the water in a bottle which they had picked up. Later, when he came to drink it, he found that something the bottle had contained had made the water salty and almost undrinkable.

February 6th—Sandstorm. The car tracks almost obliterated and very hard to follow. (In the soft sand of the desert, where your foot slips back at every step, one pace is equal—in effort—to three on a hard road.) The first three reached Sarra, 135 miles from Jebel Sherif. At

* *Reproduced by kind permission of Messrs. Collins.*

Sarra is a well, two hundred feet deep, which the Italians had filled in, with a few mud huts nearby. In them they found some waste motor-oil and bathed their feet and also made a fire out of odd bits of wood. There was no food.

February 7th—Three walking on. The tracks still hard to see. Tighe reached Sarra and sheltered in the huts, unable to follow the others. On the ground he found *one* match. It did not fail and he got some comfort from a fire.

February 8th—Three walking on. Tighe at Sarra.

February 9th—Late on in the evening of the 9th a party of French with Mercer-Nairne reached Sarra from the north. They were returning from a reconnaissance of Kufra . . . and had visited Jebel Sherif, buried Beech and the Italians, and called in at Sarra. The Sarra–Kufra track is wide and ill-defined, and the northward-bound French had missed Moore and the others. In a hut they found Tighe, weak but conscious. (Imagine his feelings when he heard the sound of their cars!) With his first words he told them of the others ahead. The French tried to follow their footmarks in the sand but in the dark this was impossible and they had to wait till dawn. Meanwhile the others had been walking on. Easton had dropped behind. During the day a French aircraft sighted Moore and Winchester and realized, I suppose, the plight they were in. The ground was too rough for a landing, but the pilot circled round and dropped food and a canvas bag of water. The food Moore and Winchester could not find; the cork of the water bag was knocked out in its fall and when they got it only a mouthful or two remained.

February 10th—At first light the rescue party left Sarra. They followed the three men's footsteps and after a time one set turned vaguely off to the west. At the end of them they found Easton, fifty-five miles from Sarra, lying on the ground but alive. Fortunately the French had with them a doctor who took Easton back to Sarra and all that day strove to save his life. But help had come too late and at seven in the evening he died. He kept his sense of humour to the end. The French made some tea for him, weak and sweet. Easton drank it and smiled. 'I like my tea without sugar,' he said.

Meanwhile another party was following Moore and Winchester. Sixty-five miles from Sarra, Winchester could not continue and Moore gave him half the remaining water—one mouthful—and pushed on. Here the French found him, near delirium but able to stand up when he heard their cars. Ten miles further south they overtook Moore, then about 210 miles from Jebel Sherif and marching steadily southwards. He felt confident that in three days he could reach Tekro, the nearest water, eighty miles ahead, and was slightly annoyed, so Mercer Nairne told me, at being prevented from proving that he could.

It has taken us three hours to reach Jebel Sherif. We have light loads, the going is excellent, Francis's navigation faultless. We have managed to stay in two-wheel drive all of the way, travelling sometimes at fifty miles an hour. We arrive at sunset and camp on the northern slope of the Jebel, which is a range of black rock outcroppings rising from a flat plain. It is too late to look for the battle site tonight. We make camp and have a quick supper and Liv puts out some traps for Hank, then everyone but Catherine climbs into one of the cars for a night hunt. Crossing the plain earlier we had seen a fresh camel-carcass and Liv thinks that we might find hyena or jackal feeding. It would be a good catch to take back to Hank. We set out across the plains swinging the big spotlight as we go. Catherine, who is in any case not interested in hunting, has decided that this is her chance to see how it feels to be alone. Travelling in the desert there is little opportunity to be really alone and she sometimes thinks that it is one of those things impossible to imagine being as it is so outside of normal experience. Watching the car lights until they are blotted out on the plain, she takes a flashlight and, half scrambling half sliding, makes her way down the slope into the long dark valley. The flash is to help her keep a wary eye out for snake and scorpion, than which she would rather come face to face with a Gorgon. The silence has a singing quality which is infinitely soothing, and the mind acts as a vacuum-cleaner whishing in thoughts and images from the cosmos about. In this still, barren and empty place all of the unused thoughts in the world seem to have come to rest, and then unavoidably she thinks of the battle fought here those twenty years ago: gunfire, explosion, roar of flaming tank or scream of the mortally wounded were a brief interruption of this continuing silence which runs at once into the past and into the future. There is a voice for the dead and a voice for the living here and a great sense of compassion. Turning at last back to camp, the mountain looms like a volcano and the stars are burning sparks shooting out of its black top.

In the desert we hunters find the dead camel undisturbed. 'There can't be any life around here,' Liv says, 'or something would be feeding. This carcass is going to mummify in the sun without a single bite being taken out of it.'

No jackal, no hyena, no fox; but recrossing the plain we pick up a desert mouse in the car lights. John lowers his rifle, which he has held at the ready.

'What a trophy to take back to barracks!' he says in disgust. But Liv jumps out of the car and tries to net the little creature with his coat. I train the spotlight on him as he zigzags long-legged across the desert, lunges and comes down on his face. The mouse pauses and then hops away to shouts and laughter from us all.

| 23RD MARCH |

DURING THE NIGHT the wind blows hard from the south carrying a gale of sand over the saddle of the hills and piping it into our sleeping-bags. By turning round, heads north and strictly downhill, with only noses out for air, we manage to sleep a little. By morning we are coated with sand and, though the wind has dropped, it is cold and we are reluctant to get up. Liv collects Hank's traps, not one of which has been disturbed, and we breakfast on black tea and oatmeal blocks, one of the best of the 'compo' items. We break camp and set out along the base of the hills looking for wartime traces. Before long we come upon tracks which seem to have been made yesterday. We wonder who has come this way and why we heard nothing in Kufra of another expedition. We investigate a camp-site where a shining can of Palethorpe's sausages, the label only slightly faded, further misleads us until we see that it is dated 1939. Dry air has preserved the paintings in Pharaohs' tombs for five thousand years. If we leave it here will Palethorpe's pig one day become the treasure of a great museum? Having encircled the first outcropping of hills we turn south where a conical hill stands alone. It has a marker on top indicating that we are on the main Kufra–Sarra track. Directly eastward of this marker is another outcropping of hills, and here we enter a narrow pass into a broad valley or bowl among the hills. There are tracks leading in and almost immediately we find first a burnt-out Italian truck, and a little further on two British trucks with three graves beside them. Two of the graves are mounded up with stones, one is marked with a rough cross made from a packing-case. Further on is another British truck, its Egyptian licence plate still readable (the Long Range Desert Group was based in Cairo)and on the fender a Maori name, for this detachment of L.R.D.G. were New Zealanders. The vehicles are riddled with bullet and shrapnel holes, the sand littered with debris, fused glass, twisted metal, pieces of wool from sweaters and gloves, bullets, fragments of grenades. John Ferguson finds an Italian coin in the sand and rubble of one of the British trucks, presumably the one which carried the Italian prisoners. Winston finds the much-battered lens of a camera. We dig carefully for fear of disturbing live ammunition. I find a tin of bully beef which we open. The meat in it is shrunken and smelly but still moist. Had it been buried in the sand instead of exposed on the surface it might well have remained fresh; as it is it has been baking in the sun, cooling off at night, for more than twenty years. Under the trucks, oil from their engines lies in black ribbons.

We try to reconstruct the battle—the British convoy coming from the south, taken by surprise, three of its trucks cornered in this valley by the Italians. We imagine the feelings of the men left alone here. Francis and John who are soldiers must feel it in their bones; and Liv and Catherine and I have had war losses. Winston, while awed, is still young enough to be insouciant. We talk of opening the graves to identify them, but feel that we have no right to. It is a place that we shall all remember. Here is silence more than sadness and we intrude upon a desperate moment which, although done with twenty years ago, and part of history, we should perhaps not have come to disturb with our probing hands and voices.

On the way back to Kufra we scorn to navigate and lose ourselves for two groping hours. We have found sand-cliffs and an ancient lake-bed which we have raced across and a land of little dunes the size of haycocks which we ploughed amongst cursing the moment we so lightly deserted our own tracks, made yesterday, for a short cut. We come suddenly upon an oasis which we flounder through, bogging and sand-tracking repeatedly. We do not see any house or tent or sign of life and the date-palms are wild and untended. Out of the oasis on hard sand again we come upon camel tracks and follow them into another oasis where we find someone to set us right for El Giof. Over-confidence is one of the real dangers in desert travel and we feel that we have been lucky, though Francis scoffs that he could always have gone to work and found out exactly where we were. 'Along the coast of Italy?' we tease.

Back at the date factory we find that the plane is in and six R.A.F. men await us, with Jack Thompson and his unwelcome five-hundred-odd pounds of radio. No Colonel O'Lone, no Paul Barringer, no Alan. Also no oatmeal. There is a touching heart-shaped letter from our children and for Catherine a letter from Alan and a box of presents: two Tilly lanterns, a bottle of white petrol, sun-tan lotion and sweets for the 'troops'. He has also forwarded down to her letters from her two boys. Duff who is studying geology at Princeton, and for whom she is making her weighty collection of rocks, writes that he has heard that slaves can still be bought in the desert and while Princeton does not allow students to keep pets there is no ruling on slaves, so would she please bring back a couple. Pretty ones of course. Pom, aged nine, writes that he will come 'emdjutly' if she wants him and school is awful as usual.

Francis is fulminating because he has had no letter from his girl and because of the radio and the concise orders to take it no matter what else we may have to jettison. We discuss doing without some of our food, water or petrol and know that we cannot. Catherine sees more than one speculative eye turn on her boxes of stones and decides to hide them somewhere at the bottom of the load in car No. 2.

We have a chaotic evening with twenty people to feed. These include the R.A.F. who have not brought food or equipment of any sort with them, and the Greek doctor who runs the small hospital here. We have to eat in relays as we do not have enough plates or implements. Garbage is piling up, mail being read and answered; Francis is plotting tomorrow's course on the table surrounded by food, half-empty mugs and tins of melted butter. The R.A.F. stagger us by daring to ask for hot water to wash in.

The stove is taken up with food preparation and the well is a hundred feet deep and icy cold. Only the women get their water drawn for them. We decide sourly that the R.A.F. is too clean anyway. But our soldiers see to their water and the friendly Greek doctor has beds brought for them from the hospital. They are taking a patient from his hospital to Tobruk tomorrow and they offer to take letters. Catherine writes to Alan, a long letter which he receives two months later on his return to New York. She thinks the R.A.F. carried it about as a mascot. While unprovisioned, the airmen did have a sort of picnic lunch with them and I have discovered bread and tinned salmon which I have confiscated without qualms.

While we have been to Jebel Sherif Hank has lost all of his steel traps for fox or larger animals. The loss is put to curious children who have doubtless had their fill of the archaic stick-and-stone snares of their forefathers. A plea to the Mutaserif is listened to with sympathy, but whatever efforts he makes to recover the traps are unfruitful. We have stayed overlong in Kufra and traps or no traps we must leave by dawn. Hank is depressed and we all feel for him.

24TH MARCH

TEA AND SHREDDED wheat and bully beef for breakfast at six-thirty. Everything washed up and packed up and ready to leave by seven-thirty-five. We've filled the airmen's thermos with tea but have no pots or eating-irons to spare so cannot leave them other food. In any case they'll be in Tobruk for lunch, so won't starve. We are off now for Uweinat, three hundred and twenty-five miles to the south-east, and almost on the Libyan–Egyptian–Sudanese border. Uweinat is an isolated mountain range where there are said to be some very fine primitive rock-paintings. The morning run is magnificent. We do a hundred miles in about four hours, stop for lunch under a boiling sun, with shade a two-by-four square directly behind the cars. With midday our luck has left us. We are in undulating dunes, roller-coasters of soft sand. All five cars have bogged repeatedly. For a while we are trapped among the crested dunes. Francis in

73

the lead is our guinea-pig, to test out just how sheer each drop is. He thinks he should have danger pay. Even standing on top of these dunes, it takes a few seconds to realize just how precipitous the drop is, especially at high noon when the sun casts no helpful shadows. We test out the dunes, we sand-track, we are careful not to walk in front of any bogged car for fear of breaking what crust there is. It is as grim an afternoon as we have had and yet everyone is cheerful. Frank walks along from one rescued car to the next victim strumming his sand track like a guitar and singing as he goes.

And now No. 4 car has burned out her clutch. We are in soft sand and making camp is going to be tricky. We find a ridge or slight rise with patches of reasonably hard sand and we distribute ourselves about on this. Two days' camp, to repair No. 4, will break what crust there is, anyway, so perhaps we are being needlessly choosy. Taffy gets into overalls, Jack Thompson hauls out his portable aerial and rigs it with the help of a couple of the boys. Liv gets the charcoal fire going. We've opened a tin of ham and are making candied sweet potatoes. The British have never tasted them and are very suspicious. To make up for this barbarian dish we also serve apple sauce, biscuits, raisins, tea and whisky. The sun is down, plummeting over the edge of the earth like molten lead. The afterglow sweeps the desert, taking our breath away, and then it is dark and the stars spring out as though a switch had been touched. Venus sets at eight o'clock, such a sparkling green and red we think at first there is another camp across the desert from us and are cheered at the thought of other living creatures in this wilderness.

It is cold again tonight and Catherine has a pain in her neck, not figuratively, she says, but positively. She says that she got it hunched over writing her diary in the car. Desert travel being what it is, we don't think she is ever going to be able to re-read this document. Her normally neat handwriting has developed the archaic look of cuneiform. Winston, who hots up the water for the two Churchill bottles every night (same water used throughout the trip), tucks me in with Randolph's and contributes his own to relieve Catherine's crooked neck. My arm is out of the cast much of the time these days and not bothering me, but I'm glad of the bottle for my toes.

THE MEN HAVE rigged tarpaulins, one by No. 4 so that Taffy and John can work without being fried alive and one in front of No. 5 for us to loaf and lunch. Francis has taken Winston and Hank and two others to make a reconnaissance and see if they can find the marked track for Uweinat. The big group is for digging the car out should they bog. They find the track about ten kilometres ahead. A marked track consists of an iron post on the top of a dune, outcropping or any available high spot. Alternately cairns of rock are used; these are so obviously heaped up by man that they cannot be mistaken. The markers are approximately five kilometres apart and each should be visible from the one before or after it. However, the iron posts cannot be relied upon as they are sometimes blown down by the wind, and sometimes stolen for tent poles by Bedouin.

At camp Liv spends most of the day under his car repairing the speedometer; he is very sweaty and hot-looking when seen at all. Catherine and I have made Bikini tops from the bright orange distress-signal flags. We want to roll back into Benghazi with impressive tans. When the reconnaissance party has returned we all crowd under the tarp and eat bread-and-cheese, peanut butter (a discovery for the British who pick at it suspiciously but declare in favour), sardines packed in oil, which we decide has once seen the inside of a petrol-drum, and tinned fruit. Frank regales us with stories about officers, none of whom does he seem mad about. 'Noo,' he says, 'sum of them air verra wet, excusin' me, Misterr Gibb sorr.' There is no enthusiastic dissent from the other men. Liv tells them that all armies are alike and they are made quite happy hearing how hard an American soldier's life can be. Winston spends the afternoon napping with a book from his 'required reading' shading his face to keep the light out. Charlie is sun-bathing behind one of the cars. He is very fair and will probably burn and thus can be his own first patient.

Unlike the wastes of Southern California, Arizona and New

Mexico, this is no living desert. In some places—and this is one of them—it is completely devoid of life, and man or beast may die, and even the bacteria are not there to decay the flesh. Eventually the wind-blown sand cleans the bones down to a glaring sculpture in white. Distorted by shimmering layers of hot desert air, a heap of bones may look from a distance like a tall white spire, or, stranger still, a white cloud floating above the horizon. Only a couple of years ago a Polish explorer left Kufra for Uweinat with a guide and a pack camel. No one knows just what happened, a fight of some sort certainly. For in the night the guide 'folded his tent, like the Arabs, and as silently stole away'. He says that they ran out of water and that the Pole would not take his advice, so rather than die with his employer he returned to his home. The Pole was found two weeks later completely mummified. No kindly Mother Nature here. We have talked of dying of thirst. It is not quickly done. Some say the victim goes mad first. Certainly every bit of body-liquid is consumed, and when that is gone pain takes over. Liv thinks the eyes must be the first to go and the worst. Catherine agrees; nothing can be worse than to be blind and in such agony that there is no room even for fear. She is rather an eye-minded person in any case, and carries four pairs of glasses about her. She has a pair of sunglasses, an extra-dark pair called elephant-glasses, glasses for ordinary use and for reading. She is always mislaying them and they turn up in various cars according to whom she has been visiting. Liv instructs her when dying of thirst to use the last bit of moisture to dampen a cloth or whatever is available to cover the eyes. As to thirst itself, that marvellously informative document *Desert Survival* (by Alonzo Pond and Paul Nesbitt) says if there is nothing to drink avoid eating, as food will not sustain you but only cause great agony. You can go seven days without food and if you are not rescued by then you are finished in any case. By no means drink alcohol, blood or urine, all of which contain a heavy residue of protein. If you have a camel available you may cut into his stomach and drink the liquid which, while not Coca-Cola, is apparently better for you than whisky, blood or urine. It is also said that if you gut the animal and crawl into the damp shady cavity thus created you will further prolong your chance of survival. Catherine and I wonder if it's worth it.

76

We also think that a rescue unit might insist on your walking home well in the rear of the party.

The sun is boiling hot but the shade pleasantly cool. Despite the lack of life in this desert an armour-plated insect with striped legs has appeared out of nowhere. I've offered it bits of bread but it seems to want my toes. I've moved twice but it only follows me around. I'm afraid it's going to want to come to Tibesti with us. Anyway, I don't understand what it lives on out here where there is nothing. Liv thinks that it may have come in the car from Kufra, which gives one to think of what else may be in the cars. Catherine says in that case we can't abandon it here but it's not to travel in No. 2. She says it looks gaunt and hungry. The boys say if I'd just stop fidgeting about they will find out if it is a carnivore. I have retreated to the car where I am pretending to read. Not that I am afraid, of course. I notice that the others have all found excuses to take themselves off, leaving our six-legged stowaway to scamper from one cot, sleeping-bag or blanket to another.

The scorpions, which Liv promised Catherine would only be around an oasis, keep themselves pretty invisible, though we have seen tracks where they have scurried crab-like between our beds at night. Catherine, since she first heard that both scorpions and snakes will curl up into the toe of a shoe, has been taking her shoes to bed with her. She says that if they were dainty little shoes it would be all right, but she keeps stumbling over them in her sleep. Hank has not bothered to set the traps out here. In some parts of the desert, such as this, you never see a mouse-track; in others, seemingly as arid, there are thousands of them. The foxes and jackals, so common in the oases, hardly ever venture into the real desert, though Hank thinks that they occasionally do, during the season when birds migrate.

Birds more than anything else give one a realization of the immensity of the desert. It seems reasonable enough that a man or animal could die of thirst; but should not a bird, figuratively and literally, be above this? But even they are not, poor things. However swift their flight they have to go sometimes hundreds of miles to find water, and all of the time fighting air so thin they must use twice the energy and develop a thirst twice as fast as they normally would. Every bit of shade, outcropping of rock, the hulk of any abandoned truck, the north side of any jettisoned oil-drum harbours a few dried-up feathers or a pathetic little mound of white bones. For some reason wagtails and swallows suffer the most. Perhaps what I first thought was inquisitiveness was a desperate search for shade, for they often come into camp. On several occasions we have put water for them, but none of us have seen them take any. Hawks and falcons manage to survive in the bleakest spots, but then they have the migrating birds to feed on. We have seen many of them on the loneliest craggiest outcroppings. Where they have roosted, the ground below is littered with castings of feathers and bones.

Taffy and John are covered with black oil and glory. They have replaced the clutch-plate in No. 4 in ten hours. We will be able to start off at dawn. Liv has fixed his speedometer, and Francis has finished *The Black Baroness*. Not knowing how long we might be over the breakdown, he has been very military over 'water discipline' and we are all thirsty. Winston has been cheering us all on by saying that if the worst comes to the worst he will let us drink the hot-water-bottle water. We watch Venus set with pleasure tonight.

| 26TH MARCH | THERE IS WIND in the night, and while we intend to get off at dawn it is just too hard dragging ourselves out |

of our warm cocoons. Everything is covered with layers of dust. We can all hear the sand on our teeth; it is gritty like sugar, but doesn't dissolve. Hank is always good for a cheering word at breakfast but I'm afraid he gets no cheering responses. The Scots are dour and so are the English, the Welsh and the remaining Americans.

Obviously, almost no one goes to Uweinat. Trail-markers which have blown down have been left down. We do not have far to go but it is a bad sand day. Archie calls it 'fat lady' sand; we are not sure whether he is thinking of softness or roundness, for truly we are in a soft and dimpled land. At midday, we have found, the sand expands and its crust crumbles more easily. Personally, I do not think it needs an excuse to crumble. The track leads us through the dunes, but, track or no, we are not the trusting souls who left Benghazi two weeks ago. We line the cars up and wait while Francis and Archie and Frank set out at a brisk military pace to test out the sand. Where they can walk without breaking through we can risk following. At that, one car takes off at a time, and we watch with bated breath as first one and then another skims over the sand to the next dune, whence the walking party has already set out to test the forward stretch. I think the dunes look like meringues but Liv just says he doesn't like meringues, anyway. We drop in the afternoon to a gravel plain ridged by watercourses which have from time to time raged down the high black mountain that is Jebel Arkenu. There are two trees here with red skinned-alive-looking bark and thorny branches. One is split in half, both sides growing; the other is stunted, but a little Napoleon to be growing here at all. We all walk around and look in awe at these two trees. Later we hear that we have come through a 'forest'. We all taste the foully bitter melons which are on the ground near by. Hank says they are poison and I believe him. In the distance we can see Mount Uweinat, pink and craggy against the sky. Through binoculars one hill is quite transparent; you can see the other hills slope down behind or through it. This is my discovery, this glass mountain. Everyone studies it with awe. Hank photographs it. He is depressed not to have a scientific explanation and says it may be a ghost mountain.

We embark again but Archie spots a little animal at the foot of the Jebel. Three pair of binoculars are out in an instant. Hank, whose eyes are binocular anyway, shouts, 'Ammotragus lervia, Aoudad, Uaddan, where's my gun, Barbary sheep!' and ten men jump for guns with the speed of a bunch of guerillas who have sighted the national enemy. We race in towards the hills, Liv on the hood of one car taking careful aim, Hank shooting out of his window as he drives with his knees. The little animal stops munching whatever it was munching and stares for a moment, and then, as the cars race to a stop almost beside her, she turns and hops up the mountain. The men stumble out of cars. Liv's long legs catch on the sand tracks as he slides off the hood, and he lands on his knees and scrambles off at a crouch to take aim. A shower of bullets ping against rock. The little animal looks a very domestic sort of goat and for a moment Liv lowers his gun and says, 'My God, I think it's somebody's pet.' Someone asks 'Whose?' and the desert echoes with the thought.

A Barbary sheep is a most elusive creature, perhaps the most in this country. This one is small and reddish and it moves by levitation, hopping up one great boulder after another without visible effort while the men struggle in pursuit, with effort that is both visible and audible. They all grow smaller, and presently only the ping of bullets hitting stone is heard. Catherine is sitting tensely beside me saying her prayers, I think. Probably 'God help all nice little red goats and confound their enemies.'

'It's for science and dinner,' I cheer her, or try to.

Catherine mutters, 'I don't like science and we've still got plenty of hash,' and then she relents and hopes that nobody breaks their neck, ankle or any other member. Whatever her prayers, it seems she has an inside track for the men come back hot, dusty and Barbary-sheepless.

Uweinat is a six-thousand-foot mountain range rising out of an alluvial plain, which latter we crossed with only two breakdowns. Both cars in question had an attack of carburetter trouble. The first to simmer to a stop, being the last car in convoy, signalled ahead frantically with horn, lights and mirror. No one, it seems, heard or saw. The stalled car sat, and its occupants simmered, until Francis, noticing something missing from his flock, turned back, unstuck the stuckee, sent him sailing on his way only to find his own carburetter clogged. Perhaps a desert djinn in this spot is unfavourable to carburetters.

From a distance Uweinat is air-brushed against the sky, all pink turrets and embattlements, Gothic cathedrals, and Norman walls. Climbing endless roads are processions of stately pink slaves, their dignity only interrupted when the mountain erupts into a leering gargoyle or five fat toes rampant into the sky. Below, the long-still avalanches of rock diminish in size as they come closer to the earth. We find Ain Zwaia nestled in a curve of the mountain's base and wonder at the dotting of brown-paper boxes. So completely are we fooled by the perfection of perspective of this place that we misjudge every distance and size. One kilometre into the base of the mountain turns into five, the

Randolph Churchill—a posed portrait

A sick child is brought to us for attention

A French patrol finds Randolph's chair

paper boxes are houses and the avalanche of rocks are boulders as much as twenty and thirty feet high. The houses are Tebu huts, cocoon-shaped and made of fine palm-matting, but most of the people in this little spa live in caves formed by the toppled boulders. In front of one cave the flag of Libya announced the office and residence of Corporal Salam Abubaker, Chief of Police. If we are seeing everyone, and I don't see how it can be otherwise for they all want to shake hands, there are about twenty-six souls in this parish and seventy-five per cent of them are children. I think that we must be a welcome sight, for not only are visitors rare but the supply truck only comes here once in three months. Liv disappears with our passports and his golden tongue into the official cave, to exchange formalities and greetings. The rest of us go to drink and dunk our heads in running water and ogle at that great invention, the tap. The wheel is supposed to be man's greatest, but Catherine and I think the tap has first claim. The wheels within wheels we are not particularly concerned with. You turn the tap and water gushes forth. This is enough of a miracle. Of course, the men want to know where the water comes from and where the pump is and a lot of nonsense.

We make camp some five kilometres away at a village of boulders, well protected from the wind, we think. We are far enough from Ain Zwaia to fool the flies, or so, again, we think. The wind for the moment is quiet, but the flies are smarter than we by far. Some of them have hitched rides, some followed probably surf-boarding on our wake, some walked and some come by camel. We swat them and talk to them as we unpack. One car has gone back to Ain Zwaia to fill up our water jerry-cans. Hank has gone off to set traps. Frank has tea on the stove, and Catherine and I are looking into food boxes. Jack is hoisting his aerial and Winston is washing his face.

After dinner Hank, Liv, John and I take one car and one gun for a shoot. We want gazelle but we will be satisfied with mice. the moon is bright and we drive straight out from the mountain. It has not rained here in years. When it does rain torrents pour off the mountain and the plain is said to be green. The dry torrent-beds look almost like roads in the moonlight. One of them leads us to a camel pasture where some moisture must be trapped in a fold or fissure under the surface, for there is wiry grass here and bits of shrub that look like shredded wheat and which the camels eat without cream or sugar. There are also stunted thorn-trees.

Discouraged at last, we turn back to the mountain, as impressive as ever except that now it is black instead of pink; the stars rain down on it, and at its base not a single light shines to welcome us home. Have we gone further south than we thought, are we coming into another mountain in the range altogether? Or have the others merely gone to bed and like good economical Scots turned out all of the lights? Hank is encouraging, perhaps afraid that I will worry. He says: 'We're right on the beam. We'll come in north of the camp and hunt fox along the base of the mountain. We're right on the beam.'

I refuse to be tranquillized. None of us has ever seen the silhouette of the mountain from this place before, so it seems to be axiomatic that we cannot know where the beam is, let alone be on it. 'We're lost,' I mutter crossly, and wonder just how cold the night will be in shorts and no sweater, how hard the sand with no cot or air mattress. The men are no better dressed than I, and I won't even be able to take female advantage and let them strip to keep me warm, without having three nude men on hand. Furthermore, being lost with a bag full of game would be one thing; I decide that there is an ignominy to being lost without having fired a shot. We come in at last to the base of the mountain and scoot along first to the north and then backtracking to the south. No camp, no Ain Zwaia, no beam. Hank continues to be cheerful, Liv optimistic and John silent. As for me, I bristle. But perhaps no one feels it but myself; I am like an inward-growing porcupine. I don't mind being lost but I want to be lost silently, so that I can enjoy the desert without undue cheer. And of course eventually we find Ain Zwaia, its little straw boxes attracting pools of starlight; its six adults, twenty children, four goats, two camels, its hordes of flies, all sleeping peacefully. From here we know the way home and we turn and skirt the mountain. Even now we almost miss camp. Among the boulders the cars are toys, dark and dwarfed. It is midnight when we come in and we are not particularly quiet, taking revenge by stumbling over our beds and rattling our wash-basins and tooth-mugs. They could have left one lead-kindly-light on.

Somewhere in the night a plane whines overhead. Probably running between Khartoum and Benghazi. It is strange to lie here and think of that bubble of comfort suspended so precariously over this hostile desert—well-turned hostesses with well-chilled martinis, children asleep under dimmed lights, crumpled mothers. As I search among the stars for that restless intruding red-and-green one, I do not envy them.

27TH MARCH

THREE GUNS WENT out early this morning and came back with two gazelle bagged by John and Frank. Hank went to work, skinning and cleaning with wonderful dexterity, put the hide and skulls to dry for his collections and gave me the meat for dinner. I have marinated it in olive oil, lemon juice, onions, garlic (bless Randolph for insisting on our bringing garlic along) and salt. The skin and skulls are hanging in No. 2 car. Catherine has taken me tactfully aside to whiff the interior.

'Do you smell anything sort of mortuary?' she whispers unhappily.

I try to be comforting. 'Hank says there is no bacterial action in this dry desert air,' I say. If anyone says a thing definitely enough I am inclined to believe it. Catherine is not convinced.

'I'm not worried about bacteria,' she says crossly. 'I just don't like the smell.'

Today is laundry day with plenty of water, cold though it be, and a brisk wind for drying. Catherine pounds her things and Winston's against a convenient rock, periodically sluicing them with water. It is a far cry from that pink washing-machine with its chromium-plated buttons. Winston holds up his end of the labour detail by supplying her with water and orangeade, and even hangs up a few pieces. The lighter pieces dry between the tub and the line. When she is through I do my lot, and in the meantime the men are all scrubbing and bathing here and there among the rocks. Liv spends the day whittling away at an old whisky-crate which he is converting into fox-traps. He is going to bait them with gazelle meat, unmarinated, and put them among the rocks and, by special permission, in Abubaker's house. Abubaker has told him that the foxes raid the house whenever there is food around. In the midst of laundry, hair-washing and general clean-up Abubaker comes to call. We give him Winston's pink orange drink and he talks of foxes and other problems. Some of the people at his settlement have not been away for thirteen years. They or their parents fled here from Kufra at the time of the Italian conquest of that oasis more than thirty years ago. Most of the original settlers died of thirst, for there were too many then and not enough water to go round. It is hard to imagine such a bleak life. They play cards, produce children and drive their camels to pastures as far as sixty-five kilometres away on the other side of the mountain. They do not appear to grow anything except one or two tired tomatoes. They have one radio, which they have begged Jack Thompson to fix. He needs a part which Abubaker says may take six months or a year to get, and we can't wait! Abubaker himself is from Kufra. He has been here seven months and he would like to take his wives, his children and his camels and settle in the Chad.

In the afternoon Abubaker will take us to see the rock-paintings. There are many of them but we haven't the time to explore. When we arrive to pick him up at Ain Zwaia Catherine makes such a hit with her Polaroid that he invites her into his cave to photograph his family. I tag along with my less dramatic camera and the men sit in the cars simmering with envy. The children all have their heads shaved with appealing little tufts of hair left, by which to yank them into paradise should occasion demand. A giggly young wife with a baby at her breast lets us photograph her without demur. She wears red flowered trousers, a crimson striped barrakan and a black head-shawl. We both think her pretty and sweet, but the second wife is rather a beauty, black and statuesque and resentful. She pulls her shawl across her face until Catherine peels off the first picture and presents it to the first wife. In a moment the second girl has dropped her shawl, and pulled it well aside to show a breast covered with gold jewelry, heavy ear-rings flashing as she throws up her head. We were both sick at not having colour film, and worried because the entrance to the cave is so dark. Catherine parts sadly with the best of her pictures but still manages to keep a couple.

To reach the cave-paintings requires a fair percentage of mountain-goat blood. Catherine gives Charlie her camera to carry, somebody else her films and somebody else her hand. She screws her eyes tight and leaps in the most petrifying fashion. Heights are not one of my fears, but I am too small to scale some of these boulders, and I keep Liv close. Catherine says for the first time she is glad Alan is not here. She says his head for heights is even worse than hers, which is only to say that he has none at all.

The paintings are more than worth the risk. They are no rough primitives, but delicately painted in terracotta, clay blue and white; cattle, men, one with a bow, women and children. The cattle are long-horned. How many thousand years since this country has been able to support any sort of cattle? Was this sand really covered with true grass, these skeletal mountains with the flesh of earth, grass and trees? Have a thousand or more years of drought and wind blown it all away? We would all like more time to explore Uweinat. But we've lost too much time on clutch-plates and such, and we must go on.

28TH MARCH

LAST NIGHT THE wind blew from the south, strong and hot. It roared in from the plain, with the thundering of an express train, turning our boulder village into a funnel of rushing air. Sand in eyes, ears and beds, cups tinkling away across the plain. A camp-bed, unoccupied for a moment, jumps the rocks and rushes away in a frenzied dance, a stumbling body and strange Gaelic curses hurtling after it. The moonlight makes these boulders menacing and ghostly, and even more gigantic than they are by day. Who pushed them off the top of the mountain? Is whatever-it-was still up there? We talk ghosts and ghouls over our charcoal fire, and when Catherine goes off to her bed behind a distant rock, which she thinks a better windbreak than anyone else's, she goes reluctantly. Liv and I make our beds close to the car, knowing that there is no such thing as a break for such a wind. As we snuggle down we hear a yelp.

85

'Fox!' Liv cries with satisfaction, tugging at his zipper. Everyone has said he would not get anything with his home-made traps. Before he can disentangle himself from his sleeping-roll the cry is repeated with increased and panicky volume from the direction of Catherine's windbreak. He finds her sitting up in bed, tangled in a cardboard ration-box and a roll of film which had rushed at her through the darkness with far-from-inanimate venom. She pulls her head down into her sleeping-bag, confining wind and rocks and ghouls alike to outer space, but obviously expecting anything to happen.

This morning everything is still and hot. We refill on water and pack up. We have ahead of us the longest lap without water, Uweinat to Tekro in Chad, three hundred and twenty miles. About twenty-five kilometres south on the plain we cross the first of the big camel pastures. Water would certainly make a great grazing land of these plains. As it is the pasture is yellow and thin. We see fifteen or twenty camels neither hobbled nor attended. I don't suppose there is any temptation for these animals to stray from the pasture until either it or they are dried up, at which point they would surely head back to the only water. Now the dunes are on our left, pyramid-shaped, every sharp sand-blasted edge in place. We have seen step pyramids cut out of the sand as though by a human hand, and now these. Catherine says nobody could have thought Egyptian geometry up without an object-lesson and here it is, where it has been for millions of years, and all the while the Egyptians have pretended to be so original. In 1932 Ralph Bagnold, a British Army officer with an adventurous spirit, made this journey with some model A Fords. He named some of the little hills we are now passing, Mud Lion, Sandara, Giant Flat Tops (there are a lot of these), Dune Gateway, Lone Tree (no tree, or perhaps we are not where we think we are). I try to draw silhouettes of these, or what I suppose to be these—but photography would be better. Drawing while one bumps over the sand is not much help to anyone. The going is good for the most part. We have not had to use the out-walker technique and have only had five boggings. It is really hot now, too hot to eat. We mix a variety of tinned fruit and have that for lunch. We have no bread and fortunately don't want it. The bread we started with from Benghazi was stale within a day, hard as a rock within two days. A fresh supply, baked in Kufra, lasted longer, as the Kufrans bake their bread with oil. But now even that is gone.

In the afternoon No. 5 has fuel-pump trouble and has to have the pump replaced. While John and Taffy work on that Winston makes us all tea and we have a party with tea, hard tack and marmalade. It is late enough for the cars to cast shadows and we crowd into this relative coolness, gratefully. Winston and Liv discover that they have gone to the same school, though years apart, and they talk of the rough old days and the professor who used to twist their arms when sufficiently exasperated. But Winston says it was all duck soup compared with Eton, where he was really toughened up for life. Thumbscrews and the rest of it. He is remarkably cheerful and unscarred, considering. He leads a gay pampered life between New York, Paris and the south of France, Switzerland and Oxford. We tell him he should renounce this playboy existence, and put his mind to journalism or politics or the theatre. He resists our efforts with his usual good nature and somehow manages to change the subject.

The pump takes an hour to fix and we are back on our way again. While Winston was tea-making I found a cache of ostrich-egg shells. Hank says they are easily a thousand years old. The children will like that. Twice we have seen old car-tracks; Francis says that these will be Leclerc's. Apart from Bagnold and Leclerc and the L.R.D.G., probably no one has been this way before us. It has a splendid solitary beauty, and if, like Tennyson's Ulysses, 'I am a part of all that I have met,' it surely belongs, a little, to me.

We are late making camp. We have travelled one hundred and forty-five miles and we settle at last at the base of a rocky castle where rules a falcon. His kingdom is a turbulent ocean of dunes to the west, a stretch of rolling sand and a line of crested dunes to the north, marching in well-spaced fashion southward. We think that this is Bagnold's Dune Gateway. The radio aerial is up; we are roasting the remaining gazelle on charcoal, and Benghazi is cross because we are late making contact. Jack taps off our news, how the cars and we are faring and where we think we are. He takes a long time, and we suspect that our report takes all of ten seconds while the rest of the time Jack devotes to exchanges of gossip with his chum, the Benghazi operator.

A couple of the boys have been ill. We have had good water, not once having to use the water purifiers we brought along. Frank solves the mystery by saying that he saw the boys drinking from the camel trough at Uweinat instead of the tap. As he turns the gazelle-meat over the embers he assures us that Charlie will give them each twenty-five pills and they will be all right. He then launches an argument as to how and whether you can really get a greatcoat into a mess-cup. It is an army regulation which Francis hasn't heard of yet and he explores the possibilities warily. The British mess-cup is a huge comforting thing which we have learned to our sorrow, for when water is low and tea rationed to one cup apiece the soldiers have it all over the rest of us. But a greatcoat is an even huger and more comforting thing, and Francis decides that it is mathematically impossible to pack the one in the other. There is a glitter in Frank's eye. He is leg-pulling again. At last he confesses. In the Army this is a ritual as old as army-issue. A new recruit or a green young officer is put to the test and watched with poker faces as he folds and prods and stamps upon his coat and cup. One intent young soldier was found by his sergeant undergoing this torment. 'Hoot, mon,' roared the sergeant, 'ye'll never get it in that way. Ye maun cut the bottons off.'—Which the poor man did, to everyone's delight. If there is a gripe in the Army, or a joke, Frank has heard it. He has a devilish look as he pokes at the charcoal embers. His curly reddish-yellow hair and beard seem to have got out of control, and his humorous eyes are reddened by the wind and sand. He is twenty and comes from Midlothian in Scotland, where his father and grandfather were coal miners. He says that he joined the Army for adventure but it is mostly polishing buttons. He and Liv have decided, on the strength of Frank's tea-making skill, to open a tea-room in the middle of the Sahara. But perhaps it would suit Frank's convivial temperament more to run a pub; it is easy to imagine him regaling customers from behind a bar —and 'bouncing' the troublesome as well.

As we sand-wash our dishes, Francis takes a census on who wants to be home, and when. Liv and I don't care much, though Charles and Ginnie Humfrey, who have adopted our children,

88

might. Winston has to be back at Oxford by the twentieth of April. Francis says: 'Not a hope—but you could make it by the twenty-fifth. I've a regimental party I must be back for by then.'

Catherine says that if Alan will fly to Faya she'd like to stay on indefinitely. The men think it would be a fine idea not to go back until July, when some of them are due for home leave anyway.

Francis takes a fix on the stars. There are no adequate maps for the area we are in now. It is up to him to get us to Tekro safely.

Francis is the product of two rigid institutions; Loretto School, in Scotland, and Sandhurst, England's West Point, but neither would care to own him now; he has sidewhiskers and shaggy hair, a wispy fur round his chin and his shorts are held up—or almost —by a safety-pin. His shoelaces have broken to random lengths. He likes schedules to be laid out and orders to be given, and as a military man has had a hard time adapting to Liv's frequent change of plans and abhorrence of trying to organize anybody. He is very dour and cross with us sometimes, and then in a moment is gay and charming and full of enthusiasm, particularly when he talks about his three favourite sports—drinking, rugger and girls.

29TH MARCH | LATITUDE 20–37, LONGITUDE 22–59. Water in the petrol-tank of No. 5. More work for Taffy. Dawn light on the falcon's castle is a run of colour, while the sand below is like Jersey cream. We pass in the lea of Jebel Hadid, stone mountains lightly iced with sand, and just as we think we have left the dunes behind we sail off from a smooth plateau into another sea of them which rolls on for miles and miles. We have trouble with the timing device of our engine, but Liv manages to repair it himself. Catherine has discovered weird pools of black glass-like twigs in the sand; Hank says these are sand tubes, caused by lightning striking the sand. The black ones are very old, the pale colours recent. We also find and wonder at flower-beds of coloured rocks and pebbles. These occur in the middle of a huge expanse of smooth sand, far from any outcroppings. None of us can even attempt to explain their being. Catherine now has fifteen envelopes of sand-samples. These are mere spoonfuls of sand, nothing to worry Hank, and are dated and approximately placed as to latitude and longitude of origin. She will turn these over to the Sloan-Kettering Institute or some group which study the micro-biological content of soils as part of their cancer-research programme.

Today we have come into the corduroy sand- or cement-quilting. The cars bounce and shake mercilessly. I've had the maps, tea-kettle, Liv's gun and my box of personal tricks, such as toothpaste, nail-file, band-aids and safety-pins, shower down my neck more than once. The only way to cross this stuff is to tack with the ripples, and that takes you in the wrong direction. We had hoped to make Tekro tonight, but the sun is going down and we're almost admittedly lost. There are hills on our left, and Francis has decided that we must cut across them to find the Tekro trail. Liv says we should skirt them, and each of us has a variety of other solutions. Catherine mutters, 'Just let's find a good motel and call it a day.'

We climb into the hills, which go up but do not seem to go down. We are on a rocky tableland. We struggle across, threading as well as we can among the rocks, and climb another gradient, more plateau, more rocks—and less light. Here the rocks are bigger and sharper and there is no space for threading amongst them; you might say there is no 'amongst'. We are in a sort of fish-trap, for there is no turning round here and no backing up. This is surely the grimmest, bleakest, windiest place in Moslemdom. We can't go over five kilometres an hour. Winston has caught or hooked his axle on rock three times and we have bent a bolt. When the last of us limp to the edge of the plateau Liv and Francis hold a conference. Here the rocky hell has come to an end, and the mountain slides away in sand, a petrifying ski-jump into a valley hidden in the dark. The wind is so strong that we can hardly stand, and we are all anxious to camp in the valley below, where we will be protected from it. Liv and Francis explore with torches and think they have found a route that one car could try. Like a good general Francis insists on going first, and we watch with our hearts thumping as he dips crazily over the edge, veers off to the right and disappears like a match in the ocean. Aside from the possibility of breaking his neck or burying himself alive in sand, there is the ever-present awareness in all of us of the dangers inherent in skylarking over a cliffside with a load of a hundred and fifty gallons of petrol on board. In a while we hear a whistle and see a light flash. Three men are climbing the mountainside and are signalling us to come on. No. 4 goes next; our car has to be jacked up to get it off the rocks so that we can get to the edge. Winston and Hank, stripped to the waist, haul rocks to build us a sort of road-bed. Below, Francis waves his light and as we at last streak down towards him he runs ahead, guiding us away from a sharp sandy precipice on the left. We are on a sloping ledge, and we must go fast to avoid sliding into the pit. When we are safely by, Archie, armed with a light, takes on for the next lap while Francis lopes back uphill to guide Hank in. We hairpin bend to the left where Archie leaves us to go back in his turn, and Frank picks us up. Like a Marathon runner he has already started ahead. Shadows leap as his torch dips and flares, guiding us down the steepest roller-coaster yet to a flat ledge of level sand in a narrow canyon. Winston, who is a keen skier, takes the descent with élan, nearly coming to grief. The rest of us climb out of our cars elated, but frankly shaky. In the morning when we inspect the night's run we know that we would not have dared it by the light of day.

There is a short-lived argument as to where we are going to camp. Hank says that, far from being in a protected spot, we are in a wind-funnel. We all agree, but as to further travel we have had it. Catherine says that she would rather curl up with serpents than explore one single inch more of this country at night. So we build wind-breaks of our tarpaulins and the strips of plywood which we carry to cover the petrol cans in the cars. Frank squats before the stove making tea. His hair is perpendicular in the wind and he looks like a 'bloomin' idol' with rubies for eyes. Beside him, Archie is stirring sand into the stew. When we hear them yell, 'Grrab yerr moogs,' I think they are saying, 'Grub, you mugs,' and decide that we must teach them to announce dinner with greater decorum.

The sand and stew are not fully homogenized but we wolf it gratefully, along with a little sandy whisky. But it is the tea that keeps us going. British army tea is quite different from anything dished up in a china pot at home. I shall try to follow the recipe when we return, but I know that I am licked before I start. I think you need a rusty gallon biscuit-tin to get that subtle flavour. The tea is dumped in, two handfuls of it, the moment the water boils. It must bubble away for half a minute, then is removed from the fire. A minute or two for the leaves to settle then, 'Grrab yerr moogs.' Catherine drinks it straight and black but the boys like sugar and lots of it. It is an opaque liquid, and if you put milk in it turns a brick-red. It cheers you, revives you and is delightfully habit-forming.

For the first time we crawl into our beds fully clothed. The wind tears around our 'breaks' and comes at us head-on. Hank is blown out of bed and Catherine, who is chasing her tooth-mug, stumbles over him. In the morning we inspect the general devastation with sand-rimmed eyes. The sand here is orange and so are we all. Even after she has washed, Catherine has a carrot-coloured hair-line, as though she'd had a gaudy and not very cleverly applied rinse. I hear her tell Liv that he looks as though he had just stepped out of a sand-box. He is apparently feeling as sandy as he looks and in no mood for light banter, for he merely grunts. Hank comes for his tea muffled to the ears and hunched against this impossible day. I think that he has slept in his glasses. His usual hearty, 'Rise and shine, friends!' is almost inaudible, but he manages a grin. I think we get on our way quicker this morning than we have ever done.

| 30TH MARCH |

THE ISRAELITES COULD not have left the Red Sea behind with greater pleasure than we leave this place. We know that we are lost and that we have somehow missed Tekro. We don't think we can be too badly lost but we maintain strict 'water discipline'. During the course of the morning Francis finds the track, if such it can be called. We are back among rocks; there is no path that a mule could tread through, but every five kilometres or so a heap of stones sits up, looking in the distance like a lumpy 'Thinker'. We follow these markers at a snail's pace, and at last we come back to sand, and down a slope between towering canyon walls to a sight which stops us, literally, in our tracks. A blue lagoon, rimmed in green trees, and beyond it a back-drop of pink-and-white cliffs. Liv murmurs, 'Zurzura,' hopefully I think. Zurzura is a legendary oasis, the Shangri-La, the El Dorado of the Sahara. It is said that none who have entered it have ever returned to their homes. A few travellers have seen it from a distance, but never quite reached it, only come back to their villages to tell of its mysterious and elusive beauty. Liv likes to think that the missing airman from the *Lady-Be-Good* has in fact found Zurzura. In the desert, as the mirages of lakes, spires and green fields appear and fade, it is easy to understand how imagination and a starved stomach could create this pleasant dream—or is it a dream? After all, the desert still has many secrets. There is, for example, the 'City of Brass'. The *Los Angeles Examiner* of 24th December 1922 reported that the French Government was sending an expedition of from five to ten tanks into the Sahara, ostensibly to test their sandworthiness, but actually to look for the fabled 'City of Brass'. The article reads:

The truth is that the mysterious city, if it exists—and the [French] Government must have fairly good evidence of its existence to go to such trouble—lies somewhere in the region dominated by the Senussi, a sect of fanatical, courageous, hard-fighting Arabs, whose influence is gradually becoming dominant among Mohammedan tribesmen of the Sahara and the Sudan. There is reason to believe that the Senussi are fully aware of the location of the City of Brass.

The article goes on to say that this city is described in *The Arabian Nights*, and that in A.D. 700 the then Caliph sent an expedition which brought back reports of fabulous wealth, of gold and jewels, of inhabitants dead from starvation and mummified in the dry desert air. The *Los Angeles Examiner*, while not vouching for the accuracy of this report, brings the matter down to modern times, saying:

The Egyptian Government, just before the [first] World War, had made arrangements for an expedition headed by Sir Don Covington, an English multi-millionaire, explorer and scientist, to search for the fabled city. This was upon information having been brought in by

93

certain Arab smugglers who claimed to have found the place, entered it and brought back treasure and relics to prove their story. These they had sold to Sir Don Covington and were to accompany his expedition as guides. However, before it could start the Senussi heard of it and warned the Egyptian Government what would happen if the party set out. And promptly the arrangements were cancelled.

If anyone needs an excuse to do anything as peculiar as to travel in the Sahara, the City of Brass is still to be found. Probably the Senussi would not mind now. I should prefer to find Zurzura, for it is green.

We look down through our binoculars, enchanted by the beauty of this place; framing the varied depths of green are columns of white-layered sandstone and across the lagoon what seems to be a village of giant bird-cages. No sign of life; not a man, not a goat. We have missed Tekro, but we may be coming to Ounianga. Liv says we must all wash and comb our beards. Desert etiquette is demanding—on meeting strangers you must never ask for water, but wait for it to be offered, and you must clean up before entering an oasis. We are admittedly pretty submarginal-looking.

As we come closer to this oasis, sailing down the canyon into very 'fat lady' sand, a gaunt black man runs to meet us—our first citizen of the Chad, if we're anywhere near on course. He is dressed in spotless white, and wears a dagger strapped to his upper arm. He tells us something which nobody understands; probably where the four-lane highway is. We ask where we are, but neither French, Arabic nor Italian makes any impression. He watches with fascination as we dig ourselves out of the sand, clean shirts and combed beards fast going back to normal. And then we are past the broken crust and into the bird-cage village. One house is in occupancy in this village, and it is covered with palm-matting like the houses at Ain Zwaia. The bird-cages are, in fact, the cane framework. When the owner wishes to move, as he does when the date harvest is over, he rolls up his roof and walls and packs them on his camel, and when he returns the following year he finds an empty framework, not necessarily the one he occupied the year before, and he hangs up his roof and walls again and takes up residence. In this place, despite its beautiful lagoon and trees, only one family has remained. An old white-bearded man in blue robe and white turban comes to talk to us in choppy French and to tell us that we are at Ounianga Segir. He points away to the south-west when we ask for Ounianga Kebir and the French 'military'. We have indeed missed Tekro, which is the official entry-post for this border of Chad.

It takes us an hour to climb the soft sandy hill by the village, but, when the last car has been sand-tracked for the last time, we come out on to a great plateau from which we look back on the spectacular lagoon of Ounianga Segir—Little Ounianga! What can Big Ounianga be? I do not think that I have ever seen so many shades of green in one place: date-trees, figs and acacia, pomegranate and thorn. The grasses are a pastel green, and the cliffs beyond the lagoon and the islands in it are pink with a copper-green wash, sweeping down to orange sand and bright blue water. The lagoon is divided by a natural causeway of palms—one side is strongly alkaline while the other is fed by springs and is full of fish.

We have twenty miles to go to Ounianga Kebir across a plain so high and smooth, by any standards we have seen for a long time, that we feel as though we are on a great elevated high-way, the widest road in the world. As we near Ounianga we sweep by and through wind-carved outcroppings, evenly ser-rated, like an endless procession of sphinx-like figures leading to some lost temple. Ounianga Kebir is advertised on the Michelin map as a 'site très pittoresque'. The French, who abhor exaggeration, have distinguished themselves in this monumental understate-ment. Here is another lake of blue, pierced by orange headlands and fringed with palms and millefeuille cliffs of white sandstone. The village of straw igloos comes to life as we roar through the last stretch of soft sand, up to a long white fort on the cliff top. Men, women and children—tall, slender Tebu, black with small bones and fine features—run out of their houses to wave and call to us. As we reach the fort the Tricolour is hoisted in our honour, and the French Chef de Poste, in kepi, well-pressed khaki, and sandals, strides out to meet us. We are no longer as neat as we tried to be but Sergent-Chef Thevrey sweeps away our apologies.

'You will stay in the fort—there is plenty of water, but little food.' We assure him that we have food with us, and we take cases into his kitchen. We will not have to open a tin or wash a dish, for, of the three Frenchmen in this little fort, one is a cook!

Before we unpack we are invited into the officers' mess hall. It is a long high room overhanging the lagoon, and is beamed with palm-boles and decorated with horns, knives, spears and ostrich feathers. A paraffin-powered icebox is a welcome part of the decor and we are offered ice-cold beer, without doubt the best beer that any of us have ever tasted. We are allotted to officers' rooms, each of which has mosquito-netted beds, a wash alcove with a drain in the floor and a barrel of water with a dipper, and, *pièce de résistance*, a balcony overhanging the cliff and the water below.

Sergent-Chef Thevrey is a jolly tub of a man, a person of great good nature and much curiosity. He is not only know-ledgeable about his domain and the people here, but about the geology and the birds and beasts of this place. He has a fascinating collection of stone-age implements and petrified bone that he has collected in the neighbourhood. He also has a trunk full of books, which are sent to him by the Army once a month, and which he reads from cover to cover. Whoever runs this depart-ment of the French Army is more of an organizer than a reader, for the books are always packed by subject-matter. Last month, the Sergent-Chef tells us, the books were entirely on hunting. This month he is studying fishing. Trout, salmon, deep sea, oriental waters; here in the heart of the Sahara, he has become an expert fisherman. When he sends this box back he hopes for a box of romances in exchange. Although he has been here in what is, after all, an exceptionally lonely spot, for two and a half years, he has asked to be sent back after his home leave this summer. Our boys find this surprising, but Catherine and Liv and I do not. Thevrey is not a lonely type of man. He has his little dog, Pupuce, half fox, but which the natives say is half gazelle, and a pretty sliver of a black girl with a gold ring in her nose. He is always busy. He runs a daily clinic, collects rocks, settles local problems, drills and teaches his soldiers, con-fers with his chef and jails troublemakers. He has a firm but bantering manner with the Tebu and they obviously love him.

At the moment he has in the jail a couple who have been in residence a dozen times before; when they have consumed too much palm wine the wife is given to hitting the husband over the head with a club. Thevrey says that if he puts only the wife in jail the husband comes the next day to say that it was all his fault—so the only solution is to put them both in until the injury is repaired, about eight days. They like the jail. It is clean, they are fed, and there is a sociable atmosphere to the fort.

The first thing that everyone wanted to do was to jump into the lake. The Sergent-Chef rocked with laughter. The last man to try had been hauled out minus one layer of skin. The lake is heavily alkaline; nothing lives in or on it. The Sergent-Chef cured the Uaddan head which hangs in the mess hall by pickling it in the lake waters. As our faces fall almost collectively he relents, and tells us that there is a spring beside the lake which offers an excellent pool. Bring our bathing-suits and he will show us the way. The spring is rimmed by palms, and separated from the lake by a narrow causeway. The water is sweet and clear and you can feel it bubble up between your toes. There are a red-bellied fish here which Liv says remind him of Siamese fighting-fish, but Hank says they look pre-historic to him. He will pickle some and take them back to Washington. There are also some entrancingly minute frogs, sixpenny-size, which Winston put down Catherine's back. She retaliated by pushing him in still half dressed and with his watch in his pocket. I hadn't thought to bring a bathing-suit, and so pop in in my shorts and drip-dry shirt. It is all a bit community-bath, but very lively. The Sergent-Chef stands on the causeway and shakes with laughter.

Sergent Salarie appears for dinner and tells us of the patrol who are looking for us at Tekro. They make a great fuss about the way we have slipped across the border. Francis mutters, 'Slipped isn't quite the word,' thinking no doubt of those miles of boulders we bounded over. Salarie is as wiry and solemn as Thevrey is broad and gay. Salarie has only been here for a month and has a special assignment to study the tribes, customs and conditions of this part of the Chad. The third Frenchman on the post is the chef, Fevrier (expected by his mother in February but actually born in March). Winston's delighted yelp of 'What will a French chef make of "compo"!' has been put to the test. He has seasoned the tinned steak with fresh watercress and cooked the tinned peas with tiny new potatoes dug out of the sand. It is superb. The Sergent-Chef serves us a wonderful Portuguese wine, brought here on camel-back. It is the only wine they keep at the fort, being the one variety which can survive the four-day camel-trek from Faya-Largeau. There is a breeze coming in from the lake, we are wined and dined, housed and happy. We go to our beds at peace with the world, and especially with the Republic of France. A day that would have ended perfectly except that Catherine, mooning on the ramparts, no doubt with visions of Beau Geste racing like sugar-plums through her head, managed to drop our best torch over the cliff.

| 31ST MARCH |
EVEN I AM amazed at what a Scot can eat for breakfast; pork and beans and sausage whipped up with eggs and things. Francis calls it 'good heavy kit'. Catherine says, 'Heavy is the operative word, never mind the good.' Our French hosts think it is *rigolo*, a comedy. They themselves drink a demi-tasse of black coffee, period. Catherine thought pancakes might be nice, and had unpacked the makings in the kitchen last night. But our supply of maple syrup was in a whisky bottle and one of the native soldiers has drunk it all up. We wonder if he was surprised at the taste, or if he put it down to the way Americans flavour their whisky. We have lots of marmalade, and Fevrier has supplied us with lovely French bread and pats of sweet chilled butter from La Manche. On the march the tinned butter we carry is more drinkable than edible, and has developed a strongly cheesy taste. We have found that the army supply of margarine stands up better to heat and bouncing.

We straggle into mess hall at various hours. Hank and Charlie are working on a trayful of fresh catch. Hank has a new variety of jerboa and some spiny mice which he caught in the fort. Sergent-Chef Thevrey calls them palm mice. They are dear little creatures with prickly tipped fur, first cousins of Mrs. Tiggy-Winkle. The Sergent-Chef is enchanted at having the mice in his house trapped, and thinks it the joke of the year that they will end in a museum. He tells Hank that there are bats here and fox, large silver ants and duck. Francis, John and Taffy have been out after the duck since dawn. Winston couldn't get himself up quite that early; besides, he has to study, so he is out on the ramparts shooting raven.

This morning a lieutenant, on patrol duty from Tekro, comes in to the post to pick up oil and petrol for a truck which he has had to abandon on the way. He tells us that he had been looking for us, and that he has alerted the Tebu in the bush to be on the look-out. We are fascinated at the idea of there being either Tebu or bush in the country we came through—we certainly saw neither. The Lieutenant says that we are the first to come in from the north. Perhaps we have blazed a trail.

'Blazed with clutch-plates and fuel pumps,' Taffy mutters.

There are perhaps twenty-five native soldiers, or *goumiers*, here. They are not Tebus, but come from various tribes, the Sudan, the Congo and even as far afield as Madagascar. Robert Byam, mess-hall orderly, is from Sarra near Kufra. He has claw-like scars down his cheeks and across his forehead. This scarring used to be a tribal custom. His people also mutilated their women until quite recently, cutting off a hand or an entire arm so that they would not be carried off as slaves. All of the soldiers are tall and well built. They wear blue shorts and shirts, and beige bush hats which we all covet. Their uniforms are always pressed and clean. In the lower deck of the fort, by the well, a small boy in a red fez does nothing but iron from morning to night, taking out four hours now and then for a nap. He uses a primitive iron filled with red coals, and a flat stone for an ironing-board. At the gate a guard is always on duty. He sits in a chair with a gun teetering on his knees, while sprawled in the gravel across the arched gate-way some of his friends play draughts. Everyone is polite, helpful and ready with a greeting. Catherine has, of course, been at them with her Polaroid. They all want their pictures, and one of them brought her a roll of exposed film begging her to develop it in her 'machine'. He was obviously puzzled when she said she couldn't, especially as she is quite incapable of explaining why. No camera has worked for her since her Brownie-box-camera childhood, and when she peels off a Polaroid picture she is as mystified and delighted as any Tebu.

The fort, built on the edge of the cliff, has an outer breast-work, four square towers and connecting ramparts. The inner court is systematically crossed with ramps and decks, and consists of three layers. Below, cut into the whitewashed walls, arched doors lead to soldiers' quarters, store rooms, prison, latrine and a home for old chickens. Across little alley-like bridges from the main deck are the mess hall, kitchen, dispensary, officers' quarters, and up zigzagging narrow steps are the ramparts and look-outs. The walls are brilliantly whitewashed and we soon learn to stand clear of them.

The Sergent-Chef has bounded into our hearts to stay. He will take us, with the aid of his favourite guide, to the plains where the largest desposits of stone-age implements and fossils are to be found. Liv, Catherine, Thevrey and I wedge ourselves into the cab of one of the Land Rovers. The Tebu guide, wiry, white-robed and ancient, travels on the hood of the car with a cushion to keep the bolts that hold the spare tyre from fracturing his spine. The plain is all of four kilometres away, and is so littered with treasure Catherine says:

'If he'd had time I'd say he had salted this place for our benefit.'

She rapidly fills a box with odd bones. Liv has found a tooth and I a piece of what seems petrified skin or perhaps tortoise-shell. The area was once covered by a shallow ocean, and along the coasts and in the swamps about it those thousands of years ago lived hippo, ostrich, giraffe, elephant and lion. We wander across the plain towards a small village on the slope above another lagoon. The Sergent-Chef invites us, brashly it seems to me, into one of the houses, calling the woman of the house by name and teasing her in a friendly way. She is a pretty girl in a red flowered sack, nose-ringed, and hair greased and plaited in tiny thread-like plaits that frame her face. The three heavier plaits which go from her forehead tightly across the top of her head indicate that she is married. She shows us her house and offers us water from the *garba* which hangs at the door. A *garba* is a goatskin which has been tanned in the sun and sewn up, leaving the neck open for a spout. Our hostess pours water into a bowl and passes it first to Liv, who drinks it murmuring:

'I can't get typhus, typhoid, para-typhoid, cholera, yellow fever, polio—do you suppose there is anything else?'

These little houses are divided, like 'all Gaul', into three parts. The straw partitions do not go all of the way to the ceiling, and are used to hang extra clothes (one brilliantly flowered dress) and the goatskins which serve as bed and covers alike. The first room is no more than a tiny entrance or wind-break, for the cane door is no great protection. The central room is oval and completely unfurnished except for the goatskins and clothes on the walls, two blackened stones on the sandy floor where the cooking-fire is made, and a bowl of date-pips ready to be ground into a meal which will be fed to the goats. The third room is obviously a washroom; we peer over the partition and see a flat stone on the floor and a gourd for pouring water. This gem of modern architecture is airy and spotlessly clean. Until we invade it the sandy floors do not have so much as a footprint, and I imagine that our trampling will be smoothed and brushed away as soon as our backs are turned.

There are a series of five lagoons in this area. Our host has promised to take us to one where there are primitive rock-carvings. Despite the fact that the bone-hunting has taken up more time than he had counted on, he says that we will make a quick run to the lagoon in question and he will show us a short cut. The native guide now illustrates the total inability of any guide to be useful in a car. Confused, as the known landmarks either don't appear or appear and disappear too fast, the Tebu waves his arm first in one direction and then in another, Hula fashion, while the enraged Sergent-Chef, too wedged in to bounce, thumps on the windshield and bellows, '*Terminez, terminez!*'

The carvings are well worth the agony. We walk along the lakeside to find them. They are primitive, camels mostly but also cattle. We pick the strange white tubes that grow like stalagmites by the lake, and are told that it is 'natron', good food for camels. It tastes like epsom salts and we leave it for the camels. Three feet of snake slither across our path. Liv wields his camera shouting to the Sergent-Chef to desist, but the latter is jumping up and down, throwing rocks. Catherine has turned to a pillar of salt and we may have to feed her to the camels. The snake, a grass-snake, doesn't like us either but you couldn't prove it to Catherine.

Back at the fort we find that our hunters have had trouble. Francis has trod unwarily on a palm-branch, causing it to spring up and shoot a thorn into the calf of his leg. The palm-thorn is poisonous, as painful as a scorpion-bite, and if not removed can result in complications, infection and a great deal of pain. Francis is grey but grimly silent. We are all impressed with the clinic at the fort which is spotless and well stocked. The *infermier* or medical orderly is deft and experienced. He has to cut open the wound but does not find the thorn, which is worrying; he hopes, of course, that it is no longer there. For this operation Francis has a shot of morphine, a local anaesthetic and two slugs of whisky, which he downs straight like the villain in the saloon scene of a Western movie. When he is stitched up and bandaged the orderly prepares an injection of penicillin, smiling in that supposedly comforting way that doctors have when they are about to torture you. From his half-world of morphine and whisky, Francis murmurs, 'He looks very happy.' With an effort he raises his head and bravely tries to say this in his primitive school French. '*Vous êtes tres joli.*'

'No, no,' I soothe, 'that doesn't mean "jolly", it means "pretty".' The orderly looks startled enough to break a needle in his patient's buttocks.

'He means "*content*",' I explained.

'*Ah, alors . . .*' the orderly grins, looking relieved, but Francis is past caring.

Francis hobbles in for lunch still white, but very stoical. The men are pretty stoical about him, too, but we don't think it suits them quite as well. Février has cooked up a mess of scrawny little Tebu chickens, giving them a special flavour, and has made us a tub full of French-fries. There is a watercress salad and radishes with bread-and-butter. The Sergent-Chef has a garden which produces quantities of lavish watercress, potatoes, tomatoes and eggplant. The first fresh food we have had since Benghazi. We can't get enough!

Jack Thompson has been working for two days now trying to contact Benghazi. He works all day and seems always to be making his most strenuous efforts at mealtime. This may explain why he is so thin. He comes in when the food is cold or finished, and we pepper him with questions. The French call him *le radio* and are impressed with his skill, as are we. He is reticent, but we have discovered that he knows a lot about birds. His father was an enthusiast, and raced pigeons when Jack was a child. I asked him what he would like to do if he were free to choose and he said he would go on more expeditions like this one. He is hard-working, even-tempered and philosophical about the discomforts of the Army. Once I saw him pouring his soup over his meat course.

'How can you?' I moaned.

'Oh, that's nothing,' said Jack. 'Once I had kippers and custard on the same plate, and nothing but a wall of hard tack between them.'

Catherine is anxious about Alan, who had promised to meet us at Faya-Largeau on the 30th if he has recovered. The 30th is already past, and there is no such thing as a hotel at Faya-Largeau and we have his sleeping-bag. The Sergent-Chef reassures her. If Alan comes, the post there will bed him down. He wires through and tells her that they are alerted to meet Alan. Still, it is worrying for her.

In the afternoon Catherine drags us all out of our naps to come and photograph the Sergent-Chef's young lady. He has invited Catherine into his *chambre de célibataire* which she describes as being spotlessly clean and neat, furnished with a large double bed and decorated with ostrich-plumes, crimson-satin drapes and a pretty girl dressed in five different shades of red and loaded down with gold jewelry. This poor lonely *célibataire* wanted Catherine to photograph the girl, Khalbila. Her camera does not take colour, so she has stirred us all up. The Sergent-Chef is delighted, Khalbila less so. She is eighteen, with oriental eyes, a gentle smile, a ring in her nose and great dignity which all of the Sergent-Chef's fussing, giggling and teasing does not ruffle, even when he digs her in the ribs to make her smile for us. Extraordinary fellow! Later in the day Liv observed his treatment of a drunk. The man had gone berserk on palm wine and interfered with dancers who were swaying and trudging to the tom-tom on the lake shore. Two soldiers brought him in, blubbering incoherently, and the Sergent-Chef pounded his head, hit him repeatedly across the face, and finally threw water at him, jumping up and down and scolding like a fat Rumpelstiltskin. Perhaps if more drunks were treated this way by their judges there would be fewer of them! I can't see myself going back for a second helping of palm wine after just one session with the Sergent-Chef.

When we take Francis back to the infirmary for a penicillin shot, we find a woman who has brought her three-year-old daughter for treatment. The child has a horrid swollen eye which the *infermier* tells us is a syphilitic cataract. This woman lives in the bush and has delayed two months before bringing the child in. Too long—she is already blind. Syphilis is hereditary here and rampant. The little girl is obviously frightened but docile, and the orderly is gentle and soothing with her.

We have duck for dinner. Catherine and I have donned dresses and perfume. Winston and the French approve, but Francis says that we are wearing the wrong brand. His girl wears 'Crêpe de Chine' and it is the only perfume he likes. At the far end of the room Winston is teasing Frank.

'How do you say "mouse" in Scotland?' he asks.

'Muce,' says Frank.

'And how,' asks Winston, grinning, 'do you say "moose"?'

'Muce,' says Frank.

There is carousing in the mess tonight, including displays of unarmed combat on the floor and a rendering by Sergent Salarie, with Fernandel solemnity, of his days as a caddy for British troops at a golf course in the north of France, including the exact way in which he stole their golf balls.

The Sergent-Chef has a toothache, and Catherine is happy at having someone to whom she can give some temporary stopping.

'The little things that make the world go round,' says Liv, awed.

1ST APRIL

THE FORT IS in an uproar. A native soldier has brought word that the Lieutenant's truck has been involved in an accident near Tekro. The Lieutenant is thought to be hurt, but the wireless connection is bad and no details are known. Salarie is busy getting together a supply convoy with petrol, water and rations. The Medical Orderly is assembling his equipment, scalpels, splints, surgical dressings and morphia. We are asked if we will take the wounded man on to Faya with us in the morning, as there is a hospital there. We plan to shift things around so that one car can be used as an ambulance. We will put inflated mattresses, blankets and sleeping-bags on the plywood that covers the petrol cans and hope to soften the bumps somewhat. But it is worrying not to know just what to expect. How badly is the Lieutenant hurt? I suppose if it is bad enough a helicopter could come up from Fort Lamy.

To while the morning away Liv joins the taxidermists, and skins a raven he has shot from the terrace. He hasn't done this kind of work for many years and decides that there are other occupations that he likes as well. He says that this is his swan-song.

Catherine and I take our personal laundry and start down the hill to the washing-spring, which is by the side of the lake near the swimming-pool. An enterprising native boy has already washed the men's things, including Francis's passport which he forgot to remove from his pocket. Their clothes are all laid out to dry on the ramparts with bits of stone and dirt to hold them down. At the spring we wait for a big black soldier to finish his wash, and when he wades out of the spring we wade in. We stand in water to our waists with laundry floating about us, and pound each piece on a great slanting rock. The fish nibble at our legs and we wonder what they make of the lather of detergent and army all-purpose soap. Two white-robed Tebu squat watching us for a while. Perhaps they are waiting their turn. Unexpectedly one of them takes off his clothes and wades out into the lake and we wonder if the Sergent-Chef has exaggerated slightly. Also we are both impressed with the fact that a naked black is so much less nude looking than a naked white. When you come right down to it, white skin is inclined to have that under-a-rock look. Certainly massive numbers of white people spend unconscionable quantities of time and money trying to darken themselves, while you never hear of dark people bothering about a bleach. As we walk up to the fort our dripping clothes dry on our backs before we have climbed to the top.

There is pigeon for lunch, nineteen lovely mouthfuls. They

were blue and downy when seen this morning, but one shouldn't think of that, and Février has made a superlative sauce. Sergent Salarie, his trucks ready, has rushed in to tear off a hunk of bread and gulp down a glass of wine for his lunch. As we are sitting around the table picking at the last pigeon, he bursts into the mess hall again, eyes blazing, and announces that the native soldiers have had him for an April Fool! There has been no accident, no wounded Lieutenant, and now there is no pigeon. The Sergent-Chef rocks with laughter, and through the rest of the meal giggles, shaking and weeping. Robert Byam brings Salarie a plate of food but the latter is not to be placated. Thumping his plate, knocking over his wine, he rages that it is a poor idea of a joke. And the angrier he becomes, the merrier the Sergent-Chef. At the moment the Sergent-Chef is out of favour with us, too, for on returning from our morning expedition he has thumbed through his book of regulations to discover that we may not remove our lovely horde of bones and artifacts from the country. He makes up to us by getting the women of the village to dance this afternoon, on the open sand by the lake. Against the orange sands their brilliant robes and head-shawls and massive gold jewelry shimmer and clash. One girl has a diadem of a gross of large safety-pins standing in a row across her head. The girls are shy in the daylight, and have to be chased into their dance by the Sergent-Chef, who runs around after them threatening and cajoling, smacking a rump or tickling a rib. They start at last, the drummer beating an oval drum and chanting a refrain which we are told says 'The white people have come from the north by the old caravan route and they are very nice and very rich and will give us plenty of money very rich very rich. . . .'

The dance is perhaps one of the less lively of the art, the feet shuffle in little sandy circles, the head is shyly bowed and the arms wave; they seem to say, 'Come or go, come or go, we couldn't care less.' This is a slightly anaemic sex dance which livens up when a white-robed male with red cartridge-belt and gun leaps into the circle, firing what we hope are blank cartridges right and left. Having scared all of the girls into fits of giggles he ends by singling out one and chasing her round and round, firing at random; the tom-tom grows louder and the waving arms, giggles and shrieks wilder. The sun is setting beyond the lake, and the palms cast their sloping shadows across the circle of dancers. We feel as though we were on a South Sea island rather than in the centre of a great desert.

The Lieutenant returned from patrol this afternoon only mildly amused to hear of the drama that had been enacted about him. He roared up to the fort in his open Dodge Power Wagon, with eight native soldiers aboard, their faces swathed and sun-goggled against the wind and dust. We thought them wonderfully dashing. They have been patrolling the northern border in this sector on the look-out for people who slip over illegally.

'Gun-running?' I ask hopefully, but he smiles condescendingly, and says that the offenders are mostly geologists from the oil camps in Libya. There is one pass which they must come through called Rocher Noir. I think that it is the pass which we missed when we came ski-ing over the mountains, so I don't suppose it is so easy to guard after all. However, the Lieutenant has just found fresh tracks at the pass—two Land-Rovers and a Dodge Power Wagon with, according to the local Tebu, two Americans, a Frenchman and a Libyan aboard. The Lieutenant says that they have never caught any geologists yet, which he says is 'regrettable'.

'We would like to compare *cailloux*, the pebbles which the geologists have come to collect,' he says, 'and then we would send them home with, of course, a severe reprimand.' I think that he enjoys this grown-up game of hide-and-seek.

We continue to send wireless messages out, and have finally received. But we can't seem to contact Benghazi. We have sent via Kufra, El Adem (the R.A.F. base near Tobruk) and Malta. It is like skipping stones into the ocean, very unsatisfactory. Winston has had anxious messages from the paper for whom he had promised a story by 26th March—and which he has not yet begun—and from his father. Catherine has finally had a cryptic message saying 'Collins presumed still in Benghazi' which she didn't like at all. She says that it sounds as though Interpol were on his trail. She is further annoyed because everyone is so unsympathetic to her desire to go on alone by camel. Liv and Francis don't want to separate the party, and the Sergent-Chef is frankly dismayed. We had planned to go from here to Gouru where we can make a base camp at an abandoned fort, while the men climb

Emi Koussi, the highest peak in the Tibesti range (eleven thousand feet). Catherine wants to start ahead and meet us there. But we have dissuaded her. In any case Emi Koussi will have to be abandoned. The only dedicated mountaineer amongst us is Charlie, who belongs to a climbing club in Scotland and would like to add Emi Koussi in its achievements. Francis and Winston have been anxious to have a crack at it, too, but now of course Francis is too lame to do any climbing, and we decide that we have lost too much time. Perhaps the climbers will have a chance at Toussidé, the Tibesti's second-largest peak, on the other side of the range.

Khalbila has presented Catherine with a very scrawny rooster which she is supposed to eat by herself—she can hardly be expected to share it with fifteen people! It has been taken down to the chicken yard next to the latrine. The Sergent-Chef has been instructed to leave it there and let it enjoy a plentiful old age. I think I detect a *coq-au-vin-rouge* glint in his eye.

| 2ND APRIL |

EASTER SUNDAY, AND we are off; regretfully but with lots of noise, shouts of farewell and blowing of horns. The going is drab at first; we seem to have exchanged a world of beauty for the hard gravel of reality. There is an occasional solitary thorn-tree which gives one the feeling of driving through a perpetual show-case in the Natural History Museum. All it needs is a caption reading 'SOUTHERN SAHARA, NATURAL HABITAT OF . . .' Still, the going is at least firm. We have done one hundred and ten kilometres by lunch. Now we are crawling over rock again, and passing dunes and rock outcroppings. In a basin, which must once have been the last of the swamps, we have found an entire petrified tree lacking only the leaves and smaller branches. It is a fifteen-inch growth, and lies along the ground as though felled by a pre-historic woodsman. Lunch over, we lose speed, though Frank says we're making as good time going up and down as forward. Where the rock is not bad the sand outdoes itself. 'Fat lady' sand is child's play to the sandy defiles which snake between these black sandstone hills. Hilltops are marked with cairns, and some attempt has been made at a sporadic road-building, for we find patches of stone laid out across the softest sand. In this country the sand is never still and the road built today is gone tomorrow. The French have probably put this track down as they convoyed across with supplies for outposts like Ounianga, helping themselves over the worst places and knowing that they would have the work to do again the next time they came through. By following their bits of road we more often than not find ourselves driving into banks of sand so deep we are up to our hubs before we know it. In exasperation we thread the hills, each looking for a better way through. One car tears off the track, giving every bit of speed he has to take a hillside, only to stick on the pinnacle like a sort of latter-day equestrian statue. The Lieutenant had told us that we could make Faya-Largeau in a day with the help of a guide, who would take us by a longer but a better route. Not yet marked, the longer route presumably does not have its crust broken, or perhaps the wind has blown the sand away from the longer route exposing firmer ground. I can tell you where the wind has blown the sand because we found it all. By sundown, tired and disgruntled, we are nowhere near Faya-Largeau. A solitary clump of palms looms in what seems to be the bed of an ancient lake, and we make camp. There is enough dead wood about to build our first camp-fire. Though there is a drizzle of rain, the night is warm and 'scorpiony' as Liv says, and a fire is infinitely comforting. We sit about and talk, and when we go to bed Catherine complains that she has softened at Ounianga and lost the habit of taking her shoes to bed with her. She says that they are dusty and smelly and it's too hot to zipper up—and anyway, why can't scorpions and serpents be more attractive-looking? For instance, if a Koala bear were poisonous you wouldn't mind so much.

3RD APRIL

FRANCIS SHOOTS HIS first gazelle near Faya-Largeau. Hank strings it up on a pole which John and Frank support on their shoulders. They look like a pair of human end-posts. Now that we are in the Chad, we are dubious about shooting gazelle without a permit, but Hank is bristling with official permissions to collect specimens for his museum.

The going is rough until we are almost on Faya-Largeau. Gorgeous stone gate-posts herald the end of the bad lands, the black hills and the sandy defiles. After the gate we are on level desert again and mostly hard going. We arrive at the first signs of vegetation and life in the late afternoon, and have a wash and change among the shrubbery. A flock of naked children, skitterng about like tadpoles, watch this operation. We follow a narrow sandy lane which surprisingly meanders through the palms to disappear into a small fat dune. Going round this little mountain we come to a wide and sandy street with adobe houses and walled gardens on either side. Architecture is varied, mostly Moorish with roof lines that are crenelated, buttressed, randomly complicated and fascinating. From over walls, oleanders and hibiscus add a touch of colour, the first flowers we have seen. In a cloud of dust and sand we circle into Place d'Ornano, a great open square surrounded on four sides by administration buildings, officers' homes, club and post office and headed by the flagstaffs, the Tricolour and the snapping-in-the-breeze flag of the Republic of Chad. We park in front of the municipal building, bringing with us, like the widening, weakening wash of a fleet of ships, a swarm of curious children with tufted heads and sack-like clothes, led by a little status-seeker in a 'Woody Woodpecker' T-shirt. We expect the usual onset of flies, pleas for chewing-gum and cool childish hands wandering over lights, door-handles and windscreen-wipers. At any other oasis, but not here. A huge black man in khaki uniform, with tribal scars running down his cheeks, strides up, cracking a rhinoceros whip. The children melt away, for which you can scarcely blame them. The parents among us are thinking of taking some of these whips home. When the air clears we are greeted by Captain Lecomte of the Marine d'Outre-Mer. A charming, staunchly built man, the Captain wears the baggy-zouave trousers and white-linen jacket which is the uniform best suited to the heat of this place. Catherine and I have our hands kissed with such debonair gallantry that we sadly regret their dish-pan look, or perhaps one should say sand-pan. We promise ourselves manicures at the first opportunity.

Alan has not arrived, and there is no word of him. A mysterious American is said to be on his way from Fort Lamy in a rented vehicle, and Catherine's hopes soar. But this turns out to be a mistake or hoax of some sort; the French are playful people. In the meanwhile we are offered the hospitality of the guest-house, a large building which can only have been built as an elephant stable and has in turn served as prison and storehouse. The walls are three feet thick, the ceilings twenty feet high and some of the doors are still barred. The corridors are wide—as they would have to be for manœuvring elephants. Whether with elephants or prisoners in mind, there are many rooms in this building. Two are washrooms; that is, rooms with sinks, shower-stalls and drains but no water and no electricity, and no doors. We spread out, setting up a kitchen and various bedrooms. There is no furniture but of course we are self-sufficient. However, four walls and a ceiling create a crying need for shelves and hooks which is not felt in the desert. Draping clothing on a fender or dropping them on the sand with a rock for anchor seems natural—dropping them on the floor of a building goes against the grain.

We are warned to lock everything up, for Faya-Largeau, a penal colony, is not surprisingly said to be full of thieves. More often called Largeau by the French after General Largeau, who defeated the Senussi in 1914, the oasis is a dry Devil's Island, surrounded by an ocean of sand. There are about three hundred convicts here. Before France gave independence to so many of her African territories the number was larger, for this was where these other countries sent their murderers, rapists, arsonists and thieves. The convicts now are mostly from the Chad itself. They wander around the streets in their convict stripes, apparently unattended. Having seen what desert any one of them must cross to effect an escape, I can only say that iron bars are not necessary; their prison is an oasis in hell. Captain Lecomte has assigned a guard to us, a sweet little old convict of whom we all become fond. Serving a term for theft, he sleeps on a mat laid across the guest-house door and guards our possessions from thieves. We step over him in the night as we come and go.

The Captain's own night watchman is an arsonist. As a man,

I think the Captain rather sympathizes with this poor devil, who burned down the house of his wife's lover. This seemed to have slowed the wife down for a while, but when the lover found himself another house she reverted to her sinful ways. Apparently too much for flesh and blood to stand, this time the husband burned down the wife and lover as well as the house. The Tebu have explosive tempers, although I think that these things depend a great deal on climate and on the deep and perpetual worry of being close to starvation. Captain Lecomte, Public Prosecutor for the French Administration, says that he had at one time to deal with eight murders in one week and always has an average of forty crimes a month. Camels are great troublemakers among these people: Look after my camel whilst I go to town. If on my return I find you unwilling to give it back to me, your need being greater than mine, there's nothing to do but kill you! This can start a long feud. Killing a man carries a penalty of one hundred camels to be paid to the family of the victim. A woman must be paid for with fifty camels, a blacksmith (originally blacksmiths were slaves and remain today low on the social register) with twenty. If the payment is not forthcoming the injured family feels free to do a little killing on its own account. This is not always practical, but a feuding family has been known to wait as long as twenty years to take its revenge, and then may not kill the offender himself but a member of his family, or alternately kidnap a child of his family and mutilate it before returning it to its parents.

There is the story of the young traveller who met a stranger in the desert. After the usual *Marhabas, Keif Haleks* and *Hamdullilahs* had been exchanged, all in the name of Allah and good will, names were finally introduced into the ceremony. Whereupon the young traveller unsheathed his knife and stabbed the stranger. Neither a thug nor a juvenile delinquent, this young man had heard the name of his family enemy, and, not pausing to ask whether the poor chap were indeed related to the enemy, had, as any fool can plainly see, carried out his duty. We are rather glad that the names Pomeroy and Collins are unlikely to have Tebu bearers running about with blood-debts to be collected and think that if we were Chaddies we would change our name every six months or so: a game of Chaddi roulette.

I find a brooding atmosphere to this place, a menacing tension which might at any moment break into violence. Catherine doesn't see it that way. Much to the disgust of the French officers she insists that it reminds her of Indo-China, which she visited as a child. She says that it is a feeling, more than any one characteristic; an atmosphere distilled by walled gardens, arched walks, dusty streets, French tropical uniforms and the long hot siesta of the day. Most of the officers here have been stationed at one time or another in Indo-China and they do not agree with her. They think of theatres and music, fine hotels and sparkling water, lovely Indonesian faces, lush jungles and temple bells. You can't expect them to have nostalgic memories of walled gardens or French tropical uniforms!

We have asked about hunting permits and have been told that, as long as we need food and don't use machine guns or leave wounded animals, we may hunt. Aside from gazelle, we may also see antelope as we go west.

The men have replenished our water supply, and both wash-rooms are full of people doing laundry and pouring water over one another. Catherine and I have one washroom to ourselves. As its wide and doorless entrance faces into the centre of the building where everyone must come and go we have to make our baths nimble, one bathing while the other stands with skirt spread wide. The cold water is gloriously welcome, for we are very hot and dusty. The north and north-west winds are the sandy and prevailing winds, prevailing right now. We are told that when the wind blows from the south it is less dusty but much hotter; the average high temperature in the summer is one hundred and eight degrees. This, then, is the cool time of the year, no more than ninety in the shade, where if you are wise you try to stay. Perhaps the hardest thing about life here for those who must live here, whether guardian or guarded, is the blowing, moving sand. It threatens the town continuously. It marches inexorably, in some places as much as two hundred feet a year, gradually covering and crushing walls and houses, allowing them to reappear years later as a pile of rubble. We have seen houses with dunes built up against their walls as though gently leaning. This 'gentle' lean probably weighs several tons, and we wonder how long the wall will take it.

The evening is fresh, but not cool enough for a sweater, as it has been until now. We are invited to the officers' mess for cocktails with Colonel Baylon, the Chef de Région. The French have a mandate from the Government of Chad to administer the northern part of the Chad, which includes the Tibesti Mountains. The Colonel, therefore, has the position of a provincial governor. Although Largeau is a penal colony, maintaining it is only a fraction of the duties of these officers. Theirs is the work of bringing law and order, education, health and civilized justice to a people who far prefer their own kind. From Largeau the smaller posts such as Ounianga, Zouar, Bardai, Wour or Oozou are commissioned and supplied. The smaller posts maintain detachments of troops under an officer or non-commissioned officer. Each has a clinic or hospital, a school and the responsibility of keeping order among a primitive people whose existence depends on the protection of their pasturage, flocks and water. Life among the Tebu is so tenuous that the trunk of a precious date-palm may be owned by one man, the fruit by another; the meat of a goat by one, its milk by someone else. In Largeau Captain Lecomte, as Public Prosecutor, is more concerned with the crimes of the people living in his parish than the criminals who have already been tried elsewhere and sent to Largeau to pay the price.

The officers' mess is a white building with arched doors and high ceilings. We sit in a little bar in comfortable modern chairs and are served with Parisian deftness. Colonel Baylon is no bluff army man, but a sophisticated and most suave gentleman. His white jacket is dazzling and tailored with razored perfection. Our soldiers have been invited to the French soldiers' mess, so that there are only six of our party for cocktails. Captain Lecomte, who has become our shepherd, has joined us, and Lieutenant Allaire, who is the Chef de Poste of Zouar and who is in Largeau for a few days. After a round of drinks we are invited to adjourn to the Colonel's garden where it will be cooler. Grass does not grow in Largeau and the ground is covered with neatly raked pebbles. It is none the less a graceful walled garden with a pool, a tennis court, palm-trees, crimson bougainvillaea, hibiscus and acacia.

Chairs are brought and we sit in a circle under a series of

arc-lights that fight with the moon for ascendency. We are served a variety of refreshments from fruit juices through the grains and wines to beer. The Colonel regrets that he cannot offer us a meal as he has lost his *maître d'hôtel* this very day. We are not sure whether his butler is a convict whose term of imprisonment is completed, a soldier whose leave has commenced or who has been transferred to another post or a capricious domestic servant who has packed his bags and departed. But we assure our host that we have dinner awaiting us as soon as our cooks have finished the excellent glasses of lemonade that they are drinking in his garden.

'The ladies! Never!' He claps his hands. At the risk of submitting us all to a very inferior meal and poor and clumsy service, he cannot allow two such charming ladies to toil over a hot stove. Catherine and I find this gallantry quite irresistible. We do not think that our own men should allow us to toil over a hot stove either. During another round of drinks the subject is explored.

Hank, who was up before dawn, which means all of a half-hour before the rest of us, closes his eyes for a little moment. Catherine joins him, but the conversation continues to bounce back and forth, and, like spectators at a tennis match, they follow it with their heads. At times I have the impression that they can see through their eyelids for they are turning so naturally with the tide of talk.

The Colonel's clap has brought two boys running. Gabriel, the cook, is instructed to whip up a little impromptu 'peek-neek'. The new *maître d'hôtel* is a big young *goumier* in shorts, knee socks and with gentle manners. His feet are of an exceptional size and he seems worried about them as he plods cautiously among us passing biscuits and little cocktail-sausages. Winston and I have appealed to the Colonel to describe tropical evening uniform to us, and he has disappeared to return dashingly attired in black zouave trousers, flaring out beneath his white jacket. Catherine has her eyes open again and is eyeing him appreciatively. Hank is explaining his collection to Captain Lecomte. To the French in these posts, Jerboa or Jerbels are merely mice; and they find a museum official travelling so far in pursuit of these little creatures deliciously funny. Fatigue and a seemingly endless march of beers have no effect on Francis, except to loosen his light hold on the French language. The Royal Scots are said to be a hard-headed regiment, and we think that Francis is well placed amongst them. No one is going to get him under the table.

The little 'peek-neek' is taking a little time. Our host has hospitably introduced us to a cocktail invented by the wife of one of his officers. He insists that he does not know exactly what goes into it. Weary as we are, we rather wonder how, if this is so, he makes it. This nameless little drink should be called the rabbit-punch. We are now a little light-headed. Colonel Baylon, who has to be on a plane at five in the morning to fly to Zouar and Bardai, is, we decide, indefatigable. Liv instructs him that he must not let the pilot set such an early hour; after all, who is running this army anyway?

'These pilots!' the Colonel grumbles, 'you cannot tell them anything. They are full of talk about wind and air currents and schedules. They are impossible. So, I leave at dawn, and I will not see you again unless we meet in the desert. I shall be returning by power-wagon day after tomorrow.'

This thought revives Liv and Francis who immediately plan a rendezvous. 'We will ambush you!' Liv cries.

'Splendid!' Colonel Baylon agrees. 'The first one to sight the other will fire a salvo of champagne!'

At eleven o'clock the picnic arrives. A long table is set under the trees and we are served a smooth mushroom soup, a soufflé that is perfection, roast lamb, tiny green beans, sauté potato balls, a fresh Beaujolais during dinner. Moët et Chandon with dessert and brandy with our coffee. A picnic to delight the heart of Lucullus himself!

The only slip-up in this delightful evening is due to my fear that I may fall asleep at table. Not only have we been rising early but our days have been long and hard. And then I am one of these people who is invariably sleepy at any meal served after eight o'clock. So I quietly ask Winston to kick me under the table if he sees any untoward signs. Later he says that he aimed at me but got the Colonel instead.

HOW CAN ONE drop into bed so bone-weary and awaken so new and made over? None of us like sleeping indoors. How spoiled we are. Catherine is quite pettish about it. She says that she is beginning to think of New York as a prison. If Alan will only turn up they will let the rest of us go home and they will stay and wander perpetually about the desert periodically visiting lovely French posts and enjoying pâté, champagne and good company. Still no word from Alan but Catherine has received a letter from Duff. None of us had thought of giving Largeau as a postal address, and we are furious with ourselves and with her. And she is furious with Duff, who has merely sent a carbon copy of a letter which she had had in Benghazi three weeks ago. 'Of course,' she says wistfully, 'he is busy studying very hard.'

'What does your son study, madame?' Captain Lecomte asks sympathetically, and Catherine shrugs and says, 'Oh, *le futball* and *les jolie filles*.' And the Captain grins and says in that case he can't possibly have time to write to his mother.

Captain Lecomte has been endlessly helpful and hospitable, whizzing us through the streets in his power-wagon, entertaining us at his club and appearing at all hours to see if we need anything. He has seen that Francis has his leg X-rayed and attended to and helped us with our many errands. We have permission from the Colonel to replenish our food supply at the commissary and to purchase the dashing French Army bush hat with which we have all fallen in love. None of us has any Chad money, which was impossible to purchase out of the country. There is no bank in Largeau—but we hear of a merchant in the market place who will change money. Supplied with dollar bills we converge upon him happily only to find that he has never seen a dollar, never heard of a dollar and is not at all sure that there is such a place as the United States. Captain Lecomte comes to our rescue. We can charge everything to him and he will take our dollars. France has heard of the United States and he is

117

sure it will still be there when he returns home this summer, when he can exchange our dollars in a French bank. He invites us to luncheon where we are served pâté with French bread, grilled doves, salad and cheese with a delightfully smooth Burgundy.

In the afternoon on our way to the market place we see a string of eighty camels plod into the Place d'Orano, part payment of a blood-debt. The market place is brilliantly white, arched and arcaded, a Moorish Agora. Within its courtyard and along its arcades is a veritable rookery of women. Black robed, sad, hawk featured, they squat before the woven platters on which they display their wares. There is nothing for sale in the market but food; dried tomatoes, onions, ocra, little heaps of henna, red peppers, fine little nests of noodles, all of the quantities are small and neatly arranged. Now and again we see a brilliant dress, but for the most part these women are in black. Black-clad women are descended from slaves. Some of them, captured as children, have no memory of another home and no real understanding of their officially free status. Traditionally the Tebu is a warrior and nomad. Farming or work of any sort he considers beneath him. In the old days while the master was out raiding or wandering with his flocks, or hunting gazelle, the slave, whose Achilles tendon had been cut to keep him from running away, was left to tend the dates and gardens. Today, with the slave trade illegal, there is little cultivation of any sort in the Tibesti. Nobody wants to work, and nobody can be forced to do so. Among these self-unemployed people perhaps the most lowly, the most looked-down-upon, are the metal workers, also former slaves. To call a Tebu a tinker is the worst insult you can throw at him. In an alley near the market we come upon one of these men at work. With a tiny charcoal fire and goatskin bellows he is forging a spearhead from the raw material—tin cans his customer has brought him. These people are also said to make jewelry and charms and to have the spell-casting powers of gypsies. It is also they who beat the tom-tom for the dances. That they are thought such a despicable bunch seems to us proof that the Tebu consider any kind of work dishonourable. Far more noble to raid a caravan, or, since that is frowned on these days, to wander with the flock, to stalk gazelle, spear in hand—for the Tebu are not permitted to carry guns—or perhaps to sit on the ground and make tea and meditate.

There are many *metisses* or half-castes in the streets, dusky children with golden curls or young girls gaudily dressed and jaunty. In fact so gaily dressed we think their income couldn't come from selling dried noodles in the market place, and say as much. The Captain shrugs, 'What will you? there is not much for a man to do in Largeau.'

In the afternoon we go to the Captain's for refreshment. From the tower of his house he points across the desert to a heap of rubble, or rocks, barely visible among the dunes.

'That,' he says, 'was a fort. It was built in 1913 and abandoned in 1932 because of the moving dunes. It has just begun to reappear. The present fort is the third which has been built here.'

We try to photograph the shapeless mass, but are sure the picture will make no sense.

Below us are many garden walls, their random angles making a pattern of light and shade. Catherine says that she has a compulsion towards garden walls, and she prefers the hidden garden to be a bit weedy and tangled. Mystery and romance simply do not thrive in the open and under a lawn-mower.

Down from the tower, we make the delightful discovery that the Captain's house is a gem of modern design—it has a bathroom. Catherine and I lose no time in batting our lashes at the good Captain and making an assignation to return to call on him while our men are busy refilling on petrol and water for to-morrow's start. It does not take much, we decide, to undermine the moral training of a lifetime. The Captain is charming, but under certain circumstances we think that it would be possible to fall in love with even a lesser man provided he owned a bathroom —streams of running water, hot as well as cold (though we would not insist on hot water; we may be sybarites at heart but we are not unreasonable)—great white towels, a stationary mirror and a toilet. Catherine says that it is as well we are leaving tomorrow, for while I have a husband to keep me in order she is both vulnerable and susceptible. In fact not half an hour after we have showered and departed she wants to go back and have another shower.

In the late afternoon Catherine and I do our commissary

shopping. Captain Lecomte irons out every difficulty, tells anyone who tries to obstruct us that they are camels, though really everyone is friendly and helpful and not camels at all. We have difficulty in choosing between the marvellous cans of French foods on the shelves. Prices are high, for this food has come a long way. We spend a hundred and fifteen dollars on fruit, juices, vegetables and rice, steeling our hearts to the pâté, the pickled herrings, the tempting cheeses and wines. Shopping done with, the Lieutenant in charge of the commissary, and the Captain, give us a glass of beer in the office lounge. We relax and talk about life. The Captain regales us with tales of his abortive attempts to get married. One girl had too outlandish a name, and he felt foolish when he used it endearingly in letters, let alone face to face. He shudders, he says, to think of marrying some pretty girl only to find that she doesn't know where to squeeze the toothpaste. His brother officer smiles cynically, and Catherine tells him that he is definitely not a serious type. This is one of the greatest compliments you can pay a Frenchman, as she well knows, and both our friends roar with laughter.

We would like, this last night, to entertain Captain Lecomte but we do not prevail. We dine at his club again. The soldiers are at the N.C.O.s' mess whooping it up. They obviously have more stamina than the rest of us, for we make gratefully for our beds at an early hour. Liv and I bed down in the garden; we will sleep well, for we're under the stars again. Fortunately this trip has made us flexible and taught us not to count on anything, for at 2 a.m. one of Hank's traps goes off under our noses with a snap that brings us upright in our cocoons. Liv's curiosity compels him to get up and see if Hank has caught a new species, but he finds nary a whisker. At 3 a.m. someone shines a flashlight in our eyes. This is accompanied by a choir of male voices rendering bawdy songs. With fascinating consideration the boys, returning from a lively evening, douse their lights as they enter the guest house, and promptly fall over every box, bag, pot, pan and jerry-can stacked in the halls. The walls reverberate and Catherine insists that the language that accompanies this débâcle is early Celtic because she cannot understand a word. She has a charitable nature. They awaken Hank, dangling a mouse in his face, and calling, 'Wake up, mon, wake up and see what ye've caught.'

WE DO NOT come naturally by early starts. There always seems to be a bevy of little things that can only be seen to at the last minute. We load up the cars and take a fond farewell of our little convict, whom Catherine says she would like to take back to Hopewell, New Jersey, to weed her garden, and we proceed as far as the public square. Catherine has at last had a cable from Alan, who is in Rome, and who will not after all rejoin us. She has a letter to mail to him and everyone wants Chad stamps. Liv has a cable to compose to the Prime Minister of Chad, at Fort Lamy. It is His Excellency Prime Minister Tomboul Bey who has made possible our entry into Chad by the north-east border. This route is generally forbidden, as its tracklessness and lack of any wells makes it hazardous to the traveller and fraught with the possibilities of trouble to the authorities. We had hoped to be able to fly to Fort Lamy and call upon the Prime Minister to express our thanks in person. But our many breakdowns and delays have eaten up too much time. We have less than three weeks before we must be back in Benghazi, and still more than four thousand kilometres to cover. While letters and cables are being despatched an officer hurries across the square to Captain Lecomte. A man is lying dead down the road. Camel theft has reared its ugly head again! Lecomte scowls and shrugs.

'I will deal with it when I get back,' he says. 'First I must say goodbye to my friends.'

He leads us out of town on to the track for Zouar, which he says is very difficult to find even in clear weather. And we are leaving Faya-Largeau in anything but clear weather. The wind whips the sand like spray into the air, reducing the visibility to a 'mere smear'. We race up the dunes which are almost literally marching on Largeau this morning. Down their far sides are valleys as hard and flat as tennis courts. Here, after pointing out our direction, kissing the ladies' hands, saluting gaily and wishing us well, our Captain turns and vanishes in a swirling foam of sand.

We immediately lose sight of the track which is obliterated by sweeping inundations of sand even as we watch it. With Francis in the lead we bang over hidden ridges, bog in creamy swamps. We have carburetter trouble and Liv must get out and clean it, with sand blowing like red-hot needles into his face, his eyes, his ears and lungs. He says he thinks we are all going to die of silicosis. Catherine gives him a chiffon scarf which he wraps around his face, but this sand would go through a stone wall let alone a bit of silk. We tie a sheet to the windward side of the hood and anchor it with our bodies, trying to protect the machinery if not the man. Our legs and backs are lashed and stung, and Catherine has the nerve to tell us that you have to pay for sand-massage like this at the beauty parlours of New York! The damage repaired, we struggle on. The cars rock in the wind and dip and roll on the boiling earth like lumbering elephants. Everywhere are wind-carved sandstone cliffs. There is no pretence of knowing where we are. It is plain that we are witnessing the Creation, for here the crust of the earth is still bubbling and bursting; soft boils of blue-grey matter seem to plop-plop all about us and an unholy smoke steams up into the laden air. 'Realize thyself, amoeba dear' has not yet been spoken. The moment has not yet come. Life cannot exist in this place—not here. We cross vast plains of talcum powder, the 'fesh-fesh' of the Arabs. Caliche, Hank calls it. We race across it with almost hysterical speed, fearful of its delicate crust. We stir up atomic blasts of dust that mushroom into the sky, completely blotting out each of us in turn so that the car behind cannot see what has happened to the car in front. The earth may open and swallow us alive in this dreadful place, but there is nothing to do but race to the end, whatever end it be. Catherine says that this is the only time, so far, that she has been really frightened, and Winston says that it smells of vanilla! We come through this smouldering inferno with only one bogging, during which Liv manages to push out a small window-pane at the back of our car. After this we wrap out heads in towels in order to breathe at all. Now the crust is thinner, a greenish-white meringue which breaks under our weight. There is a nightmare quality to this day that leaves us with nothing to do but laugh. By evening we figure that we are no more than twenty-five miles from Largeau, having made a loop around the town. However poorly our dashing military friends think of their post, we think of it nostalgically as a little metropolis, a gem of civilized living from whose bright lights and gay faces we have been banished.

We make camp beneath a wall of dunes. Liv and Winston and Francis go off to 'recce', saying that they will be back by the time tea is made. They want to see if they can find the track. The wind has dropped with the sun and we are all tired and very doubtful of this manoeuvre. We say they are probably nipping back into Largeau for an evening at the club. Actually, we have been impressed by the lost world we have come through, and we don't like to see any of the men go off alone.

Two hours and one gallon of tea later the 'recce' party is still not back. There is no moon, the stars are bright, but the desert is a big place. We are not in flat country here where our camp lights might be expected to be seen from any distance. Hank is pessimistic in an optimistic way. He says I'm not to worry if they don't get back tonight, he himself doesn't think that they possibly can. He points out that they have food and water with them so there is nothing to worry about. But then it's not his husband out there! I tell him as much and we blow our respective tops at each other and then feel ashamed, like children caught sticking out their tongues, and rather bashfully make friends. Hank sets up the spotlights, one aimed at Jack's aerial, one sweeping the sky. Catherine and I stumble up the highest dune with a torch and are appalled at the extent of blackness beyond. At eight o'clock Hank fires off a Very pistol but there is no answering rocket. Then, just before nine, a flare streaks across the sky to the west. We shout with relief and Hank shoots off an answering signal. We train the spotlights westward, sweeping the horizon. But there is nothing there, no glimmer of light, no looming shape. We wonder if they are stuck or need help. And then with a rumble and blare of horn they come racing in over a dune from the opposite direction. They have been stuck, more than once, axle-deep in fesh-fesh, and had finally to jack the car to get out. They pretend to be shocked that we could have thought that they—of all skilled desert navigators—should be lost. They say that they had neither fired their flare nor seen ours. They laugh at us and tell us scornfully that we have wasted our ammunition on a shooting star.

123

THE STARS ARE not propitious. Perhaps they did not like being shot at last night. We are up early but start late. Winston's 'points' have to be taken out and cleaned. Francis keeps looking at his watch, a nervous tic he has developed since his watch has not worked in two weeks. There are small hairy dunes here which Hank explores for spoor. Liv and I drive up a crested dune and almost lose our car. We have reached the summit and got out the binoculars to see if we can spot any cairns. The sand is firm, but beneath the crest it drops away a hundred feet in a breath-taking concave. We walk as close as we dare and spend about ten minutes scouring the horizon when suddenly it dawns on us that the wind which is whipping the sand up and over the dune is at the same time eating it out from under the tyres of the car. We watch with horror as the car gives a little shrug and settles down, only to repeat the gesture before we can even get to it. Frantically we haul out the sand tracks and force them under the tyres; pushing, rocking and worrying at the car. Soon it is in up to the hub-caps. The wind is whipping up a frenzy and the car seems in danger of vanishing. As a last resort, we let most of the air out of the tyres and with a mighty effort our old crate heaves herself free and slithers downhill to solid sand. While reinflating the tyres Liv admits that this has been one of his least brilliant experiments.

Two hours later we find the Zouar track. It is marked by periodic cairns, iron posts or split petrol-drums. In the late afternoon we sail by a long island of trees and scrub, an oasis abandoned to gazelle. We see a dozen of them dancing on their hind feet and give chase to some larger antelope. Two cars with eager guns race off leaving the rest of us sitting in the sand waiting. Winston has been sick all day, and we get him to stretch out under a car where there is shade. We have all eaten the same food so decide that he cannot have food-poisoning. I look up heat-stroke in the first-aid book. He has all of the symptoms except that of seeing things through a purple haze. We are about to settle for this when we discover that he was an asthmatic child and particularly allergic to household dust. We decide that what he breathed-in yesterday was to household dust as a tiger is to a kitten. We have diagnosed. In this party when one of us feels ill the rest hover with saturnine concern. Each of us has his own infallible opinion, bottle of pills or house-sized bottle of paregoric. When the Army gets dysentery it takes twenty-four pills, all at once. When Catherine and I try to hold the sick down to a mild diet of boiled rice and tea we are promptly sat on. Frank firmly but gently told Catherine at one point that she was trying to starve a poor bloke. 'I dinna like to go agin a lady,' he said, 'but good heavy kit is what a mon needs, especially when he's feelin' poorly.' Good heavy kit, in particular, means beans for breakfast.

Tonight we have fresh gazelle. It is not as tender as the Uweinat gazelle. Frank spends the evening curing the head. He wants a trophy. Catherine, who has been sponging blood off the hood of No. 2, says she hopes everyone is not going to want a trophy. She says that No. 2 smells like a butcher's van and now it's beginning to look like one. She says that she is cross and is going to take her bed into the desert. In the morning Liv tells her that she looks like an Eskimo in his kayak; only the dogs missing. She is all good humour again and says that the moon has done it. It came on at midnight like an arc-light in the sky and washed her brain in an emulsion of lovely thoughts.

'The sun magnifies little things,' she says, 'but the moon makes them small again, as little things should be. The sun is for being, but the moon is for thinking. It is a pity we have to sleep at night.'

| 7TH APRIL | WE ARE UP at four-thirty and on the road before six. Francis for once has no cause for darting glances at his silent |

watch or tapping his impatient foot. We think he is looking a bit righteous, but agree that this is the prerogative of the person who awakens first and has the pleasure of turning the rest out of bed.

We are on firm gravel and the going is good. Towards eight o'clock we see in the distance three bushes which seem to be sweeping down on us, and remember our rendezvous with

Colonel Baylon. It is, in fact, the French! Our command bellows out, 'One to the right flank, Four and Five to the left.' Winston takes a frontal attack on the Colonel, whom we now see standing in the centre French car. There are three open Dodge Power-Wagons (*Les powères*, the French call them). The French party are all standing: the Colonel, Captain Alix, three N.C.O.s and a dozen or so *goumiers*. In bush hats and goggles, their faces swathed in scarves, they look like something from outer space. Having decided that the ambush is a draw, we bring out mugs and bottles.

The French set up a table covered with a white plastic cloth and offer us vermouth and a perfectly chilled white wine. Foolishly, I ask if they are carrying a refrigerator. The Colonel is delighted. 'Come and see,' he says, and leads me to *le powère* where, beside a goatskin of water, is tied a canvas sack. There is water in this and bottles of wine. The evaporation of the water through the saturated canvas keeps the wine cool.

We toast our respective nations, presidents, reigning families and patron saints and then we toast one another, one another's family and friends. The Colonel asks solicitously after Alan. Catherine pouts and says that he is still in Rome—she thinks perhaps he has found a *jolie petite blonde*. The Colonel looks horrified.

'*Oh, mais non, madame*, surely he has stayed to see the Pope.' We take yards of photographs, still, instantaneous and moving. And sadly we part company; the French roaring off to Largeau, we towards Zouar. We have consumed one bottle of whisky besides the vermouth and wine, and all before eight-thirty in the morning. We look all right and we act all right but I think that, like Dorian Gray, disintegration must be setting in somewhere.

Nor is the day ended. At lunchtime Francis discovers that he has lost his spare spring which was lashed to his bumper. While we lunch and nap under our cars he goes back over the track doing seventy-five miles in two hours, but not finding anything. It is worrying, for springs are vulnerable in this sort of travel and we expect them to pop at any time. It is hot and windy, our teeth are gritty and our eyelashes harbour little beaches. Catherine says that she never did like sand and she doesn't know why she didn't think of it before. At home she refuses to go to the beach, even for a day. We take turns breaking down and bogging. Francis prowls and scowls at each delay. Really, we are not so different from babies on a four-hour schedule. Give us our pablum on time and we are very cheerful. We are quite charitable, after black tea and sausage, towards the foibles and needs of our fellows. But after an hour or two of engine trouble, somebody looking for a bush, a load having to be rearranged after a monumental bump, a vehicle lost either before or behind us, frowns reappear, sour looks increase in frequency. With five vehicles delays are multiplied that many times. The moment for tempers to be cooled by the application of sardines and orangeade makes itself felt like clockwork.

We visit back and forth. Sometimes Catherine rides with Liv and I with Hank or Winston, or Taffy rides with Hank and Catherine piles in with us. I sit in the middle, as my legs are short and mesh with the various and sundry gears with greater ease. It is hot and the floor is unbearable. I have long since hung my sneakers out of the window and for the most part travel with my feet on the windscreen. Our engine is popping and overheating continuously. Francis and Winston have disappeared over the horizon where, on the flat gravelly plain, a lump of sugar stands up against the sky—or perhaps it is a building, put up by a prehistoric Frank Lloyd Wright.

Because of all of the bogging this afternoon each of us has sought his own sure-to-be-firmer route, and as we speed along there is no one in sight. Suddenly, as though the rock ahead of us were a magnet, all five cars appear from different points on the compass and converge upon it. It proves to be the giant rocky flat-top called by the Tebu Eli Atroun. The desert curves up to it deceptively, and only at the last minute does one see the sand dip into a circular moat at the base of this mysterious citadel. One could easily zoom by and entirely miss any encampment there, but we see No. 3 drop over the lip of sand and we all follow. We set up camp here and with the last of daylight explore the base of the cliffs. We find gazelle, fox and hyena tracks and bat droppings. High on this rocky castle a falcon has a look-out. We also find pot-shards and pictures scratched in the stone, and Frank finds a stone ball, chiselled to a perfect roundness. We decide that is is a prehistoric polo-ball.

Francis's leg is bothering him. We bathe it in salt water and Liv boils up Hank's mouse-tweezers and removes the clamps that the doctor in Largeau put in. Francis is very stoical. Catherine holds the torch for this operation and shudders. She is certainly unlike Liv, whose great ambition is to remove an appendix. As we are given to travel in remote places he once begged instructions for performing an appendectomy from a medical friend, and says that he has the whole thing blueprinted. None of us is enthusiastic at this news. Catherine says rather caustically that there is not much choice in her opinion between dying of a burst appendix or from being chopped up by your over-curious brother.

The light of the moon as it rises over the cliff is eerie and lovely.

| 8TH APRIL |

THERE ARE GAZELLE everywhere. Thank heaven the men are sated and there is no more shooting. This is much more of a living desert than anything we have yet seen. There are occasional solitary trees, occasional clumps and finally a thin forest of acacia. In Largeau we heard of gardens which the Tebu cultivate, coming from twenty and thirty miles each day, but where the mosquitoes make it impossible for them to live. We think that these gardens are somewhere near by. If the trees will grow, so, surely, will other things. We see camels grazing, and once a child with a herd of Nubian goats, but not another sign of human life. Going through these groves is difficult, as the sand is soft and churned. We cross a caravan trail and find a littering of feathers where a great bustard and an Egyptian vulture have fought and ripped each other literally to pieces. In the distance black hills loom, and as we come in to them we find a real road bulldozed through the sand and stone. We lunch on sardines and hard tack in the shade of overhanging rocks and are joined by a lordly Tebu travelling on a brilliantly caparisoned camel. Later in the hills we meet a party of tribesmen carrying spears, which we barter for. Catherine tries to trade with beads she has brought for the purpose, but these boys want money, and are not too pleased to see that ours is paper. In the end they accept our paper money, looking torn between scepticism at its worth and fear that we are djinns to be there in the first place.

128

Looking for the mouse

Where did we pack that trap?

Miggs Pomeroy and Catherine Collin.

We call on the Kaimakan. Left to right: Winston, Mr. Susi, the Kaimakan,
Mr. Bufarwa, Liv, Miggs, Catherine, Francis Gibb, Dr. Hank Setzer.

We pass a well where a wooden cross marks the death of an entire patrol. This patrol, nine Cameroonians and their camels, left Largeau for Zouar two years ago. Losing their way in a sandstorm they missed the first well, and when they came to the second well found it silted up. Here they should have turned back. However, they pushed on to the third well, which they found also dry. By then they had not the water to go either back or forward and here they died. We look at the well with sober thoughts. Further on we pass an abandoned fort. The sand slants up to the ramparts and it looks like an old tub in a heavy sea.

In the afternoon the road winds down from the hot black hills to the Zouarké valley and Zouar, a straw village commanded by a great square fort, bravely flying a tattered Tricolour. Long adobe buildings flank the fort: barracks, the house of the Chef de Poste, a guest-house with walls five feet thick, a garage full of *powères* and, behind barricades of barbed wire, row upon row of petrol-drums. Lieutenant Allaire, who with his crew haircut looked rather American when we met him over cocktails in Faya, is now in what I would call a sub-sub-tropical uniform. He wears black Mohammedan trousers topped by a loose white cassock whose open sides are held together by tabs. The Mohammedan trouser is a unique garment, roped at the waist, long in the groin and unfitted, the leg is slender only above the ankle where it fastens. It is said to be designed to catch the infant Messiah who tradition holds will be born to a man. The French Army, we feel certain, has adopted this costume for coolness only. In Faya the officers wore sandals, which we have decided is the only way to be shod in the desert. Sand which gets in can also spill out, whereas our boots and sneakers sometimes fill up so completely that they become too small for our feet. At Zouar bare feet are standard issue. We ask Lientenant Allaire if he is not afraid of being bitten by a scorpion, but he says that he has been bitten several times. He shrugs. It is not pleasant, but not fatal.

We are shown the well and our quarters and invited to return to the Lieutenant's house for drinks and dinner. Like the guest-house in Largeau, that in Zouar has two wash- or what might better be described as drain-rooms. Also like the 'drain' rooms in Largeau these are without doors. We decide that whoever comes to these places are not women, and men are not particularly concerned with privacy. The cars roar off to the well and come back with an abundance of clear cool water. Catherine and I lather ourselves from head to toe and rinse in unstinted gallons.

Lieutenant Allaire's house is a Moorish ranch-type. All of the rooms open on to a long, arcaded entrance, and in the rear a second arcade serves as pantry and gallery and between these arcades the sun never penetrates. His living-room is comfortable, cool and modern, his tastes obviously sophisticated. There are Misurata rugs on the stone floors and none of the crimson drapes we have seen elsewhere. On the far wall over a refectory table he has drawn, in charcoal, towering replicas of the Bardai rock-carvings—a gazelle, a mammoth, a running and rather apelike man. Like everyone else in this country he collects stone and stone-age implements. One lovely axe-head is cut from stone of a rich ox-blood red. He mixes drinks for us and tells us that he has learned, while on camel patrols through the mountains, where to look for these primitive relics. Allaire is a young man of austere good looks who moves with the indolent grace of an athlete. Catherine says that she finds him a bit *farouche* and that she has always wanted to meet someone to whom she could apply that description. He is hospitable, as all the French are, but basically I feel that we are an invasion of his citadel and that left to his own devices he would have thrown us all in his deepest dungeon. Over drinks he admits to us that he does not like going down to Largeau but prefers his own post. When Catherine asks him where his home is, he says, 'Here, where else?' He has been in this isolated valley for two years, and would like to return after his summer's leave.

Over the rim of his glass he watches us cynically as we argue among ourselves about our next move. We will base in Zouar. So far, so good. After that everyone has a different idea of what he wants to do. Hank wants to stay here and collect. The Lieutenant tells him that there are baboon in the rocky gorges that hem in this valley. They are difficult to find and impossible to catch. He shot a mother once, planning to keep her young for a pet. At his shot the entire pack stampeded away, one old male catching up the fallen baby and lumbering off with it. This is unexpected country in which to find monkeys and there is something ancient and mysterious, something left over from Eden, in their being here at all. They are shy almost to the point of being invisible, but the Lieutenant says that they will, upon occasion, raid the post, sweeping down from the mountains like a thunderstorm and leaving devastation in their wake. Hank is wildly enthusiastic and the Lieutenant promises to take us to a *guelta*, a pool high in the mountains, where we may find some. He asks however that we do not shoot gazelle. His predecessor was so enthusiastic a hunter, he tells us, that when he himself inherited the post there were no gazelle in the valley. After two years of protecting them they have come back. The Lieutenant runs five miles for exercise in the early mornings, for Zouar is too hot a place for any exertion later in the day. He likes to see the gazelle when he is out and says that he can come quite close to them.

Winston and Charlie are still bent on mountain climbing. The Lieutenant tells us that Toussidé is an interesting climb, though not as high as Emi Koussi. Some of us may make the attempt, some go to Bardai—a post further in the mountains—and from there to Oozou where warm springs bubble out of the rock, forming natural swimming-pools that sound delightful. Catherine is determined on going on by camel. Everyone tries to dissuade her. We don't want her to go alone, and none of us are anxious to go with her. The Lieutenant teases her and says that he will arrange a camel ride around the post for her. A half-hour should be sufficient to last her a lifetime. She will have ridden a camel.

'But I have ridden a camel, I don't even like them,' she wails.

This brings down the house, but we know we will have to take a camel trip. I for one am too weary to argue.

Dinner is served by a *goumier* whose awkwardness causes the Lieutenant to grumble, 'When I come back to this post I must bring a Japanese cook and houseboy.' Through a haze I hear Catherine tell him that he is spoiled, that his boy is not awkward and that good servants have become obsolete in a world of push-buttons and automation. My lashes weigh a ton and I let them drop, thinking that I have carried them too long in any case. It suddenly dawns on me that this lovely refreshing moment of silence has lasted too long and I open my eyes to find the Lieutenant staring at me with an expression of delighted amazement. I think he is impressed at my being able to sleep and eat at the same time. Catherine, who has watched the whole comedy with amusement, insists that the sight of a sleeping lady at his side has evoked memories. I find myself blushing while everyone else grins amiably and the Lieutenant laughs outright.

This evening we make contact with Benghazi and exchange Morse messages with the children. We had hoped for a voice contact, but the connection is not strong enough. We have to be content with dotting and dashing our love to one another. Thompson is rapid with his messages; he sends ours almost simultaneously with our writing it out, reading it upside down as he taps.

During the day the guest-house is as cool as a tunnel, but by night the air has heated up and seems trapped within its thick walls. Liv has taken our beds and Catherine's on to the roof. In the village the tom-toms are being beaten. An exciting rhythm, jungly and African, and high above it we hear a lilting warble as the edge of the drum is struck. It sounds like pipes. From the nearby dump the petrol drums bang at intervals as the metal contracts in the cool evening air. The night is fresh and the stars are bright and we are at home.

SUNDAY, AND THE Lord would not
like the sight of us. What laundresses
Catherine and I have become! Everything dries as you hang it up, which is as well, for the wind sprays our no-longer-snowy linen with a fine yellow dust. Between labours we have plotted and planned, conferring back and forth with one another and finally arriving at a plan satisfying to everyone. Francis, Winston, John, Charlie, Archie and Frank will take two cars and drive to Bardai, a post deep in the mountains to the north. They will camp at Trou au Natron, a volcanic crater, the first night, and will attempt to climb Pic Toussidé (3263 metres). If they have no trouble they will go on to Oozou to see the springs. They leave in the morning and will return on Friday. That will give us Saturday to organize and pack up for take-off on the following day for Sebha and home. Winston must be in Sebha by the 21st in order to make the weekly plane that sets down there. He will in any case be overdue for Oxford. The rest

| 9TH APRIL |

of us want to reach Benghazi by 25th April. From Zouar we need a minimum of ten days for this trip.

While the men are off climbing Toussidé and splashing in the springs of Oozou, Hank will stay here to collect, Jack to mind the radio, and Taffy, who has been ill, to rest. Liv and I have succumbed to Catherine's badgering and will go up the Zouarké by camel. Our sceptical young Lieutenant, who thinks that we are all mad, none the less agrees that this is the only way to really see the Tibesti. In the desert a Land Rover can go almost anywhere, but in these embattled mountains there is a country only to be seen on foot or by camel. The French use camel patrols constantly. In fact one is now preparing to go out from here, with Sergent Boisson in charge. He will have sixty men, a hundred camels, and will be gone for nine months. Catherine looks wistful at the news. We think there is something wrong with her.

We discuss our camel trip with the Lieutenant, who promises to find us a guide, and suggests that we follow the valley up to the Trou au Natron, where Hank can meet us with our car and we needn't have the tedious ride back. Catherine says that she does not want to come back but to go on. However, we are firm with her. The Lieutenant says that this trip would take him a day and a night, but, looking at us as a Western rancher might look at a dude, he allows as how it will take us a spell longer.

In the hot and dry afternoon we are off to see a *guelta*, to swim, we hope, and perhaps to see some baboon. We take a guide some twelve miles on the road to Bardai where we leave the cars and hike in. The sun is brutal and we've a forty-five-minute walk or scramble over rocks hot enough to bake a dozen *pizzas*. A *guelta* is a pocket in the rock where water has been trapped during the annual rainy season and which is sufficiently protected from the sun by overhanging rocks to remain cool and avoid excess evaporation. There are said to be *gueltas* all through these mountains, but it would take a year's exploring to find a fraction of them. We climb over boulders and through a narrow pass to find a body of water about thirty feet wide by a thousand long. It is set in a deep canyon and its surface is smooth and green. Disappointment and civilized fastidiousness vie with heat and dust and sweat —and lose the battle. Frank, who is an excellent swimmer, sets the pace by plunging fearlessly into this turf of algae, and soon we are in water that is deep and cold and, according to Liv, even sweet to taste despite its stink. Frank climbs the rocky cliff and makes a couple of fifteen-foot dives. We are cool and refreshed. The walk has set Francis's leg to throbbing, but now he says it is better, and I wonder if we are not perhaps bathing in penicillin.

Back at the base Catherine, who was supposed to rest and write letters and bits of journal, has decided to police the kitchen. Everything we have, every pot and pan, knife, spoon, dish and mug, is encrusted with dirt. The last leg of our trip we were on 'water discipline' as we had started out from Faya primed with tales of thirsty deaths. Francis had not countenanced any dish-washing except in sand; and baked beans and sausages when mixed with sand form a sort of glue that resists the hardest scrubbing. With a towel about her middle, ten gallons of water and two boxes of soap by her side, the plates and pans and implements stacked on the dirt floor, she sets to work. Having removed her shoes to keep them clean she wiggles her painted toes in the mud-puddles that form on the floor and feels very 'po'-white-trash'. When we return everything is so spotless that Frank says he hardly dares walk into the kitchen.

'You and my sister'd get on fine,' he says. 'Everything so clean there's nae comfort in the hoos.' Catherine's only comment on her effort is that her manicured toes have come unmanicured. Winston thinks the idea of anyone painting their toes before coming into the desert is funny anyway, and says he would like to have taken a close-up of the toes in the mud.

We are all exhausted from our afternoon's sport. Frank is no longer so sure he wants to go mountain climbing. He says he thinks he will just 'bide a wee'. I expect he will have bounced back to normal by morning, though I'm not sure that I will have.

The French sergeant and Lieutenant Allaire come for dinner which we serve al fresco in the 'public square'. We have asked them to bring their own eating-irons and we give them ham for dinner, noddles with cream sauce and spinach and fruit. The moon is bright and conversation lively. A guide has been found for our camel trip. He will appear tomorrow afternoon at three. In the morning Allaire will take us to look for baboon. Each in his own way, Catherine and Hank are satisfied.

WE AWAKEN to the bugle and the sound of running feet. In the first light of day, before the sun has topped the mountains to the east, Lieutenant Allaire has his men running cross-country as mercilessly as though he were training them for the Olympics. Getting out of bed on a flat roof-top presents difficulties. If we dress here we are on a stage. If we go down into the house we must climb downstairs on the outside of the building and cross what amounts to a public square in our pyjamas. Catherine and I hunch down in our sleeping-bags to dress, looking like two giant caterpillars humping along.

The mountaineers are off by eight o'clock and by ten Allaire has polished off his morning duties and is ready to show us the playground of the baboon. We drive up the Zouarké past towering wind-carved monuments of rock, to a place where we leave the cars and climb through a boulder-strewn canyon. We smell the *guelta* before we get to it, and not mere algae this time for a donkey has strayed here and fallen in. Its bloated carcass has sent up a reek that almost stops us in our tracks. Sheer rock skirts this little pool, and the Lieutenant, finding foothold along a thin white trail where the apes have climbed, leads us nimbly up the cliff. Hank and Liv, Taffy and I follow gingerly. In the rear Catherine crawls along, using her hands like suction-cups and talking to herself, or perhaps to God, as she comes. A final scramble brings us to a ledge from which we can look into a second pool, a deep cavern of water which flows still and dark into the mountain. The rotting smell from the pool below comes up to us and, all about the ledges and outcroppings of rock, monkey-droppings foul the air. Fetid and feral, there is no doubt that this is a favourite sporting-ground of these uncouth animals. We do not see a ripple, or a sign of life. Hank and Liv and I dare all, and jump into perhaps the coldest water I have ever felt. I doesn't take me long to clamber out but Liv swims off, disappearing into a deep fold of rock. When he returns it is to tell us that he has swum through the mountain to a pool on the far side which still smells of ape, though not of donkey. Taffy is sitting on a high peak looking saintly, with his 'Brigham Young' beard and his pale blue eyes. Catherine is taking pictures and Lieutenant Allaire, very Californian today in short shorts and sun-goggles, watches us with a curious expression. I drip-dry in the only accessible patch of sun, near the entrance to the canyon and overlooking the 'dead-donkey pool'.

'I must be getting used to the smell,' I say, for somehow it does not seem quite as bad as it was.

'It is quite possible,' Hank tells me, 'that you have nasal fatigue.' Catherine chokes over that, almost dropping her camera, and decides that it is an expression she is going to take back to New York with her.

The return trip is frightening, even for those of us who have good heads. Catherine takes one look over the side of the cliff and balks. It almost looks as though she will have to take up residence with the baboons. In the end Allaire, the only truly goat-footed amongst us, leads her down, coaxing each step out of her as she clutches at the cliff-side with one hand and at him with the other, totally oblivious of her billowing skirt.

Back at Zouar over cold beers with the Lieutenant our spirits flag, and demoralization sets in to such an extent that we want nothing but sleep. The idea of organizing food and equipment for a camel trip is almost more than we can face. In this we reckon without Catherine. She is every bit as glassy-eyed as we, but she is like a bulldozer in gear and we don't know how to disengage her. Then of course we have our pride, Liv and I, and we don't like our host's cynical leer. He obviously doesn't think that we are going to get off. However, he makes us a loan of his handsomely crimson-fringed *malamala*, or camel saddlebag, as well as a spanking new goatskin for water. Liv says unappreciatively that an old one would be better as it would have had time for the taste of decay to wash away. Allaire tells us to take plenty of padding if we intend to ride, and Catherine says that she certainly isn't going by camel on her own feet.

At three sharp our guide is there, a tall white-draped Tebu, his black face as haughty and beautiful as a fallen angel's. He has a string of camels and a boy to help him. The camels roar and grind their teeth and spit at us. Catherine can definitely have them. Allaire has come to help us load up. Julius Caesar could not have swept the Gauls from his path with greater disdain than the Lieutenant lends to our affairs. First all of our neat packages must be undone, and cans and bottles, pans and mugs are thrown helter-skelter into the *malamala*. Catherine and I have taken some trouble to make up tasty menus for our trip but the Lieutenant pokes amongst our provisions scornfully, shaming us out of the onion salt and the Worcester sauce.

'You are too fond of your comforts,' he says, as he throws out the tortillas and sweet gherkins. 'When I go out with camels I take only rice and pasta. For meat you can always slaughter a goat or shoot a gazelle.'

Over the camel's hump Catherine and I lock eyes; a delightful young man but no one to go on a picnic with.

Actually we don't see that removing the onion salt has helped much. Aside from saddlebags filled with tins of food, pans and eating utensils and bundles of warm clothing, our camels are lavishly decorated with sleeping-rolls, air mattresses, *garbas*, a plastic jerry-can of water, a gun, cameras, insect repellent and blankets. On top of these heaps, on two of the beasts, go Catherine and I. On the carved wooden pommel of Catherine's saddle hangs a pink-and-blue watered-silk necessity case which causes the Lieutenant to blink in defeat. The third camel is a pack-camel. I realize with some consternation that Liv is to walk.

It is five before we set out, Catherine and I feeling alarmingly aloft. Hank has taken the movie camera from Liv and follows us in the Rover up to the rocky pass over which we climb out of the Zouarké into a valley where the car cannot follow. Liv retrieves the camera, confirms our date for two days from now and clambers over the rocks after us. It is a perfect hour of day. The heat has passed, the sun is low on the pink mountains and gorges all about us; the serrated and wind-carved pinnacles, the sand floor of the valley, are creamy; the tufts of grass and camel-thorn a painted green; the wild mimosa in full bloom. We have been travelling for three weeks in a crowd of convivial but noisy people, with comfortable but noisy cars. Now suddenly we are alone, the three of us with our quiet guide, Shehai Ocoremi, and the little white-clad boy. They stop for a moment, turn towards the east and fall down to their prayers. The camels move on, never breaking their swift pace, which, for all their appearance of lethargy, is a man's fast walk. Their pads are smooth and round and milky-white, and slightly hypnotizing to watch. At dusk we are admittedly stiff from this rollicking pace, but, conscious of our late start, would like to go on. We have crossed into yet another valley, over yet another narrow rocky pass. Shehai tells that we must camp here as we are close to the end of pasturage for the camels.

We perch limply on some nearby rocks, rubbing our backs and hips to restore normal posture and circulation, and bickering over who forgot the cocktail and how we are going to survive without it. Shehai and the boy unpack and hobble the camels, lay out our sleeping-bags, and start a twig fire. We urge him to hobble the camels further from our equipment, for no sooner are the packs off their backs than they urinate freely. From the dark of the valley two figures appear carrying a small goat, which we are offered. We decline with many grateful sounds and a present of tea. Somewhere in the valley, without light and without water, is a small Tebu encampment. Our guide converses with our visitors, one of whom walks with the strange flip-flop that shows that his Achilles tendons have been cut. Shehai squats over the fire, his bony black knees as high as his head, humming. He cooks up our dinner of tinned spaghetti and meat balls and offers us two glasses each of a sticky but delicious green tea. We lie back on our sleeping-bags and watch the stars brighten.

11TH APRIL

SHEHAI HAS THE fire going and water for coffee bubbling while the moon is still high in the sky, and we are packed up and off before dawn. It is cool travelling and the sunrise is spectacular. The sky is awash with bits of coloured cloud. We go over another rocky pass and down a long valley where the mimosa is gnarled and old and without any flower, but where the air has a lemony perfume whose source we cannot find. Everywhere are great clumps of Euforb with its poisonous fruit and its clusters of purple-and-white-starred flowers. Liv is carrying his gun in hopes of finding something new and strange for Hank. We see baboon in the distance at the foot of the mountains, and more than once gazelle. This seems to be a camel range. There are many, unhobbled, grazing on the thorn and wiry grass. Camel in foal are let out, to have their young and range until they have finished nursing. As a camel nurses its young for two years, camel-raising can't produce a quick turnover. Every time we spot one of these wandering animals Shehai's boy, whom we thought was along as a sort of assistant camel-driver, trots off to investigate it for its brand mark. He has, in fact, joined our caravan to pick up two or three camels for his grandfather.

I am not fond of camels. Wonder-beasts though they be, they are still unlovely. They have ticks, halitosis, flatulence and a rocking gait which tends to wear the skin off one's behind. However, the camel is still the model-T, the hot rod and the Cadillac of this part of the world. Although it is hard to think of the Sahara without camels, there must have been a time, not too long ago, when they were not known here, for there is no sign of them in the earliest cave-paintings and carvings; and yet there are plenty of recent pictures of these ugly, surly but very useful beasts on every waterside rock-face or shady overhang where Tebu shepherd-boys lie about tending their flocks. In America these same boys would be lounging about the corner drug store, reading magazines and talking about various late or old model cars. Here they lounge about in much the same spirit, but scratch pictures of old and decrepit, or fast and modern, camels, according to whether the lad is a realist or a dreamer. Some of the tribal aristocrats still breed the prized white racing camels, and would no more think of putting them to the strain of the six or seven days without water that these animals are capable of than we would try to drive a fine car without oil. We saw a few of these sleek, well-groomed camels around Zouar, and although we never saw them raced Shehai says that they are only used for stud and racing, and that they can easily outrun a horse. This may be true, but where he gets the information is a mystery, as there are no horses in the Tibesti, and he admits that he has never actually seen one himself.

Apart from usefulness, camels possess the virtue of long-suffering obedience, though a maltreated camel is said to bear a grudge for ever against his persecutor. I was told of a man who misused his animal for many years until it decided at last that it had had enough; it knocked its master down, knelt on him and pulverized him with its shoulders. They are apparently never shown affection or kindness, and only rarely consideration, and that merely to get more work out of them. Catherine insists that they do have an appealing look about them. They have truly beautiful eyes, patrician noses and teddy-bear hair. The young are sweetly tufty looking, and have eyelashes so long that you can see them at fifty paces. But even she is daunted by the smells, the grinding yellow teeth and string of sounds that are nothing short of blasphemous, the vindictive glares and the carefully aimed spit.

At eleven Shehai has called a halt. We are glad to come down from our tortuous roosts, and Liv's calf muscles are aching. But from the point of view of efficiency this seems an early hour to stop. At our protests Shehai shakes his head, unpacks the camels and lays out our beds. We are to lunch and rest, and lunch and rest we do—for four hours. We are under a big thorn-tree, the camels are out of sight, the *garba*, hung on a branch, produces a yellowish but cool water. We have hard tack, cheese and mackerel marinated in white wine. Shehai has made tea, which is hot and sweet and refreshing. He has put down his own bed and is reading, one bony finger running along the line of print, a French novel called *L'esclave*. Catherine speculates aloud as to whether it is red propaganda or a seductive bit of trash; the desert, the Arab way of life, beautiful slaves hidden behind bleak walls, have inspired more than one writer to purple prose. Later, when Shehai is off looking for the camels, she has a quick look and finds that his book is an historical novel about New Orleans before the Civil War.

We nap, we read, we scribble in our diaries. The heat is heavy; we explore a bit without any real enthusiasm. In two places we have found rings of stone, the remnants of stone-age houses. In the early afternoon we see a small black figure far up the dry river-bed on which we are camped. As she approaches we see that she is a small black woman carrying on her back a girl almost as big as herself. Laying the girl in the sand at our feet she squats down and exchanges a litany of greeting with Shehai. The sound of her words is musical if incomprehensible, though even our unaccustomed ears recognize the repetitious melody of a greeting formula as they chant it back and forth. When this is done the sounds change and presently Shehai translates for us from the Tebu into French. Her child has been attacked and severely beaten by an older woman and she seems to be paralysed. The mother shows us the bruised and swollen places on arms, ribs and at the back of the neck. The child is feverish and quite supine. We think she is probably concussed. We give her aspirin and try to explain cold compresses and rest with the hopeless feeling that it means nothing, though it looks as though nature is guaranteeing rest. Shehai, bored with the situation, has turned over on his side to sleep again. The mother, mournful and beautiful in her anxiety, is grateful for our pills and rather shamingly full of faith. It is a struggle to raise children in this country. A diet of dates, douma palm-nuts, goat's milk, occasional goat meat or, if one's man is handy with his spear, gazelle, is not a diet to build strength. The people are ignorant, isolated and indolent. Where they could grow gardens they do not. The French supply clinics and travelling doctors and surgeons, help which the people continue to resist. Mortality of children up to seventeen is high. Malnutrition, syphilis and trachoma and bilharziasis are rampant and, strangely enough in this high dry climate, so is T.B. At Zouar we saw children with great welts and scars on their chests and abdomens from the red-hot pokers applied by witch-doctors whom their parents would rather send for than the medical man at the Post. The treatment is said to chase the devil out of the thin little chest. It often chases the child out as well. A survivor can be expected to live to a ripe old age, for he is tough.

We have offered to take the child back to Zouar, but the mother is unwilling. She wanders off, leaving us alone; the child lies still on the sand. The *garbas* swing gently in the breeze, Shehai sleeps, a morning dove calls. Before the mother finally comes back we begin to wonder anxiously if this little bundle has been left at our doorstep. She has carried her child twelve kilometres this morning. Now she takes her up, refusing any help, and sets off for an encampment twenty kilometres down the valley.

It is after four before we get on our way again. Now we leave the valley behind us, travelling up the long twisting river-bed where the rocks are every colour of the rainbow and trees and bushes along the bank are fewer and fewer. Shehai stops at a clump of berry bushes, leading the camels to it as guests to a table. While they tear eagerly at the small red berries he hands us each a branch. This berry looks like a redcurrant, is sweet and peppery at once. Catherine has picked a branch for fly swatting. We have a repellent called 'Off' which is briefly effective. The flies nudge one another for wing space on our backs, arms and legs. Catherine says that I look embroidered. If they would just stay on my back I would not mind so much. But these are flies who like eyes. Presumably they are after moisture for they also like lips and nostrils. Entirely aside from the crawly discomfort, we have all seen too much trachoma to take this invasion lightly.

Sometime in the course of the day Shehai's apprentice has attached two camels, increasing our string to five. Liv gives himself ten minutes aboard one to discover that he never wants to ride a camel again. Back on foot he sets the pace, outdistancing us a good deal of the time, cutting straight across country. We see him disappear over the edge of a ravine or glimpse him scrambling up a rock-fall or striding intently along a ridge. Then unexpectedly he rejoins us. He seems to me to be even thinner and more wiry than when we left home. Perhaps his pointed beard has something to do with it. He looks like a Goya painting, some saint who has spent lonely years in the wilderness, or perhaps a Spanish grandee who has managed to acquire the same ascetic look during a life among the flesh-pots.

We think that there are few places where our camels cannot go, but we are wrong. The country has become rough and dangerous and we must follow the winding white ribbon that cuts up the narrow defiles, along shelf-like ledges overhanging deep canyons and across endless plateaux of volcanic pumice. In the distance all about us the mountains are blue and dreamy. In the canyons a hundred feet or more below us the rocks and cliff sides are oxydized to numberless shades of pastel: lavender, pink, green and blue. Our camels are unbelievably sure-footed. Catherine says that unbelievable is the operative word, and that these steep narrow paths were not in the travel brochure. Along the cliffs loose rocks and pebbles strew the paths, inviting, we think, disaster. Half of the time Catherine has her arms about her pommel and is positively croaking with unashamed terror. Behind me,

I dare not turn my head to look, I hear Liv cheer her on with ill-timed comments.

'If your camel goes over the cliff,' he says, 'I'll see that Shehai loses his licence.' And later:

'It's only a thousand feet down, and there's some sand at the bottom. It's not all rock.'

We career down from one plateau and scramble steeply up to another. We would both gladly get off and walk, but there is only one way to disembark from a camel and that when it is on its knees. Here there is no room for camel-kneeling. Gangling, knock-kneed, weak-ankled and smooth-padded, they do somehow find the right footstep in these rocky paths. They teeter like drunks in high-heeled slippers, but they never stumble. Aside from the mountain-climbing, which we had not counted on, we have become quite used to the rollicking gait of these creatures. The important thing is to have lots of padding under one; because the camel's hump protrudes through a central hole in the wooden saddle like a knife-blade, because the saddle is for the most part wooden, and because the one bit of padding which these saddles afford is undoubtedly stuffed with cactus. We now know just how the sleeping-rolls and blankets should be lashed to the load for greatest comfort, though perhaps 'greatest' is a strong word to use here. Perched on high, with gun and camera slung over our pommels and sitting with a Victorian uprightness to save our weary back muscles, we feel that we must look like those old postcard pictures one finds in the attic, of hardy colonial ladies accompanying their husbands into the bush. Actually they were far hardier than we for they wore those bits of ancient torture: corsets and long skirts, high-necked blouses and all sorts of hats and veils. The hats and veils are not a bad idea. We are in shorts and open-necked shirts. On her camel when the going is not mountainous Catherine has become so at home that she has taken to manicuring her toe-nails, propping one foot against the pommel and leaning over to pare and prune and paint it red. She admits that leaning over gives her a backache. But then so does sitting up. A friend who has ridden camels in the desert a good deal has since told me that it is a great relief to turn round and face the tail. Something we never thought of.

It has been a pleasant tepid day; cool in the morning, with the noon heat kept at bay by our long rest. Now in the late afternoon the skies have opened, and racing down from the mountains a cold wind whips about us. We are on top of a flat rocky table in space; behind us by half a day's march is the last tree, ahead by another day's march pinnacles of mountains which might provide a cave. In a moment we are wet through and chilled. Shehai, to whom Allah sends all things, lopes on unmindful of our misery. But Liv, in his Western mind well aware that God helps those who help themselves, orders the camels down so that we can wrap ourselves in coats, bed-rolls and air mattresses. We have brought heavy down-filled winter jackets and at the end of this tropical day they are more than welcome.

The sun downs early with mountains closing in to screen it suddenly away from us. There is still light in the sky but the world is grey about us. The rain has done its worst by the time we find a camp-site in the lea of a high rocky ledge. We have come upon three round stone huts, dark and quiet in the failing light. If there are people here they are already asleep. Shehai smooths away rocks and pebbles, lays out our beds and makes his fire. He tells us that there is a *guelta* near by and he will refill our jerry-cans and water the camels at dawn. Even Catherine is somewhat disillusioned at this beautiful man who falls on his face to pray five times a day, has a plebeian cold in his patrician nose and is given to making noises that compare unfavourably with those that the camels make. Nor does he believe in going behind bushes. His long white robe covers a multitude of activities. His dish-washing would fail every *Good Housekeeping* test. His little blue teapot, while too small to actually put his long leather toes in, he none the less uses for washing his feet.

Over hot steak-and-kidney pud we become aware that Shehai has awakened the neighbours. There are shadowy shapes and the sing-song Tebu chant. Someone has offered us a kid. It bleats pitifully and we decline with thanks. Not so Shehai, who prepares to slaughter it as close to the dining-room table as makes no matter. Liv firmly relegates him to outer darkness to do this deed. Though we have offered him our food he will not eat it without knowing what manner of meat it is or who killed it. We think of suggesting to Armour & Swift's that if they wish

Playing on the beach

Winston washing dishes

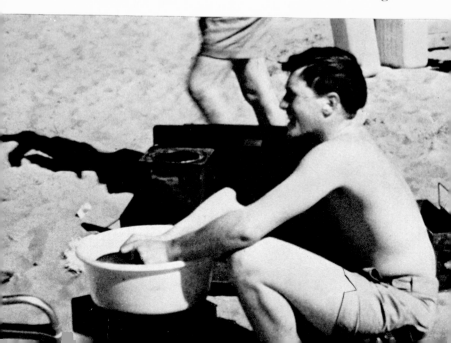

Miggs on a camel

Out in the midday sun

to capture the Mohammedan market for tinned meat they include on the label the name, address and religion of the butcher. There seems an indecently short interval between the last child-like bleat and the smell of roasting meat. Across the fire Shehai and his boy squat, tearing at the meat with hands and teeth. The stone huts are quiet again. We go off among the rocks to wash and make ready for bed. We have decided that we have stepped back in time to the stone ages. Shehai, as he turns eastward this night to chant his praise to Allah, belches and yawns mid-stanza, replete with his unaccustomed feast.

WE AWAKEN TO a smouldering fire, no camels, no Shehai. A stone's throw from us two black-draped women squat like monkeys close to the ground. We stagger off to wash and dress behind giant boulders, and are delighted to find them covered with carvings of camels and people and occasionally gazelle. There is no telling how old these carvings are. We were not wrong; these people are stone-age people. They build their houses as they have built for thousands of years, a circle of stones placed one on top of another without mortar of any sort, and topped off with still-green Euforb branches. What rain or wind or blowing sand comes to this place comes indoors as well as out. They crush date-pips or nuts in stone bowls, using as pestle any round stone that comes to hand, and in their lonely animal life they seek an outlet for the human spark—they make pictures with a bit of stone on pieces of rock. Yesterday we saw more than once the small ring of stones where a house had been. And today we see the graves that we have been told to watch for. Heaps of stones, some mounds neolithic, some made yesterday.

Our two visitors have returned to their houses and come back bringing us goat's milk that is dusty and warm, in an enamel bowl made in Hong Kong. The women are slight and frail, batlike in black, their eyes red and rheumy. We know that the milk is important to them, the bowl more than a koh-i-noor. We give them a tin of raspberry jam and, turning out the last of our pancake batter, make a king-size cake which they accept with much the look of suspicion that we feel for their goat's milk. Shehai is not back from the water-hole and we invite ourselves to visit our Tebu friends in their houses. With signs and gestures we follow them. All about the houses is a system of asymmetrical landscaping. Here where nothing grows they have made themselves several little gardens of pebbles and brushed sand, outlined with geometric precision. Some of these outdoor rooms are filled with a special kind of pebble, some with goat manure. We cannot guess at their use or meaning. We stoop to follow the women into their house. Inside I can stand upright but Liv and Catherine cannot. The woman who is carrying the pancake and tin tosses them both into a sling or hammock which hangs from the ceiling, and which seems to contain all of the family's worldly goods. A couple of tin cans are evidence of contact with civilization and obviously treasured as cooking utensils. Plaited straw, a stone bowl and a heap of goatskins complete the furnishing of the house. The sandy floor, like that in the straw hut we saw at Ounianga, is immaculately swept, the hearth two blackened stones in the centre of the room. Smoke is no problem as it rises straight through the loosely twined branches of the roof. I wonder why they have bothered with a roof at all, it is so loosely made that it cannot offer much protection. Perhaps it is a convenience from which to hang things, for beside the hammock hangs a basket and a *garba* of water. To live in such poverty, so close to starvation and yet without squalor, is surely an achievement.

There are no men about and only two children, a chubby baby wearing a ring in only one ear, and a little girl who could not be more than five, bravely hustling a flock of goats down to the water-hole. The men will be away in the valley with their flocks or in the mountains hunting gazelle or mouflon. In the absence of their men Tebu women have complete authority over affairs at home, including the disposition of any livestock left to them, and, not so very long ago, of their slaves. They are greatly respected and run to somewhat of a matriarchal culture. This is unusual amongst Moslems who tend to consider their women unable to manage anything except childbearing and cookery.

With Shehai's return we are soon on our way again. The Tebu women squatting by their houses wave shyly, and we think somewhat hopelessly, to us. In this place of black rocks, black huts, their black faces half hidden in black cowls, the shadow of the mountains looming, we think of these women as serving in a special purgatory from which they have no hope of rescue. In fact, as the day drags on and we climb into country that is wilder and more forbidding by the moment, Liv announces that we are all dead and roaming in hell; we just think that we are on a camel trip of our own free wills. Catherine and I admit that our backs ache unbearably, and Liv says that his calf and thigh muscles will never be the same.

We have seen a whole troop of baboon, a nursery of female and young with a lumbering old male in attendance. We have also seen a good many gazelle and lost considerable face with Shehai for not shooting any. This morning Liv, who has gone on ahead, has spotted something new and strange. We round a canyon's end to find him sitting on a bit of outcropping, his hand up to forestall speech, and at the same time pointing to something just out of sight to us, round the rocks. Shehai enthusiastically unbuckles the gun and hurries forward—but even with his speed too late; the animal has gone. Liv is not sure what he has seen, and is surprised to have seen anything in this place where there is not a blade or twig to live on. The baboon will travel far for food and so will gazelle. But this animal was small and, Liv thought, some sort of marmot.

'The illusive *na*?' I ask hopefully, using my one and only Tebu word. 'John and Frank were talking about it the other day. The Tebus call it a *na*, Hank calls it a hyrax. Frank said, "And what is that?" and John said, "I dinna noo, but Hank says it looks like a momot." And Frank said, "So it's mommoth ye're after is it? Ye'd better take something bigger than a shotgun or ye'll nae be comin' back alive." '

Liv laughs but looks wistfully towards the rocks as though he'd like to spend the day here stalking—for Hank has not got a 'momot' at all. According to Hank, Frank is not so far wrong, for the Rock Hyrax is a distant relative of the elephant and mammoth. While we have seen signs of them before, until now none of us has seen one. Hank is anxious to have one for the museum. But this particular *na* has seen as well as been seen, and evidently has no intention of ending its days stuffed full of cotton in a museum drawer. It is a pity that we cannot give it more time, but we have a long way yet to go. Although as leader of the expedition Liv has the right to rule comings and goings, he has been long-suffering with the perpetual impatience of some of the boys to hurry on. He himself would have preferred to dally, to get the feel of a place, talk with a farmer or a king, or sketch a valley at sunset. Now we have Hank waiting for us at the Trou au Natron, and our fine, feathered French friend Allaire has misled us atrociously about both distance and speed. We think he never made this trip by camel, but quite possibly did by helicopter.

It is plain that Shehai is disgusted with us. As we move on at last he explains patiently that the *na* can be eaten only by children. This seems to be so of most of the small animals and birds of the Tibesti. Man eats gazelle, antelope, mouflon and hare, children eat 'less serious' game: small birds, mice, jerboa, fox, jackal, lizard, hyrax and coney or gundis. Of course, in time of famine these taboos are forgotten, and everyone eats anything he can find. Asked when especially there is famine, Shehai shrugs haughtily. 'For some,' he says, 'it is always famine time.'

From our camel-tops we scour the ground for artifacts or interesting pebbles, though we are tantalizingly high for such a pastime. By the time we have said 'Um!' and called to Shehai to stop the beasts, the pebble is far behind, indistinguishable among a million others. But Shehai has a certain unexpected sympathy when he discovers what the great white ladies from far away want and often, without prompting, finds us some choice piece of jet or mica. He has sharp eyes, and if he had the will could undoubtedly find us a *na*. We are climbing again today, up steeper canyons, across more endless-seeming pumice plains. Quite suddenly in the distance beyond our sight he has spotted movement, and calls out a long and echoing 'coo-ee'. From far away we hear a warbling response, and Shehai speeds up the camels. We have gone a mile before we see the warbler, running nimbly over the rocks to intercept us on our path. She is there when we come up; a girl in black, like the women at last night's encampment. But, while they were old with flesh that hung like dried haddock from their faces, this girl is fresh and pretty. She squats on the rock and exchanges with Shehai the singing litany we had heard before. 'God be with you and all of yours,' she sings.

'God be with you and all of yours,' Shehai answers.

'God be with your mother and your father.'
'God be with your mother and your father.'
'God be with your brothers and your sisters.'
'God be with your brothers and your sisters.'
'God be with your wife, God be with your wife, God be with your wife' (in case there are more than one, but not to be prying).
'God be with your man.'

Only then can she ask Shehai where he is going, who we are. What the news of the valley is, or of the last settlement we have passed.

Shehai is obviously bored with this girl and yet it was he who first coo-eed her, and he would not have dreamed of refusing to respond to the ritual. Only the questions obviously irk him and he hastens to push on. We wave to the girl, but she has no answering wave for us.

Hank will be at the rendezvous today but there is not a hope that we will. We have already travelled a day longer than our good Lieutenant prophesied, and we have been travelling fast. Shehai brings the camels to a halt by a lonely thorn-tree growing in the floor of a canyon. It is eleven o'clock and time to rest. Liv protests.

'No rest today,' he says. 'We want to get to the Trou by nightfall.' But Shehai shakes his head.

'Tomorrow, maybe.' He points at a blue pinnacle in the distance. 'Tomorrow we will climb that. Trou au Natron is beyond by another four hours.'

Catherine says that she doesn't believe the mountain to begin with and how are we supposed to get the camels over it? Liv says that tomorrow is too late and that we must hurry. But Shehai is not moved. He unpacks the camels and, smoothing away stones and pebbles, makes a place for our beds. 'We must rest,' he says. 'The camels must feed, they must stay in the shade, the sun is bad for them.' And he makes a fire and puts on his little pot. Liv pours water into a basin and washes his socks and feet. He is cross with Shehai and gives him a lecture on efficiency and then we all go to sleep; that is Shehai and Liv and Catherine and I go to sleep, the flies do not. They have had a long morning's ride and now they take a little exercise, skin-diving. They enjoy their busy days and only give up when the sun goes down and the mosquitoes take over the night shift. By being adamantly Western Liv manages to get us back on the road by three-thirty. We continue to climb. Each mesa seems higher than the last. On the sides of the canyons there are often thorn-trees, which we learn to dread, for the camels love to rub against them and it is a feat to swing your legs out of the way in time. The thorns look big enough to sew leather with and we suspect are poisonous as well.

Shehai is moody. He says that we have not rested long enough, and one of his camels is sun-struck. A novel idea which we do not buy for a minute. His little assistant disappeared in the early dawn today; apparently he had found the camels he wanted and has taken them off home. It has been a hard day and none of us are sorry when it is done. We make camp in a canyon. Shehai worrying over his camel and Catherine over her legs. She says that she can't straighten them out and she thinks that she is getting the camel bends. We have found some instant cocoa among our rations. It is very reviving. We have a smooth ledge of rock for our table and on the canyon floor Shehai's fire burns brightly. Sun-struck or not one of the camels is definitely off his thorn-bush and moons and glooms about the fire instead of going off with his fellows. Liv had started out on this jaunt without an air mattress. He says he knew he would have to blow up ours for us anyway and three were more than he could take. In which he maligned us quite monstrously. And tonight he is sorry—so, I might say, are we. If there is sand in this gully it is invisible beneath the clutter of rocks, and even Shehai's valiant efforts have not made a smooth place for the beds. We contrive a sort of triple bed by lying the two mattresses sidewise and the three of us sleeping tight packed. I am reminded of the fact that Japanese wives are trained not to move in the night unless their husbands do and then to turn simultaneously. I call this to the attention of the other two—for I am not only in the middle but being the lightest am flipped into the air like a pancake when either of the other two turn over. The night is cold and deliciously bright and sleep comes down like an ether cone.

WE CLIMB OUT of the gully under our own steam. Catherine says that she has had her fill of camel-alping, but that is just what she thinks. The Land Rovers may not be limousines, but they are beginning to seem so to us. After an hour's scrambling Shehai suggests we get back on board, he says that we will have real climbing later and should save our strength. One look at the mountain ahead of us and we abjectly agree.

This trip has been a series of giant steps up higher and higher plateaux, not one of which can we go straight across but must thread and twist and circumvent to avoid crevasses and pits, gulfs and chasms. At four thousand feet we cross a sandy valley and climb to yet another plateau. Ahead is the menacing mountain we are to climb. Surprisingly, in this wilderness, we come upon an old man and a boy. The boy carries a *garba* and a goatskin, the man a staff. Shehai has stopped to exchange a litany. When this is done he and the old man and the boy stand together facing the east and pray aloud, going down at last on their knees and three times touching their heads to the ground. When this is done we move on again. The old man walks with us a while, talks with Shehai, shakes hands solemnly with Liv and never once looks at Catherine or me atop our camels with the other chattels. The child does not come with us but squats down with his water-skin and his goatskin, so small and thin and so alone in this immense loneliness, and with so few chances of living anyway, that one wonders. These people are nomads. They know where the grass is greener—where there is any grass at all. They know where the water is. So why do they come into these mountains to live? The huts we visited are built in a wasteland of rock, while only fifty kilometres away is the Zouarké valley with its trees and pasturage. Perhaps Liv is right and this is purgatory. Who then is sharing it with us? Who was the old woman who offered us goat's milk this morning? Messalina perhaps! This place would be fitting

151

punishment for her. And the fat baby? I thought he must be still nursing to be fat, or perhaps wet-nursing on the goat—for chubbiness is not common among these people. Considering the high mortality among children perhaps his is a soul that has not sinned greatly and will not then be long for this place, A gruesome thought, but a gruesome place that gives rise to it.

The camel's pace is fast, and for all its rocking is still smooth, a rocking as regular as a metronome. The camel's feet, round and white, lift and fall, lift and fall. Shehai walks ahead with a swinging pace that seems without effort, his white turban brought around his mouth to keep the wind, or perhaps the sun, away. Far ahead Liv lopes, exploring now to the right, now to the left, occasionally picking up a stone or coming back for camera or gun. A dramatic skyscraper pinnacles above us and we disembark to scramble up this unlikely Alp on foot, sometimes even trotting to keep ahead of the camels. The path is narrow, the slopes steep and the animals loom much too quickly on our heels. Walking with camels is like taking a stroll with dinosaurs. They tower over us with wicked sneers, they do seem to have a well-developed hatred for the human race. The path is slippery with loose rock and shale. We scramble and puff, indignant as each seemingly last pinnacle merely hides another and higher peak. After two hours of climbing we struggle over a scarp to a high and unexpected plateau. This surprising mountain does not have a descending slope. We are six thousand feet up and we have, Shehai tells us, four hours' fast walk to the Trou. It is windy here and cold with an intermittent drizzle. We put on our coats and mount the camels again, grateful for a rest and rather sorry for the poor devils who have carried all of our gear up this steep path and now must carry us. The sun-struck camel has his own ideas on this score, and he roars and spits and grinds his teeth and refuses to budge. He is a small tough camel used as a pack animal and not even heavily burdened, carrying as he does Shehai's gear: blanket, prayer-rug, bag of dates and tea, the volume L'Esclave and the little blue teapot. Still he will not move, and behind him our mounts are stationary. It is close to normal rest-time and he may have that in mind—but Liv is firm that we have no morning rest today but push on to the Trou.

Shehai has added his curses to the camel's not inconsiderable vocabulary. He tightens the rope fastened about the animal's lower lip until the blood spurts out and the creature screams with pain and anger. Still it will not budge and Shehai, seizing up a rock as big as a plate, heaves it, catching the camel a sickening blow on the side of its head. Behind me I hear Catherine muttering about reporting Shehai to the R.S.P.C.A. and me as well when he hands me a fistful of stones which I am to fling at its hindquarters. We beg Shehai, now beside himself, to tie the camel to the end of the string—especially desirable since the furious camel has now reared back until his head is on a level with my naked and cringing legs. Liv, already in the distance, is no support to us, and neither is the R.S.P.C.A. who have not any influence in the Tibesti. In desperation, Shehai finally takes our advice and attaches the sun-struck, rock-struck, fuming beast to the rear and like magic we move on again. Catherine says that her own rear feels very undefended and suspects that her camel feels the same way and that is why we suddenly commence to move so fast.

There are occasional stunted trees and bushes in this high country. Shehai picks a lavender-coloured flower which grows on a bush that looks like a laurel and which he says is good for camels with the colic and for women in childbirth. He also picks us branches of a yellow flower with a mimosa-like bud and a sweet and lemony scent.

We are all tired, and we wonder how Liv keeps up the pace. We have travelled almost eighty miles and most of it climbing. Ahead the land continues to rise. While we don't have another mountain to scale we will have to climb a long escarpment. Without asking I know that we are all thinking of the luxury of riding back to Zouar in Land Rovers, the cosseting comfort of lots of soap and water. Never mind if the water is cold and has to be ladled by hand. After four interminable hours Liv calls out, pointing to a distant escarpment. We distinctly see an ant on top of it, soon joined by two other ants and perhaps a half-hour later we are able to distinguish several animated toothpicks. When at last we lumber up the final slope we see that three cars are awaiting us and all of the boys. There is a mad dash for cameras. Frank and Archie have the stove set up and are brewing tea. Winston shouts out that we make a wonderful shot but that he's dropped his camera six times in the last two days and doesn't think it's done it any good. He runs it hopefully none the less.

It is a wildly hilarious reunion. The party from Bardai had arrived only two hours ago and decided to wait with Hank. They are all in good form though Francis is already tapping his toe and looking at his long-silent watch. Hank is trying to stamp away the cold as he drinks down some boiling tea. He is cold, wet and somewhat disgusted, for which we cannot blame him. Expecting to meet us the day before, he drove out from Zouar bringing a guide but failing to bring food, warm clothing or a sleeping-bag. The night must have been perishingly cold and I'm frank to admit I would have gone home and tried again another day. His frustration cannot have been helped by the fact that he found the place ratless and mouseless and did not bring a book with which to pass the time.

While we have tea Shehai has a fire going and is making up his own favourite brand which Hank's guide shares with him. Shehai will start back down the mountain as soon as his beasts have had their four-hour nap. He has unsaddled them and they stand looking sadly down the way we have come. There is nothing for them to eat here and they stand there haughty even in their misery—perhaps it is they who are in purgatory, paying surely for the sin of pride.

We are on yet another plateau but a small one and we walk across it now to its edge. Here the land drops two thousand feet into the Trou au Natron, a magnificent and somewhat terrifying crater completely surrounded by cliffs. The lip of the bowl is twenty-five miles in circumference, and from where we stand it is eight miles to the far side. Below, on the floor of the bowl, are several black volcanic cones rising out of a snowfield of natron. There is a steep narrow path going into the crater, but there is no one so goat-footed amongst us that he would care to try it. And yet it is used by the Tebu who go down to collect the natron (sodium nitrate) which is fed to the camels much as we feed rock-salt to cattle. Hank's guide says that two families live in the crater but Shehai shakes his head. Perhaps he is afraid that we will want to go down to see them. He need have no fear.

The drive back to Zouar takes us five miserable hours. Gone is our peace and solitude, our feeling of belonging. We have to crowd eleven people into space which will seat six comfortably, nine uncomfortably. Hank rides back with Francis and we take his guide with us, starting him off in the rear of No. 2. The descending track is bumpy and curving. Closed in the rear the fumes of petrol mix with the smell of our camel-contaminated sleeping-bags, dirty lunch dishes and Hank's formaldehyde, and prove too much for the guide. We hear him groan, and dragging him out to put him up front with us we find that he has gone quite olive green. Four of us packed hotly into the cab is something to endure. On the mountain trail before we come down into the Zouarké we meet a convoy of three *powères* in charge of a lieutenant who stops to have a cigarette and pass the time of day. His has been the discouraging task of delivering from Bardai motors and spare parts for five Zouar *powères* which have burnt out their plates. In the course of this trip one of his own cars burnt out and had to be abandoned and he is now on his way back to Bardai with two cars which he does not expect much of. 'All of our cars have rebuilt motors,' he says. 'Twenty thousand kilometres is all we can hope of them.'

He refuses a second cigarette and we part, going down into the hot Zouarké where our No. 5 has its own spot of engine trouble—oil where there should be none. It bogs, and we all pile out and confer. John fixes it up in a hot sandy hour and we go on, only to lose Winston when he hares off after a herd of gazelle. It is night before we come into Zouar, have our promised baths and creep gratefully to the roof-top.

14TH APRIL

I LOVE THE early mornings at Zouar. The bugler—not a very good bugler, but British-trained, according to the Lieutenant—awakens us with reveille. It is barely light but by raising myself on one elbow I can see the crenelated outline of the fort against the topaz sky. Soon the long-legged native soldiers run by, doing their morning exercise. They chant rhythmically to help themselves along. Their voices are deep and their chant has a booming sound. The French in these outposts put up obstacle courses which look worthy of the International Horse

Show. This morning they are ordered to sprint the last hundred yards to their barracks; two fall, causing a hazard for those behind, and the exercise disintegrates merrily. With this entertainment over I roll back into my bed and watch the tips of the mountains change colour, ready to receive the sun. A raven hops ponderously on to the roof, and in hope of scraps peers over the balustrade at our table, set out of doors below. Ravens are sacred to the Tebu and are never trapped or hunted; they are comically sure of themselves, and the only nosier birds are the little white-crested chats, which will hop right into the cars.

The bugler reappears as the soldiers parade for the raising of the Tricolour. I notice this morning that the torn flag has been replaced by a bright new one. The Lieutenant says that it takes no more than a month for dust and wind to tear a flag to shreds. The flag now flying bravely over the fort, the soldiers disperse about their daily jobs and I suddenly realize that the sun is up, the world is awake and that I'm on a roof-top in the middle of the compound in a pair of conspicuous red-and-white-striped pyjamas.

One aspect of this trip which has turned out far less embarrassing than we had expected it to be has been the bathroom department. What do you do, Catherine and I worried, accompanied by ten men in what the books call a featureless desert, when you need a bush? There were occasions when the nearest dune meant a mile's walk, and once reached it had shrunk to a molehill. Too often it proved not to have a sequestered side but to be a sort of stage on which, one felt, every opera-glass was trained. However, on the whole, the desert is peppered with friendly boulders, dips and dunes. When all of these fail one simply sends the others a decent five miles ahead and later follow their tracks. Very rarely were we unable to find a camp-site without some shelter—rocks, palm-tree or dune—and of course there was always the furtive night. Forts and guest-houses all had their latrines, and each, like the rabbit-hutch at Kufra, was at least distinctive. At Ounianga a long black tunnel led to a throne cut into the embattlements. A stack of comics was kept here and a fat lizard with pink skin haunted the walls. At Zouar an Egyptian vulture perched on the wall in front of the outhouse. A man's world, none of these places could boast a door. But we found singing in the latrine quite effective.

As to bathing, except for Francis's fiercest moments of 'water discipline', when all washing was forbidden we managed complete baths in a cup or two of water, and even rinsed out our clothes frequently. Clothes would dry almost instantly, even at night, and we would feel fresh the next day if decidedly tattle-tale-greyish. Light colours suffered the most from being washed in too little water, and for the sake of appearance and morale plaids and reds and bronzes are better travel colours. Something the Bedouin, who wash only at birth and death, have long discovered. Sneakers we have all decided are an abomination in the desert, except perhaps when scrambling over rocks; the sand scorches through them at midday and they are no protection from the cold at night. It is best to have boots for cold weather, sandals for hot. Other necessities for desert travel are lots of cold cream or suntan lotion, and perhaps for the men the wind-up razors which some of our men carried. Actually only Winston and Francis shaved, though Liv trimmed his beard into fancy shapes.

This morning Catherine and I collect jerry-cans of water and every available bowl for a last wash. Sunday we take off for home. We sit on stools beside the wash-drain and soak, wash, rinse (normal); soak, soak, wash, wash, first rinse, second rinse, third rinse (camel trip). Catherine wishes aloud for tubs full of running water and a scrubbing-board, and I suggest rather pettishly that while she's wishing she make it an automatic washing-machine. After all there's no need to stint, is there? Outside we hang things on lines strung between cars. Fifteen minutes' drying time in the hot wind is all that even the heaviest trousers take. The men have their wash strung out on Thompson's aerial. Hank uses it as well to dry skins and skulls. He has got his baboon at the *guelta* of the dead donkey. All of the lack of bacteria in the world does not eradicate the smell. He says that the creature was full of parasites both inside and out and that its hands and feet were almost shredded with thorns. I asked if it were male or female and Hank said, 'Dog.'

'I mean the monkey,' I said.

'The baboon,' Hank told me patiently, 'is a dog.' I feel that I have joined Catherine's non-scientific category in his mind.

Curried gazelle for dinner. A work of art we think. We have invited the Lieutenant for dinner and a French Army Captain

Doctor who has just come into Zouar on a tour of posts. The Captain joins us but reports the Lieutenant ill; he thinks hepatitis, but is not sure yet. A military plane comes to Zouar once a week and he can be flown out if necessary.

It is Taffy's birthday. We haven't been able to make a cake but have devised a sort of shortbread dessert with an ample lathering of stewed apricots. The Army have broached a case of these which they have been hiding in the bottom of their loads. The fruit, overlaid with dust, looked as though it had been powdered with brown sugar, and had to be washed in many waters before it was edible at all. The dinner is almost too successful. Everyone likes it and there is not enough for seconds. Like a magnanimous host whose new cook has let him down, Francis sighs with exasperation, touching off my fiery desert temperament, and I find myself calling him pompous, pig-headed and humourless, to which Francis responds in kind, finishing off by saying that he doesn't approve of humour anyway. Catherine stops us in our tracks by saying that she hadn't intended to tell us but one of the French officers thought that Francis and I were married and that Francis was really a very complacent husband to let me go around with Liv so much.

'Now after a scrap like this you'll never be able to convince the French that it isn't so,' she says, and on this sobering note we quickly make friends again.

For Taffy's birthday we have opened a bottle and ply him in place of a proper cake and presents. We all rejoice, and Taffy glitteringly so, muttering musical Welsh nonsense into his beard, his eyes sparkling. He has a great advantage in that nobody can understand him and we must all guess at the inner workings of his heart. Catherine and I are not at all sure that these are saintly workings, but with his bushy beard and his gentle smile he has us guessing.

We are all weary, but there is so little time left I cannot bear to go to bed. After dinner Liv, John Ferguson and I leave the others to put Taffy to bed and go out for a shoot. John perches on the roof of the car directing the spotlight with one hand and clutching his gun with the other. Our first kill is a hare which takes five out of the six cartridges we have brought with us. We catch some gazelle in the spotlight, just to watch them. They look so enchantingly bewildered that we wonder we ever brought ourselves to shoot them and resolve that only if starving will we ever do so again. With our last cartridge we shoot a fenic—a desert fox. At first we thought it a hare, it is certainly no bigger, but its action is different, as it streaks instead of hops across the desert. If Hank had not wanted a specimen we would not have shot it either—it is far too beautiful with its thick creamy coat and enormous ears.

Back at Zouar the entire post is asleep, Catherine on the roof, the men indoors and Hank under the only tree. Liv sees what he thinks is a hyena worrying at one of Hank's skins and stalks it with his gun, but it proves to be the Lieutenant's police dog. Rescuing the skin—a gazelle—and several other skins which have been stretched out to dry on the ground, Liv puts them all on top of No. 4 car. It is the wireless car and the least likely to be moved.

| 15TH APRIL | THIS IS A day of much talk, repacking and reorganizing. We leave tomorrow. |

Francis is giving Winston lessons in navigation, Liv is reorganizing his movie film and Hank is skinning the fenic, which he reports to be a female who has recently weaned three cubs. We are going to send out a gang of children to see if they can find the den. The children here will do anything just for a handshake, let alone a bit of candy or food of any sort. Yesterday Catherine gave two undersized urchins a pot full of stew which our spoiled men had refused to eat, having, they claimed, eaten all of the gazelle they ever intend to. She told the children to take it home to their mothers, but they hunkered down on the ground before her and ate every last drop, share and share alike, then cleaned the pot and gave it back to her.

She is rummaging through supplies to find Bisquick, a magical mix with which one can make pancakes, dumplings, cakes and baking powder bread. Unlike Largeau we cannot get a supply of bread here and it will be hard to cook on the way as we are out of white petrol. Our oven cannot be used with other fuel. The Army's supply of hard tack is at an end; either eaten, traded or dumped when we were not looking. The Army does not seem to like hard tack as much as the rest of us do. As she rummages, Catherine talks about flies, brushing and swatting at them angrily.

'Remember visiting Jim and Hazel,' she says wistfully, 'when Hazel saw a fly in the dining-room and rang for the butler?'

We remember only too well, and with both nostalgia and mirth. The cool golden room in far-away Pennsylvania and the butler's look of consternation. 'McGill,' Liv mimics, trying to make his voice appropriately female and outraged, 'there is a fly in the house!' Our laughter disturbs a cloud of flies, but they don't go far. They know by now that our aim is poor, our hatred ineffectual.

Catherine finds the Bisquick at last, and we make an appointment to visit the sick Lieutenant this afternoon and borrow his oven. In the early afternoon Winston and Francis go off to swim in a *guelta*. Taffy is repairing No. 5 so they take No. 4, all unaware of Hank's skins still drying on its top. There has been much controversy as to which *guelta* they will go to; the one covered with green scum, with the donkey carcass or with the monkey business? They pick the latter but in the end cannot face going in. The stench, never lovely, is even stronger and no nose, they say, could be fatigued enough to stand it. And of course when they return there are no longer any skins on the top of the car, they have been jolted off somewhere in the Zouarké valley. Hank is quite frankly beside himself, especially over the baboon which was hard to get and may not be replaceable. A string of cars goes off up the valley to search, and we're all much relieved to have it return with the baboon-skin intact and one badly torn gazelle. In so short a time some animal had found it and worried at it hopefully for what nourishment there was still in it. One gazelle-skin and one skull are gone for good. However, the baboon was recovered intact. Hank has, I feel, not without justice, lost some of his scientific detachment and would, I am sure, far rather take Winston's and Francis's skins home than all of the baboons in the Tibesti.

While this is going on Liv and I have visited Sergent Boisson in his mess. It is he who will leave shortly on the nine-month camel patrol of the border. He will take a medical orderly with him, call in at the oases, hear and try to solve local problems, study the tracks of border crossers and generally spread the word that the frontier is watched. He has come to Chad from France a few months ago and is looking forward to this lonely venture. Catherine says that she wishes that she could go. We tell her that it is a safe wish and that we do not believe her. Tough as we are beginning to suspect her of being, we saw her wilt and fall easy prey to Liv's fantasy of a trip through purgatory. Another few days and he would have had her doing penance. She merely shrugs at our teasing and says that one would naturally have to get used to that!

In the afternoon we walk over with our baking ingredients to call on the Lieutenant, now very feverish, pay our respects, arrange about picking up our petrol and if possible borrow his oven. This oven consists of an oil-drum half buried in sand. A soldier is sent into the yard to build a fire in this contraption while Liv and the Lieutenant go over the details of our departure.

Catherine is right that Allaire is *farouche*, moody and impatient, in a moment making one feel that one has no business disturbing his kingdom and in a flash charming with the warmth of his smile and quick laughter. He inquires minutely of our water supply which he says is hopelessly inadequate. We are carrying three hundred and forty litres, or about five litres per person per day. We must travel seven hundred and twenty kilometres without wells, a probable journey of five days. Allaire wants us to take ten litres per person per day, and plan on the trip taking us ten days. This would mean one thousand two hundred litres or sixty jerry-cans. We have only seventeen. Allaire shakes his head. 'You may not leave Zouar,' he says, stalking up and down his living-room with his temperature ticking at one hundred and three, 'unless you carry more water or make a stop-over at Wour, about one hundred and fifty kilometres to the north. It is thirty kilometres off the track and not easy to find as you must go through an unmarked pass into the mountains. However, we will brief you. Fill ten petrol-cans with water before you leave Zouar. Refill at Wour those water-cans you will have used by then and put water in all of your empty petrol-cans. You will probably have used another ten. If you are dying of thirst,' he grins, 'you won't mind the taste of petrol.'

Protests are unavailable. If all goes well we do, he admits, have enough water. But in the desert one cannot count on all going well. Two years ago Allaire tells us that he gave these same instructions to an English party who thought that he was being over-cautious and dictatorial. Taking the matter in their own hands they slipped away in the night. Later they developed engine trouble, split up to look for water and failed to join forces again. The French automatically send out patrols to look for travellers who do not appear at a given destination within four days of their estimated travel time. This party was within a day of dying of thirst when the Lieutenant caught up with them and brought them back to Zouar to recuperate. This kind of behaviour by tyros is what makes the French adamant that no car may travel alone in the Chad, why guides are obligatory in some parts of the Tibesti. It also explains the Chad Government's reluctance to allow anyone to come into the country from the desolate north. Like the ocean the desert is friendly while all goes well, its very emptiness giving one the opposite feeling to big-city loneliness —a luxurious oneness with the world and sky. But when something goes wrong one is suddenly in the wrong element. A poor swimmer will thrash frantically in deep water when his only salvation is to keep his head and make with slow strokes to the shore. And in the desert a small misfortune can be turned to a tragedy by one panicky decision. A mechanical breakdown can cause a two-day delay in schedule. One is sure that by setting off again before dawn and driving hard all day one can make up the lost time. One thinks there is really no point in economizing on water. After all, working on a car under the blazing sun one needs more water, not less. The car repaired, one sets off at dawn as intended but by eleven, when the sun scorches and distorts landmarks, one finds that the track has somehow been missed and all about the sand is soft. Nothing to panic about certainly, the track is sure to be on that hard-looking gravel crest a mile or so to the north. Sand tracking in the heat is thirsty work and one drinks, but without much relief, for sweat like an open valve runs the water right out of one. By evening the gravel crest has been succeeded by yet another, and nowhere is there any sign of the track. This is being lost—short of water and probably less than half-way to the next supply, if indeed one could find it. At this point there is only one right decision and apparently in the desert it is the hardest to make: Turn back, follow one's own tracks to the last well, and start all over again. There are many tales in the Tibesti of travellers dying of thirst. And, as Colonel Baylon said, which did not cheer us, 'In the desert one does not lie down quietly to die of thirst, one goes mad first.'

Having so graphically given us our orders about route and water, Lieutenant Allaire explains to Liv about picking up our petrol supply. This supply, trucked in from Fort Lamy by Mobil Oil, has been here for about two weeks. In every instance where Liv has arranged oil-dumps the supply has been on hand, and accounted for with military precision. Finally the Lieutenant asks for our passports and *carnet de passage*.

'Carnet?' says Liv, as though this were a new French word for him.

'Yes,' says the Lieutenant, 'you know, those sort of books which you unfold—you need them when you cross borders with cars—not just in the Chad but anywhere.'

I can see a veil of childish innocence drop over Liv's face as he admits that it just happens that carnets are one thing we are short of. As a matter of fact the two army vehicles have the rather naive attitude that being Her Majesty's personal property they do not need carnets. Liv has quite frankly forgotten ours, Randolph apparently gone off to his tulips carrying the papers for Winston's car and only the Collinses' vehicle is in order. Catherine, doing a little mental telepathy stunt with Liv, seems to have got the message, for she does not mention her superior status. Perhaps she is afraid that we will all be detained, and she sent home in undesired glory.

I must say that after the first shock the Lieutenant takes it well. He shrugs, says we are mad, stamps our passports and offers us a drink which he says he is not allowed to have but he needs badly; it has been a hard afternoon!

Liv goes about his tasks and Catherine and I whip up a most enormous Bisquick batter. The Lieutenant prowls tiger-like, says we are making a repugnant mess and that this conforms with his ideas of American cooking. In the yard the drum is raging hot, the coals glowing. The soldier shovels them out and puts our trayful of dough in with the aid of a long shovel. Then he closes the end of the drum with an iron sheet propped up by a pole.

Half an hour later he brings us our first golden loaf, carrying it gingerly on his shovel. Breaking off a piece, the Lieutenant admits that American cooks have had poor publicity, and he accepts with evident pleasure a present of a couple of boxes of our magic mix.

Behind the fort is a walled garden shady with casuarina, acacia and the graceful date-palm. We had thought it a cemetery, because so often in arid countries the secluded green corners are reserved for those who no longer need them. We have promised ourselves an exploration, and once the petrol is seen to, and the bread put away to cool, Liv, Catherine and I walk along the walls to a little gate that we find unlatched. We push it diffidently and find to our joy no cemetery but a garden, neat plots of lettuces, peppers and tomatoes, carrots, celery and fruit-trees squared off with trim irrigation ditches leading to a central well. Drawing water at the well is a small muscular man with two teeth in his mouth, both on the lower jaw. He carries a slingshot with all the dignity of a Beefeater his halberd.

'The exterminator,' Liv murmurs. Visualizing a fine last catch for Hank, he asks if there are any mice in the garden. The gardener nods enthusiastically.

'Oh, yes,' he says, '*ils marchent à minuit.*'

'Besides marching at midnight,' Liv asks, 'do they do any damage?' This seems a matter for thought. The little man looks puzzled, shakes his head, gestures vaguely with his slingshot and says at last:

'No, no, they don't do anything. They just march, at midnight. *Ils marchent à minuit.*'

We visualize a Tibesti 'Waltz of Flowers' with mice compelled in spite of themselves to march at the sound of the nightly tom-tom. Walking away from this bit of green wonderland, Liv says:

'Do you know, I hate to leave. I'd like to spend at least two years here. It is a wonderful country and delightful people.'

'You mean,' says Catherine, 'that you want a garden full of mice that march at midnight?'

'Yes,' Liv admits, 'and trees full of birds that nest in the sky. Do you know that these people believe the Egyptian vulture nests in the sky? I thought they must mean in the mountains, but

Shehai says, "No, no, up there in the sky." Perhaps they think that clouds are giant birds' nests. Anyway I like the idea.'

SUNDAY AND NO reveille, no obstacle races, no flag flying, but I did see a goat tiptoeing along the ramparts. It is hard to leave but we get about it busily. We pack up our cars, the boys fill up on water, grumbling at the order to put water in ten of the petrol-tins. They believe they are going to be poisoned. Catherine tries to tell them that a form of petrol was what their mamas dosed them with when they had nasty colds as little tykes, but they do not take kindly to the notion. Of all of us, only Winston is in a good humour. Nothing either depresses or suppresses him, he is impossible to keep down.

Shehai of the disdainful profile has returned from the Trou and comes to see us all freshly robed and turbaned. He is going to take us to call on Uadei Kihidemi, King of the Tibesti, sometimes called Sultan, sometimes the Derdai. The title of King in the Tibesti is alternated among three families who inherit in strict rotation. An attempt to assassinate the present king was made when as a young man he made his way down from the mountains to take up his royal duties. The incumbent of one of the other families apparently did not want to wait out the new king's life time for his own turn, unless that life was to be a short one. However, the young king, like any other boy who survives the Tibesti, was tough; no royal nursery had sheltered him from the common lot of his own people. A spear through his chest, he dragged himself into Zouar and lived another forty years to rule his people, protect the ravens and receive us this morning. Shehai brings us to a village of adobe houses where a group of men are hunkered down in the shade passing the time. They unwind as we drive up and come forward to shake hands, deferring to a tall shy man of about sixty with a dignified carriage and a rather sweet childish face. This is the King. He wears a spotless white turban, a blue cotton gown and a pair of sneakers. He seems pleased to be called on and we are all sorry that we have not come sooner. He is delighted with the instant pictures which

165

Catherine gives him and poses, with the unconcern of the great, for stills and movies alike.

Liv says, 'You should visit Libya, sir; one should know one's neighbours.'

The King bows slightly. 'I would like to, but have had no formal invitation.' Adding wistfully, 'I also need permission from my government.'

According to Dr. Briggs's book, *Tribes of the Sahara*, the last independent Derdai or King ruled in 1914 when he was defeated by the French and fled to Kufra. He surrendered in 1920 and was reinstated to rule under the French until his death in 1939.

We are sorry to take leave of the King, who has not only received us graciously but who we feel would be a mine of information about his people and their ways. However, we have left it too long. Our party is made up of too many young men with 'Tibesti and Back or Bust' engraved on their hearts. We can only keep them happy by keeping the wheels rolling.

We return to say our goodbyes to the Lieutenant, in bed now and squirming because the Captain Doctor is about to give him a shot of penicillin. Catherine has asked for the torn Tricolour which flew from the fort on our arrival and which has since been replaced. She would like to fly it, she says, from her own flagstaff in New Jersey when the Lieutenant comes to America this summer. Further cause, if he needed it, to convince the Lieutenant that we are mad. The flag can unfortunately not be found and as we at last say goodbye the Lieutenant gallantly wrenches his mind from the penicillin needle to promise that he will bring the flag to America with him.

It is midday before we leave Zouar. In the end we are all reluctant to go. This is a fascinating Never-Never Land where we have been offered every hospitality and warmth. We drive down the Zouarké, past the last acacia, and thread through the monumental wind-carved rocks. Towering above us top-heavy like giant champagne glasses they also make me think of those Nilotic tribesmen given to standing on one leg. We lunch, dejectedly, under the overhang of one such monster. There are carvings in the rock above our heads, the ubiquitous camel and gazelle. Now that we know about the four-hour tea-break that the native traveller is given to we can readily understand the need for some sort of entertainment, and hence the vast number of carvings wherever there is a receptive surface. I have managed to drop one of our precious loaves of Bisquick. We dust most of the sand off and eat it none the less, for bread is something we are going to be short of. In the afternoon we pass some impressive needle-rocks soaring out of the sand. These monumental rock sculptures are the Aiguilles de Sisse. On top of one we make out a cairn-like heap, a neolithic grave. Some idea of the size of these rocks can be had from the fact that three cars roar in close to explore one, while the rest of us sail by without seeing the cars. In five or ten kilometres we stop, confer and wonder how we have lost the others. Beneath these rocks a car is a pebble, no more.

We are on a well-travelled route on broad, hard desert. But we know that the detour for Wour will be difficult to find. We have been told that we will see palm-trees close to the base of the mountains to the north and after that we must turn north to find the stone pylons that mark the beginning of the Wour track. However, we must not turn too soon for the ground will be very rocky and treacherous. We never do see the palm-trees, but late in the day we see acacias and unwisely turn towards them, getting badly bogged in soft sand. Sand-tracking out we spot, of all miraculous things, a Tebu all robed in white. He tells us that he just happens to be going to Wour. There doesn't seem to be anywhere for him to have come from or anything for him to have been doing in this desolate place. But we are grateful of a guide; the sun has slipped behind the mountain and we are anxious to reach Wour before nightfall.

Our guide is more efficient than we have been led to believe guides are, but then perhaps he too is in a hurry to reach Wour. He directs us in towards the mountains, where after much bumping over rock we come to a graded road. We wind through rolling hills of black rock, dropping down at last to a valley of palms, where in the dark our lights pick out the French fort stark against a cliff of stone.

Sergent-Chef Pollux gives us the kind of welcome which is synonymous with the French Marine d'Outre Mer in the Tibesti, and insists that we use his quarterrs for eating and bathing and to set up our kitchen. He has bedrooms for four of us, but the rest will have to camp out. We are all too aware now that our nights under the stars are numbered and ask if we may, instead, sleep on his roof. He looks horrified, but is far too agreeable to object.

The Sergent-Chef's quarters are hung with woven barrakans and Misurata rugs, with assegais and lethal-looking machetes and knives. We sit gratefully about his table after we have eaten of our own supplies and drink his wine. This post is the loneliest we have seen so far. The Sergent-Chef is the only European at the post, the others being *goumiers*. He tells us that most travellers who come in for water do not spend the night, but fill up their cans and return to the main track, and so he seldom has anyone of his own world to talk to. He has no vehicle here and is, in fact, leaving by camel in the morning for Bardai which he expects to reach in four days. While he is lonely and homesick for his wife in France he is also busy. He keeps his post immaculate, and the classrooms for his soldiers are full of carefully worked-out bulletin-boards of instructions on the ways of life in France. He also indulges in the local pastime of collecting rocks and artifacts. The central courtyard of the fort is astir with chickens of all sizes, and the Sergent-Chef has a collection of lizards which the French call *fouette queue* (Whip tail). We wonder if these are not in fact miniature dinosaurs. Landlocked in the Tibesti and bereft for thousands of years of their normal supply of vitamins, might not the species have shrunk so? This is in any case what Catherine thinks, and furthermore she thinks they are repulsive and when she sees two of them skitter across the dining-room floor, and slip into a pair of boots which are standing by the door, she almost faints. She is too polite to do much more than turn green, but I see her fold her feet up under her, and in this uncouth half-kneeling position nervously finish her dinner. The Sergent-Chef has graciously given us two of these creaures to take home to the children. He has offered Catherine one for Pom, but she says no she doesn't think they would get through Customs, and I don't think she said 'Thank you'.

The roof is cool and we spread out, each choosing his own spot. The wall of the cliff rises above us and the stars come down to meet it. Here we see the Southern Cross for the first time, slightly tipsy, standing on the rampart above Winston's head.

SOME THREE THOUSAND camels pasture in the neighbourhood of Wour and depend on its well for water. In fact we were not able to fill our cans last night as a herd had drained the well almost dry. Even today the water is cloudy and full of sand. As this is in any case emergency water it does not matter too much. We fill up the petrol-cans and hope that we won't have to use them.

The French hold out little or no hope for the adult generation of Tebu who do not seem to want to learn, or to try, new ways of living. On the other hand they believe that there is promise in the children, and a settlement of any size has its one- or two-roomed schoolhouse. This morning, as the children go by, Liv stops to talk to them.

'*Tu vas à l'école eh?*' he asks with his most obnoxious early-morning heartiness.

'*Oui, monsieur,*' a little boy answers dutifully, sounding like a primer himself, '*nous allons à l'école.*'

'And what do you learn?'

'Lessons, monsieur.'

'And do you like that?' Even I think that is an inane question, and am not surprised when the little Tebu refrains from any answer.

'*Alors,*' Liv tries again, '*ça va?*'

The boy shakes his head sadly. '*Non, monsieur, ça va pas,*' and walks off to his school.

We are getting ready to leave. Winston's carburetter is acting up, and on the level area before the fort there is much argument, shoving and towing about before it is finally persuaded to clatter into life. It sounds terrible and we only hope it will last out the trip. Winston has lived up to his father's boast that the boy can take one of these cars apart, but there have been no signs of putting it together again. He drives it much as a Tebu drives his camel, though we have never seen him throw a rock at it we think this is only because he is so incredibly good tempered. By now he has unhinged both doors and jacked the roof up with a wedge to provide greater ventilation. He keeps his washbasin full of water nestled in the spare tyre on the hood, and floats water bottles and canteens in this contraption to keep their contents cool. When riding with him one is very likely to get a shower of water in the face whenever one goes over a bump. Altogether Winston is ingenious and insouciant. If the car does not hold up he will thumb a ride, and leave it with the many dead cars of General Leclerc, to show where Winston Churchill, too, crossed the Sahara.

Sergent-Chef Pollux is in long baggy trousers this morning for his camel trek to Bardai. He looks crossly up the valley at a group of Tebu who are wandering through the trees towards the fort.

'You see them?' he mutters. 'They know I am going away today. They have had weeks, months, to bring me their problems. But no, they must wait until I go away. Every time—even if I go only for a few days—they come just as I am leaving. You'd think they would realize that it might be annoying. . . .' He shrugs in exasperation. Inexorably the little group of men with their donkeys, camels and problems gather before the fort and make themselves comfortable under the palms.

We say goodbye and Liv and I, Hank and Catherine start ahead to the first stretch of open sand, twenty miles away, to take horror movies of our miniature dinosaurs. The open desert, with its lack of telltale landmarks, is the perfect place for trick photography. One dinosaur (very close up) is to attack Catherine (very long shot), who is to throw up her hands in horrified despair and run away. I, as stage hand, am to hold the lizard and aim it in the right direction.

This simple little plot is harder to direct than a troop of Hollywood stars. Catherine is only willing to do her part at such a long shot that we are not at all sure she is on screen. The lizard on the other hand keeps escaping me and scuttling off into the shade under the car, where he burrows so swiftly into the sand that at one moment we almost lose him completely. We are afraid the plot is quite ruined; our actors, far from upstaging each other, do not seem to want any part of being on stage together.

Coming up a long scarp Catherine has to get out to shoo a camel out of Hank's way. Hank drives on to the top of the hill and we pick her up. In moving to make room for her I hand her the old chocolate box in which the lizards are travelling. Catherine, all unaware, crows greedily:

'Chocolates!' She pops her hand in, smack on a slimy fat head. They aren't really slimy, but she says they are and the shriek that she lets out brings Hank back from half a mile up the road. He finds Catherine still shaking, the box back in my lap and Liv so doubled over with laughter that he can hardly get his head out of the steering-wheel. For his part, I don't think that Hank has ever laughed quite so hard. Poor Catherine is bedevilled by beasts, alive in our car and dead in hers—or for the most part dead. Once she claimed that one of Hank's rare fleas escaped from its box and found refuge in her sleeping-bag. Gone are the days when she would tactfully wait until Hank was out of earshot and ask me if I could smell anything. I think that she used to be afraid that it was her imagination. Now we all know. No. 2, pure and simple, stinks. When we take down the tailboard at lunch-time to get out the mugs and plates we are assailed by a potpourri of mice, jerboa, pickled fish (from the spring at Ounianga), gazelle, fox, fleas, ticks and—strongest and richest of all—the baboon. A dog baboon at that. Catherine is philosophical by now. We have all followed in Winston's footsteps and removed our doors, and she keeps perilously close to the wide open spaces and hopes for nasal fatigue to set in.

Towards dusk we round a dune rippled by the wind in a thousand spiny waves like a mammoth dragon's tail. Coming towards us is a caravan of many camels. We swoop down upon them and ask them where they're from and where they are going. We are like puppies who have accosted a cobra, for they are not glad to see us and they scowl at us angrily, especially when we ask to see their spears. They tell us shortly that they are carrying dates from Libya to Chad, and for a box of tea they trade Winston a bucketful. The dates are as hard as nuts and not too clean, but the men pitch into them despite Liv's warning that they have not been pasteurized and will give them dysentery. We offer presents and take pictures, but, for the first time in our experience of the Tebu, these men want none of us. Their anger makes us wonder if they are perhaps gun-running, a profitable business among the Tebu who are forbidden guns.

The Kourizo Pass is a narrow canyon winding between low sandstone cliffs. This is the pass that has often been described as the gateway to the Tibesti, and appropriately enough the northern approach to the pass is barred by a mighty dune. We rush it, praying that we will not disappear into its secret depths like Ali Baba into his cavern or the Piper of Hamlin into his mountain. And for once not one car bogs but we sail over and down to camp in sight of the pass itself.

We have a message from the Humfreys tonight, suggesting that they bring the children to meet us at our last night's camp, and even offering to bake us a cake. We accept gratefully and everyone gets on the band wagon with suggestions of things they would rather see even than our children and a cake, such as a case of cold beer. Catherine would, of course, like to see Alan, and more messages go off into the blue for him.

After supper we sit round the charcoal stove on which we have an oven full of bread. The night is cold, and Winston hops over in his sleeping-bag to join us for a round of 'kikapoo joy juice' while we wait for the bread to brown.

18TH APRIL

YESTERDAY WE PASSED a few burned-out cars and today there are more. Like the famous Elephants' Graveyard, this seems to be the place where Leclerc's mortally wounded Fords and Chevvies came to die, World War II's Jacques Leclerc was an assumed name—a *nom de guerre* under which he hid his true identity in order to protect his family who were still in Occupied France. Here in the silence the broken hulks seem to speak for him—a hero and a myth in our own day. He had Frenchmen and native soldiers with him, some artillery, not very well matched, one or two armoured cars, and what must have looked a very riff-raff collection of transport from what we can see of those that fell by the wayside. Until he came, the Kourizou Pass had been all right for camels, but Leclerc blasted it open to allow his heavy trucks through. Yesterday we were grateful for those scars in the rock as we climbed easily over the pass. We think of Montgomery's classic understatement when he said of Leclerc, 'I can make use of that chap.' Liv says that he could, too, and that Leclerc makes just the kind of road-blazer he needs.

Northward from Kourizo begins a road which Liv discovered and built—or so you would think to hear him talk about it. Actually it is no road, but a track. Historically it is, I think, as old as the first camel, for it is one of the ancient caravan routes which link the Mediterranean to Central Africa. Liv ignores all of this, and sees in it a great future highway, which will one day carry the bulk of African trade to the Mediterranean ports and Europe. He has read everything available about trade along these routes in the past—the camel caravans with their cargoes of salt, gold, slaves and ivory.

For many years after the war the T.A.T. (Transport Africain Tunisien) sent heavily laden trucks on convoy through Sebha and Gatroun to Faya-Largeau and Fort Lamy. These convoys carried anything and everything from tins of fruit to drums of oil and bolts of cloth. It is two years since the last of these trucks has gone south, though the authorities keep talking of reviving the service. In any case, Liv does not think this good enough for the world of tomorrow. We discuss the pros and cons of railways, salt-water canals or six-lane highways; ending inevitably with the nays having it. Now he is seeing the real problems of this route at first hand—the series of great plains of soft sand, the sharp steppes of broken rock, the uncompromising dunes. I sense that he is feeling glum about his future transportation empire.

We have a good morning run, mostly on hard sand. The track is well marked and we wonder at the over-cautious French with their tales of lost travellers. By comparison with the country we have crossed, the going here is tame. We think our shock absorbers have gone, for we bound over the slightest bump, and those behind say that they have seen all four of our tyres off the ground at the same time. Hank grumbles about his 'bicycle tyres', John says that No. 5 is about to come apart, Winston's car sounds as though it had long ago. Aside from the engines and bodies, our loads have suffered as well. Our own is now dimly viewed through dust-encrusted glass, dishevelled, bent and tossed about to look like a Salvation Army depository of unwanted junk in a poor part of town. Winston's car looks very dashing from the outside, but those who have looked into the interior are dazed at the breakage of his unlashed load. Hank's load is perhaps the neatest of all. He keeps his and Catherine's air mattresses inflated, and packs them in on top of the load, so keeping everything firmly in place. The army cars have had their own breakage; one spring, two Tilly lanterns, one hurricane lantern, one compass, two plastic jerry-cans and a variety of lesser things. Like any army's, their attitude towards property, theirs or that of others, is nonchalant to say the least. What is broken or lost or dumped can always be replaced out of a magic and never-failing stockpile.

In the afternoon we have come upon that amazing bit of sur-realist construction—a Nissen hut in the middle of nowhere. This is one of the T.A.T. shelters and should contain barrels of water and petrol to be used by any needy traveller. We find a bit of very stagnant water in a rusty drum, and some petrol. The walls are crowded with chalkings, pencillings and scratchings in every con-ceivable language. One neat scribble is signed and dated by Barbara Toy, the desert writer, who says she is proceeding on two-wheel drive only. Catherine, who is our most non-mechanical member, says it sounds to her as though she were proceeding rampant by bicycle. Frank and Archie have added to the well-autographed walls. We explore a bit, but decide that the artifacts are too modern for charm, and go gratefully on our way.

We make camp on the shores of an immense sand lake. You can almost see the waters receding those ten millions of years ago, pouring in waterfalls and rivers from every slope and shelf, and leaving the land to dry and dry and for ever dry. In the moonlight on this cold-starred night they seem to come back, those ancient waters, to haunt the desert with their lapping and gurgling, and in the morning the sand is all rippled about.

Several of the boys have been ill, we think from Winston's unpasteurized dates. Catherine washed them for him and put them to soak overnight, which made them less like wooden pellets but no more hygienic. We are trying, both Catherine and I, to keep these boys on a rice diet until they are better. But the Army is really not susceptible to female influence. 'Good heavy kit is what a mon needs when he's sick,' Frank insists, as he dishes the invalids extras of pork and beans. We think of Randolph, and how needless his worry that we might change the mighty ways of the British Army. We feel that we have made no inroads at all, and that we will return them to the Empire unimpaired and uncorrupted. So far at least they have refused to take suggestions, let alone orders, from women, and as to our medical ministerings, one would think we were a pair of witch-doctors.

Jack contacts Benghazi, asking after his dog and his laundry. The British Army in Cyprus, monitoring these conversations, must, I feel, be outraged. Francis and Winston work late on their navigational charts and books. The rest of us hover about the charcoal fire where another batch of bread is baking.

19TH APRIL

THIS MORNING THE wind is hot and from the south. With an early take-off we hope to make good time. We have rocky hills to climb and stretches of hard gravelly sand. The trail is marked and the going good until Francis and Winston, driving together today, hare off at a tangent and get us lost. We suspect the former of letting the latter practise his navigation. As soon as we realize what has happened we race after them to stop and turn them about. It is a tantalizing chase, for Francis stops the minute he sees that we are too far behind and waits for us to catch up. But before we have come within shouting distance he, seeing that we are on our way, takes off once more at full speed. We are now careering over unmarked hills and dipping down into valleys of dry quicksand in this will-o'-the-wisp chase. Tempers are at boiling point when Liv finally brings us all to a halt and goes out after Francis alone. An hour later he is back with the offenders with whom he has come to verbal blows that seem to echo in their stony expressions. Each in our own way raging inside our mobile matchboxes we spend the rest of the morning retracing our steps to that place where we lost the trail.

At lunchtime we rig a tarpaulin between two cars and all twelve of us crowd under it. When lunch is done and we want to stretch out on the sand to nap, our shade-patch is so small that some of us have to lie under the cars themselves; one way to learn about the innards of a car, though I'd just as soon be ignorant. Often in the desert one needs only to step out of the sun to be cool. Today one needs to step into the sun to realize that the shade is in fact a degree or so less scorching. Wind beats at the tarpaulin, bringing it down upon us twice. I lie in the shade beneath our car, resting my head on my arms, watching the heat waves distort the petrol-drums which serve as trail markers, and near which we have stopped. Suddenly, at eye level, a tremendous, evil green dragon slithers with terrifying speed towards the drums, where it as suddenly shrinks and disappears. As I rub my smarting eyes I hear a lethargic voice from the human heap under the tarpaulin say, 'One of your lizards got away.'

I scramble out, bumping my head on the axle and calling Liv from his slumbers. We have not only to dig for this beast who has gone to earth, or rather to sand, beneath the drum, but once it is un-sanded it gives Liv quite a race across the desert before it can be retaken. These animals are every bit as unlovely to look at as Catherine thinks them, being green with yellow spots, squared-off mouths and horned tails. But they are none the less extraordinary. They are vegetarians, living by preference on flowers and leaves, they dig themselves into the sand to keep cool, and for all of their ponderous look they have a fantastic streak of speed. As we take our little pet back to his chocolate box I tell Liv how in this land of illusions and tricky perspectives they can be mistaken for dragons.

'St. George,' he says, 'is said by some to have met his dragon in Libya. Perhaps it was one of these, and he was just telling a very tall fish story.'

We are back in Libya, or think we are. The border is in dispute, though not strenuously so, since neither side sets great store by a few more square miles of sand and rock. Perhaps when Liv's highway is opened it will all become more important, though he is, he says, both disillusioned and discouraged. He has estimated that it will cost a hundred million dollars to built even a moderately good road through this overgrown sand-pile, and probably another hundred million to try to find out what has happened to it.

It is late afternoon when we arrive at a second Quonset hut, or 'desert refuge', surrounded on the outside by sardine and tuna tins, and embellished inside by the usual flowering of autographs. Frank logs the advent of Frank White of Scotland and the Pomeroy-Tibesti expedition. Over the door is a scribbled word

176

of welcome and the pious and fatuous hope that all who pass through will sweep the hut. Beside it is a note giving directions for finding a well some five hundred yards from the building. As a PS. someone has added that there is something dead in the well. As this helpful bit of information is undated, we have no way of knowing whether the body in the well is of ancient or recent vintage and decide that we will at least risk camping in the vicinity.

It makes a nice camp-site—a sandy floor with palm-trees, a scattering of boulders and two metal discs which cap the well, and a drum in which to put water for animals. We do not detect a body, either recent or ancient, and Winston, armed with a bucket, has himself lowered into the deep well to dredge out sand and start the flow of water. We are impressed with his social consciousness until he admits that he has really gone down to cool off.

Jack makes voice contact with Benghazi and, after having made sure that his laundry has been sorted, puts our children on the air. They are utterly confused by the 'over to you' routine and the frustration of being unable to interrupt.

20TH APRIL

THIS MORNING CATHERINE says that she doesn't want to get up, but will let Hank lash her, complete with sleeping-bag, to the top of the car. So far, except when Hank has trapping on his mind, she has been the first out of her cocoon. So much so that at Zouar Francis had occasion to tell her kindly to remain in bed, as she always made straight for the kitchen, and the rattling of pans disturbed the men. As we approach civilization we suspect that she is remembering breakfast in bed, and white trays daintily set with pink porcelain, thin slices of buttered toast and frothy glasses of orange juice. We catch her sadly pouring our precious drinking-water for a swallow she has found, but which Hank and Liv tell her will not be able to drink as swallows need to skim their water from pools and lakes.

Catherine, more often seen in her New York apartment wearing something hand-stitched in Italy, has decorated her French bush hat with a bustard's feather, and wears her tattered sawn-off trousers with aplomb. She carries around a clutch of glasses for her sensitive eyes—pale, dark and darkest—and has acquired what is probably a permanent stoop from looking for pebbles. I tell her that I am awed by her endless curiosity about everything and her surprising reserve of stamina. She retaliates by insisting that I record that I have as much of the monkey and the jackdaw in me as she has—that I too am always snooping into cairns and dunes picking up bright objects, and that anyone who has chosen to spend their life with her brother should not talk about other people's stamina. And then of course she says polite things about Liv, to whom she is really very partial.

'It is just that there are times in life,' she says, 'when one wants to sink into a torpor, and that would be just the moment when Liv would bound in and announce, "Pack up everything—we're going to Mogadiscio." '

She knows very well that under the excuse of a career our battings about the world hide a secret work—Liv is compiling material for his book *Pomeroy's Encyclopaedia of Little-Known Facts* which will contain items like the beetle that flies at 400 miles an hour, or how a dried chameleon's head can protect your child from evil spirits. How could a wife do other than fight the torpor? However, he has promised that when we are old we will retire and he will write a different book which will be called *101 Things a Stupid Old Man Can Do*.

We reach Gatroun by midday. A spindly oasis some seventy-five kilometres long, with many tracks leading into it, but no way of knowing which is the right one. Pick the wrong set to follow and we will be in soft sand up to our hubs, as we well know. But today we are in luck, and our choice of tracks leads us to a small clutter of huts and up to a charming, rundown mud fort well marked with signs of battle, guarded by a pair of 1910 French guns and flying the Libyan flag.

The Turks and Italians have both had forts at Gatroun. The present fort was vacated by the French only four years ago. As we drive up several police and Customs officials come out to greet us, and lead us into a small dark room to question us and examine our passports. They are much puzzled by our lack of carnets and not quite as philosophical as the French have been. They are further disturbed to find that Catherine's visa, acquired four months ago in Washington, is no longer valid. There are entries on her passport which show that she has been in Chad for much of this time, but as she has never been officially out of Libya it seems to be a puzzle. Exactly where is she, and, if she is indeed here, how did she get here to bedevil a poor frontier post? They say it will take a couple of hours to figure out. While we are talking, the Mudir arrives to greet us. The Mudir of Gatroun is black and robust, with a smile that flashes with pleasure and welcome. He sits on a barrel in the police office and exchanges with Liv the ritual greeting.

'*Keif halek?*' (How are you?) says the Mudir formally.

'*Queis el Hamdullilah. Keif halek anta?*' (Fine, thanks be to God. How are you?) Liv answers gravely.

'*Labas, labas. Keif halek?*' (Fine, fine. How are you?) the Mudir asks happily.

'*Queis el Hamdullilah. Keif halek anta?*' Liv repeats. I suspect that he doesn't know what 'labas' means.

'*Queis el Hamdullilah. Keif halek?*' the Mudir counters.

'*Queis el Hamdullilah. Keif halek?*' Liv says happily. The rest of us are getting bored with the script, but the Mudir is just getting warmed up. He bounces up and down on the barrel and screams with delight,

'*Labas, labas, Keif halek?*'

Winston says, 'Why don't you two sign off?' and Hank says: 'Even I know that much Arabic. What does "labas" mean anyway?'

'I don't know,' says Liv, 'but it seems to be his favourite expression. I think I'll try it the next time around.'

So the next time the joyful little Mudir asks Liv how he is, Liv answers, '*Labas, labas!*' and that seems to make such a profound impression on everyone in the room that they give us back our passports, always excepting Catherine's, which seems to need further study, and to top it off the Mudir has invited us all to his house for tea.

The Mudir's house is in a tiered adobe village below the fort. We walk past the deep open well and a fenced-in bit of garden where the Mudir's horse lives in solitary splendour. No oasis that we have heard of supports more than one horse, and this is used by the local governor for occasions of state. In the old days when the fiercer desert raiders used horses for combat, large caravans of camels were necessary to carry water and fodder for the horses. The horses were only ridden for an actual attack. A horse in the desert is a great rarity and a great luxury.

On the street before the Mudir's house men are at work making adobe bricks. They have dug a hole in the street itself, which is in any case a sand track, and to this hole a string of men bring buckets of water from the well up the hill. Having thoroughly saturated the sand in the hole it is dug out and pat-a-caked by hand into a wooden mould, to form bricks roughly one foot by eight inches by four. These are laid out on the street to dry. It seemed to me that it would have been more efficient to do this work nearer to the well where there is plenty of space and not the distance to carry water. However, I suppose that it is six of one and half a dozen of the other, for in their present position the bricks are no doubt handy for building.

The Mudir's house is built round a small courtyard. He has gone ahead of us to order tea and to put on, over his pink-striped gown, a brilliant red burnoose handsomely embroidered in gold. There are cool straw mats on the floor and across one end of the room a red-striped barrakan. We discuss among ourselves the fine points of whether or not we should remove our shoes, being frankly reluctant to let so many hot sweaty feet escape from their covering in so small a room. The Mudir shakes his head firmly as we gesture to follow his example in this, and we move gingerly across his clean rugs to hunker down as best we can. The twelve of us line the walls with the Mudir, Berka Mohammed Salah, and the Customs officer, Mohammed Gneidi, and a chap in blue with a white turban who proves to be chief tea-maker, roughly in the centre of the room.

To start off the reception and pass the time while the tea is making, the Mudir brings a tin bowl of water which he places on the floor before us. We are uncertain as to whether local protocol calls for our washing our hands or drinking, and as we anxiously look for a clue a fly explores the rim, skidding on the damp tin and sailing off into the water.

'Shoo,' says Winston, but too late, the fly can no longer get airborne. The Mudir claps his hands in righteous indignation and personally carries the bowl out of the room. Against the sunlit wall of the courtyard we see his ample shadow mime, finger dipping into the bowl and sodden fly flicked to the ground. Flyless he returns the bowl to us, smiling and this time presenting us with a glass. We are obviously witless creatures who cannot figure out what to do with a bowl of water by ourselves. He illustrates, pouring the first glass and holding it out to Liv, who gallantly offers it to Catherine. Everyone joins the Mudir in insisting that the honour is Liv's and fiendishly watch him drink. But our joy is short-lived, for the Mudir makes us all sip of the fly's bathwater. We try to think that the fly was a brand-new one and had never crawled through the acres of trachoma that any other insect in the village would have done.

The chap with the turban has in the meantime been buzzing in and out, and now appears with a trayful of small tea-glasses containing a green tea both hot and strong enough to murder any bacteria previously swallowed. Fast on this a tray of biscuits and sweets are passed. Mohammedans have quite an incredible appetite for sweets of all sorts. Tea is drunk down with a murmur of pleasant acknowledgement and a quick swallow for it is only the first of a ritual three servings. The second glass is equally strong and sweet with the added aroma of mint. The third has peanuts thrown in. This is not a favourite cup with Westerners who, coming upon the peanuts unexpectedly, are apt to be suspicious. I have lived in Libya long enough to know about the peanut, but I can tell from other expressions about the room that it is a toss-up as to whether it will in some cases stay down. I hasten to explain that it is not a fat worm they just swallowed, nor somebody's discarded olive-pip. There is a little sigh of acceptance and the last of the tea is swallowed. Before taking our leave we photograph the Mudir and his friends, trying our every wile to persuade them to smile, for the Mudir especially has as beatific a smile as any of us have ever encountered. But merely to focus a lens is to freeze these men into the most austere dignity.

'*Affwan, affwan . . .*' they say to our thanks and good wishes and smile their golden smiles, only to draw themselves up in granite pose as out of the corner of the eye they see that Liv is peering through a lens.

Back at the fort the police have decided to stamp Catherine's passport. They give us the mail to carry to Sebha, including a letter which they have written the immigration authorities there and which we tell Catherine undoubtedly recommends her imprisonment or deportation. In a sense she says that she is deporting herself pretty soon anyway so as long as it isn't prison it won't matter.

We lunch on biscuits and peanut butter sitting on the cannons before the fort, and after many handshakes take off for Sebha. For a hundred kilometres the sand is hard and we are able to make good time. For variety in this sandy vacuum, Francis suggests that we keep open formation, driving abreast in a straight line. It is more difficult than it seems. Catherine, who is driving for the first time since she broke our speedometer before Kufra, says she prefers having another car ahead to follow. Spread out like this, without a landmark of any sort to give direction, her eyes incline to waver from right to left and the car with them. This makes the other drivers nervous and they commence to wobble, trying to keep out of her way. And then to tell the truth our rabble takes discipline hard. Winston is bored and has decided to take movies. Like a jet peeling away from its fellows he zooms out of line, weaving back in and then out again, leans out of his car grinning happily with camera buzzing. He got close-up shots of Liv asleep in No. 1 and Hank looking tensely unhappy in No. 2. What he does not realize apparently is that he is indulging in a dangerous sport. Between Catherine and Winston they have completely unnerved Frank, in No. 4, who is a learner-driver. Gallantly Frank insists that Winston's is the greater blame, and he and Archie draw lots as to who shall have the pleasure of clobbering him. Frank wins the toss and when we stop to cool the motors there is a moment of hot high tension and a brisk exchange of blows.

There has been little soft sand but now suddenly we are crossing a sand sea. Catherine is visiting with Liv, and I with Hank. Not as accustomed to his driving as she is, I am suddenly amazed to have him take off at full speed following a solitary set of tyre tracks to the east of the direction we have been heading.

'These bicycle tyres won't take the soft sand,' he explains tersely; 'this fellow obviously knew the short cut out of the sand-sea.' I ask if we hadn't better wait and consult with the others, but Hank shakes his head. 'Can't stop or we'll go right in.'

So we race off roughly in the direction of distant Ghat where a tribe of ironworkers live in houses dug down under the ground and which I have always wanted to see, anyway. Behind us headlights blink, signal-mirrors flash and horns bray. Hank never for a moment slackens his speed. I look back and see three cars pulled up on a distant ridge while No. 5 with Francis in the conning tower, flashing and waving, comes after us. Where the sand is black it is sure to be hard, and sighting one of these patches Hank pulls up to wait. There is a little exchange of repartee between the men and we reset our course towards the west where we promptly catch up on our sand-tracking practice. I don't know where Hank's track was going, but he was certainly doing all right on it. Now my husband and my good sister-in-law in the rear tell me that the sight of our flight was so delicious that they could not drive for laughing and had to send Francis to the rescue.

'And what was so funny?' I asked, nettled.

'Well, we thought that Hank had either been struck with a sudden desert madness and gone quite berserk—or that you were eloping.' And as to my own family thinking either of these alternatives funny, I take it unkindly, as indeed I think Hank might.

We make camp on a hard ridge near another of Leclerc's wrecked vehicles, send off messages to Alan in Benghazi, and make a quick dinner of 'compo'. As night falls we hear a motor in the distance and see lights across the desert five miles or so away. We signal them rather hoping that they will signal back and join us. Excepting our rendezvous with the French this is the first time in six weeks that we have seen signs of any other vehicle in the desert, and we feel friendly and curious. But apparently our fellow travellers are more blasé than we. They neither return our signals nor make any move to come nearer. On the other hand we have been seen by other eyes and presently an old man, a veritable Abraham on his donkey, led by his favourite son —anyway perhaps he is a favourite and perhaps a son—looms out of the night and squats down amongst us. They want a blanket because they are cold, some tea and biscuits and anything else we might have lying about. We supply these wants and add a bucket of water for the donkey, who won't drink, and a tube of ophthalmic ointment for the boy whose eyes are sadly in need of a miracle.

For Winston this is probably the last night. His plane leaves tomorrow from Sebha. Of course, there is always the chance that

183

we will get stuck and not make it—but it seems unlikely that we would all get stuck. One car could always go on ahead. We are coming into civilized desert again what with camp lights five miles ahead, and while we don't like to divide up, we have decided that we will if necessary. If Winston misses this plane he will be two weeks late at Oxford instead of one and have to think twice as hard for a good excuse. We sit about with out nightcaps in the cool of the day and the peace of the stars and talk of this and other things. Francis and Winston are miffed at the fellows across the desert for unresponsive yokels and plot out a strategy of attack upon them. Winston was in favour of a pincer movement, but Francis, with the authority of Sandhurst, refused to divide his forces.

BEFORE THE DAWN the enemy has

| 21ST APRIL |

materialized in the form of a gigantic oil truck which, without so much as waving, roars by the derelict vehicle where Catherine is bathing herself. We all think they are blasé indeed and Catherine says if they are so smart they could have gone on the other side of her hide-out instead of her side. We tell her that she would probably have felt worse if they had waved.

We watch the old man scramble on to his donkey, our blanket, which we no longer want, still wrapped about him. With his boy in the lead he starts off. We watch them totter a quarter of a mile to the south-west, then for some unfathomable reason point north-east, and finally meander off through some scrub in an entirely different direction. Nobody ever keeps a straight line in the desert.

This morning a flock of doves whirr out of the shade of a wizened tree to follow us. They fly low in the wake of the cars and I wonder if we make a stir that helps them fight the drag of desert air. Their wings beat at such a frantic speed one aches to communicate with them and offer a lift. They do at times zoom up ahead of us, and then surprisingly settle down in the sand as though to wait, taking off again in our wake. Do they want company, or water, or food? Or do they think we are another flock migrating northwards and are perhaps following them?

We pause for a while at a cone-shaped construction about eight feet high with rock-lined paths symmetrically laid out around it.

We explore, and everyone advances a pet theory as to just what bit of black magic this is. We decide it must be the remains of a primitive settlement. The cone is an oven and it is even likely that a scarred stone on its lintel was used for sacrifice. The plot is ruined when Charlie kicks over a 1960 beer-tin, now empty, and various other durable signs of twentieth-century culinary art. We have come upon an abandoned oil camp, perhaps used for seismic exploration. The rows of stones were the neat streets of tents and air-conditioned trailers, the sacrificial cone a bakery.

Hank says that he can think of no use for the million square miles of Sahara except perhaps to bury our atomic waste. 'Better than the sea,' he says, 'where it will destroy life and contaminate sea food.' Catherine wants to know why we don't bury it in our own deserts but Hank, who knows the American deserts from sandy shore to sandy shore, says that we have nothing so vast and lifeless at home. 'Our deserts are living,' he says. 'They are inhabited, they have flora and fauna.' And Catherine is quite rightly silenced; flora and fauna and inhabitants are pretty drastically missing from most of the Sahara.

For one delighted moment we think that our travel troubles have dissolved. We have come upon a road-bed. This is at least a place where bulldozers have forged across the desert packing the sand and scraping the rock and leaving a solid corduroy trail that promises to shake every bolt out of every car. We crawl along, occasionally abandoning the road for the less predictable but smoother sand beside it.

We had been advised by an earlier Tibesti explorer to bring beads along for trading and making friends. We would not like to throw his well-intentioned advice in his face but certainly we had no success with the supply that Catherine brought with her from New York. Everywhere we saw girls decked with beads, and suspect that our informant had flooded the market in his own time. Now, as we come into the oasis of Zuila, we see two little girls watching a herd of goats. They are tiny and pathetically ragged and Catherine wants to stop and give them beads.

'They'd love them,' she says, and Liv puts on the brake. But these little girls are not the pushing sort who want to be the centre of attention. They and their goats scamper away in fright leaving Catherine leaning out of the car, her hands, full of beads, stretched out towards them.

'They'll come back,' she says, tossing the beads to the side of the track. 'Poor little things, they'll pick them up later.'

We get in gear and Liv, looking back, mutters, 'You've reckoned without those thrifty Scots and thieving Welsh.' No. 4, dubbed Friendly Four because it always brings up the rear to see that everyone is safe and sound, has pulled up. Two nimble figures have jumped out, retrieved the beads and hopped into their places once more. Catherine is outraged, until we suggest that the boys want the beads for their girls, which rather gets round her. When we stop in the oasis we see that the boys have decorated their hats with these trophies robbed from defenceless little children. Catherine looks shocked, and Liv tells the boys he has a feeling their new hat-style is not going to go down well with the regiment.

In the oasis itself the road we have been following so happily disappears, and we have to ask directions. A nut-brown man working in a barley patch drops his hoe and rushes out to shake Liv's hand with such enthusiasm that Catherine thinks he must be some old friend from Benghazi. They are talking in Arabic, and Catherine says in an aside to me: 'Don't tell me what they're saying. I'll tell you. "Pomeroy you old faker, what are you doing down here letting the American Information programme go to pot while you gallivant about the countryside with two women?"'

Liv tells her to shut up because he can't think, but even he is overwhelmed at the quality of his reception. He asks the way for Sebha now, and his old friend points to some palms where a bed of ivory-white sand winds towards the north. Not knowing how to say 'soft going' in Arabic, Liv compromises by asking if the sand is bad.

'Sand?' cries his friend, 'what sand? There's no sand *here*.'

A hundred yards further on among the palms we are up to our hubs.

Beyond the oasis there is no road but later at the next oasis, Gaddua, it starts again and this time does go through the oasis. Gaddua has a deep well, manned by a Rube Goldberg contraption which is motor driven. Here the grain grows tall and thick. We ask a farmer working in a field whose land it is, for we are impressed at the first motor-pumped well we have seen. He shakes his head. A rich man from Sebha, he thinks, but he is not sure. He has probably never seen his employer. It seems to us a pity to grow grain on such good land where oranges, lemons, peaches, apricots and tomatoes could be grown so much more profitably both for the owner and the people of Libya.

The road leading out of Gaddua is another corduroy master-piece. As we bounce along, more fearful of our springs than we have been in the roughest desert, Liv has a brainwave. We are no longer going to build a multi-million-dollar highway, but only a half-million-dollar land freighter. It will float across all obstacles— like something horrible in a science-fiction movie—on wide, low pressure rollers, and will carry a thousand tons or more. I think it is to be pulled by a tractor or caterpillar and will average fifteen miles an hour with never a stop until it reaches Fort Lamy or Brazzaville. We aren't too sure of that as we don't have a map of Africa with us. This gruesome monster will do the trip from the coast to Central Africa in one week, and will cut all existing freight rates in half. Liv isn't too sure about this point either as he doesn't know what the existing freight rates are—except that they are much too high—but it makes exhilarating conversation.

By noon we are beginning to despair of Winston's ever making his plane, when like a cloud on the horizon the fort of Sebha materializes. It sits atop a conical rock high above the town, a fort to withstand the fiercest siege. As we come into focus a plane circles and settles down at its feet, and we put on a burst of speed and race across the desert to the airport.

Winston's plane, for such it is, if one can be so possessive of a commercial flight, will not take off again until five in the after-noon. We have time to find the local hotel for lunch and to locate a camp-site for the night. Sebha, capital of the Fezzan, one of the three provinces of Libya, is a fast-growing oil-rush town. At the base of the fort, the corduroy road we have come in on joins a smooth black-top which bisects the town. On either side are modern buildings, glistening white villas behind garden walls and, wonder of wonders, a petrol station brilliant with tanks and signs. At a crossroads we stop to ask directions of a policeman. Liv gets down from the lead car to shake the bewildered man by the hand, and ask after his health and that of his family in a sort of Bedouin litany, before coming to the point of asking just where the hotel might be, and I wonder whether we have perhaps been in the desert too long. Certainly the populace of this busy metropolis eye us as though we had. Of all the wonders of civilization I think the neat shining cars full of clean-shirted passengers in jackets, ties and starched dresses is the most telling. The impact of civilization on such as we is not how welcome we are, but rather how disdainful and disinterested these clean untroubled people are towards us—the off-beat, the stained, the outsider—and rightly so. While we have as usual stopped outside the oasis to change to clean shirts and slacks, it must be admitted that it is weeks since any of our clothes have looked spotless. Laundry has been done in cold and often dirty water and nothing has been ironed and our footgear is extremely dirty. Our hair is bushy with sand, the men's beards are wild and untrimmed. On top of this our complexions range from brown to scarlet, with Winston's eyebrows a show-stopper of platinum against his red face. The cars are encrusted with sand and dust so that you can barely see through the windscreens, and No. 2 is streaked and spotted with blood. Definitely, civilization has not much to expect from us.

Alan had told us that in true frontier-town fashion Sebha boasts a casino. This appears to have been wishful thinking on his part. It does boast a delightful small hotel run by Haj Morsi, formerly pin-stripe-suited manager of the Berenice Hotel in Benghazi. He is a friend of many years' standing, and we fall upon each other with pleasure. The good Haj is no longer in a business suit but in voluminous white Turkish trousers, embroidered white vest, blouse and skull-cap and sporting a trim white beard and moustache. He has put on girth and bonhomie, we think. When Liv teases him about his dramatic get-up he beams, patting his belly, and says: 'Ah well, one must do something folk-lorish here in the desert. I shall be known as the Hemingway of the Sahara.'

While lunch is preparing the Haj brings us bottles of ice-cold beer and we sit in the lounge and look at month-old magazines and papers with a lovely sense of peace and discovery. Winston has disappeared to a shower, and returns at lunch-time in fresh shirt and long trousers, already mentally on his way home and for the first time preoccupied about all those books he has not read.

Lunch is a banquet, commencing with a spinach soufflé baked

in a light egg batter, stuffed veal, fried potatoes and young peas, salad with a marvellous hot sauce, fruit cup, cheese and crackers and finally thick, sweet, black Turkish coffee. In the four years that we have lived in Libya we have not, at any hotel, had as good or as well served a meal.

Catherine and I now commence to disintegrate and show every known feminine weakness. After lunch we let the others go to find a camp-site, arrange for Winston's tickets and announce our presence to the police. We have been offered a room and bath where we can bathe in hot water and rest on inner-spring mattresses. Stars or no stars, this one night we will sleep at the hotel. Later, bathed and refreshed and with a sizable laundry to our credit, we go to see Winston off. We photograph each other for the last time, fondly embrace and wave him off into such a cloud of red dust that it is a wonder the plane can lift above it into the clear bright sky beyond.

Among the people with whom Alan corresponded in his two years of really epic efforts to organize this trip was General Badi, Chief of Police of the Fezzan. We call on him now and are most hospitably received. The police club is a modern building with a swimming-pool and a garden with unexpected fountains and flowers, where roses and hollyhocks, like visiting royalty, are given the tenderest of care. The General and his officers entertain us in an open loggia where we are served orange drinks, in crystal pop bottles. Beset by flies, we talk of our journey. The General has a letter for Catherine from Alan, and asks after him, with real regret that he has not come with us. He tells his officers with some pride of the long correspondence from New York. We ask him about the Dawada tribe, whom Alan especially wanted to visit. These people, one of the strangest and smallest of Sahara tribes, live at Mandara, hidden behind so formidable an erg that they can be visited only by camel, except for a short period after the occasional December rain, which sometimes packs the sand hard enough to allow a Land Rover to cross it. The Dawada live on shrimps which they fish from the salty water of their oasis lagoon. That there are shrimp in the desert was such a source of wonder to Alan that he was determined to visit these people, despite the fact that he is quite violently allergic to shrimp. We would all like to go calling, but today is the twenty-first and we must be in

Benghazi by the twenty-fifth. As in Zouar, we are feeling the pinch of time—we need at the very least another two months. The mention of camels has brought a gleam to Catherine's eye, but Alan will be in Benghazi in a few days and the competition undoes the camels.

On the way back to the hotel Catherine says rather wistfully that she would like to send a message of love to Alan, but is afraid that the Army would not approve. We tell her that if the Army is willing to monitor Jack's laundry they will undoubtedly take her love in stride.

Hank and the 'troops' have a beer party tonight and Liv, Francis, Catherine and I have steak for dinner, tender and sweet, and ice in our whiskies. We eat in the patio under a full moon that looks too theatrical to be true. Haj Morsi brings us to sharp reality by presenting us with a bevy of police forms to be filled in, giving parentage, birth dates, marriages and occupations. All of this is entered in a little book that leaves carbon copies for the hotel files after the top copy has been torn out for the police. Looking back over recent visitors we see a Frenchman who has put his occupation down as a forger, and decide that even the police are due for a little entertainment. Catherine and I say that we have always resented being 'housewives', and Liv puts my occupation down as 'Living Doll'. As the police seem to have let the forger through I don't suppose they will even notice my new occupation. Liv and Francis go back to camp for the night and Catherine and I, now that we are bathed and the laundry done, crawl rather regretfully into our ceilinged beds. Camp has been made at a government experimental station where there is shade, sheep and such determined mosquitoes that the men have to wrap up heavily and might as well have been sleeping under a roof themselves.

| 22ND APRIL |

AT BREAKFAST THIS morning Morsi endears himself by greeting me with, 'And how is the Living Doll this morning?'

He has also won Catherine's heart. She has been poring over his startling collection of petrified wood, and he has presented her with a log three feet long, complete with broken branch and knot-hole. It cannot weigh a smidgen under a hundred pounds. Hank looks as though it were the proverbial straw and his the back it is going to break. Aside from this we haven't added much to our load at Sebha, where for the first time we've been let down on our promised petrol. We hope to pick some up further along from an army dump. In the meantime we've been to the market.

The Tuaregs make bead bracelets rather like American Indian work. They are a small-boned people, and the bracelets we buy will never fit anyone but Julia and her little friends. Catherine has also acquired a rug worked with a design of camels that closely resemble turtles, and several pounds of a wonderful date confection.

Riding with Hank one day he admitted to me that he did not mind Catherine's little weaknesses for collecting, but when one deals, as she does, in rock, he kept hoping that she would keep them small. So far, bits of stone and pebbles, artifacts and arrow-heads—for which she has an absolute nose, once finding five in one day—have made up the bulk of her treasure. She does have one great statuey thing, a mammoth's shinbone, and—apart from the Haj's log—about a quarter of a cord of petrified wood. Hank has developed an unexpected streak of philosophy, though he did tell me that he finds Catherine a nervous traveller. Liv and I are surprised at this as we find her somewhat placid and easygoing. He explains himself by saying that when driving along, Catherine is either writing in her copybook or rearranging her boxes of pebbles and soil samples, doing her nails or creaming her face. She never sleeps and is almost never idle. I think that painting her toe-nails as we bounded over the precipice of a crested dune was almost as amazing to him as her resistance to his theory of nasal fatigue. He is proud of his bunches of skulls and his aromatic baboon-skin, but Catherine believes that a nose is a nose is a nose.

An ambitious, surfaced road is being built from Sebha to the main east-west coast road some four hundred and fifty miles away. The last hundred miles approaching the coast has been com-pleted, but out of Sebha we have three hundred and fifty miles of corduroy on which fifteen miles an hour is reckless speed, there are detours across soft sand, and work-crews block the way and raise dust everywhere. To make matters worse No. 5 has a loose bolt and we think we have too—anyway, something is loose. We decide to make an early camp, contact Benghazi and warn them that we may not come in on time. We have been hoping to reach Agedabia on Monday night where the Humfreys will bring Alan and the children. Tuesday is Regimental Day and Francis wants to roll into barracks by noon.

We have started from Sebha late and not gone more than twenty-five miles and we are hot and disgusted. While waiting for No. 5 Liv and Hank have found a racing breed of tick which move across a palm-frond with the speed of the desert gazelle. They have captured a pride of these little creatures for Hank's tick friend back home. We get to bed early determined to be off before dawn.

| 23RD APRIL | THIS DAY, LIKE every day in which we try to beat Allah at his own game, seems doomed to failure. We are up by |

moonlight, so are the road gangs, so is the *ghibli*, the sandstorm, so are the gremlins that eat nuts and bolts and puncture tyres. Within the first two hours we average fifty miles per hour but now the wind is working up a frenzy. With sand in our eyes and dust pouring into the cars and carrying with it an oppressive heat, we tie handkerchiefs across our mouths to help us breathe. No. 4 has not been seen for a long time. No. 5 goes back to investigate and disappears into the rearguard silence.

We are in open desert somewhere between the bulldozed road and a detour trail. The *ghibli* is so fierce we can hardly see fifty paces ahead. Hank says that he has seen a car proceeding northwards on the road and thinks for sure it is No. 4. So we send Winston's car, now driven by Francis, back to tell No. 5 that No. 4 is found. Waiting for the others we amuse ourselves by cursing the *ghibli*. Catherine says that we are seeing a waste of a hundred million tons of marketable face-powder. This dust is finely textured and covering the face and arms hides every blemish, and freckles, moles, lips and eyebrows as well. She insists it is exactly the colour of Rachel No. 2 and boxed with a drop of oil of Arabia could be sold under some romantic trade name such as Desert Dust. But Liv says it is obvious that we'd make more money selling vacuum cleaners to nomads, and says that his own sales resistance would be way down if a vacuum-cleaner salesman happened along at the moment.

Francis has returned to say that No. 5 has sheered off its steering bolts. The car going north has been seen coming back and proves to be one belonging to the construction team. It is now four hours since we have missed No. 4. It is decided that Francis will go back to continue the hunt for No. 4 and keep in touch with No. 5. Liv and Catherine, Hank and I will proceed to Hon to wait for them. We go through a mediaeval walled town all turreted and ramparted and then cut across the desert to Hon. Hon is white walled and arcaded and very very sleepy. So indeed are we. We visit the police and buy mint tea and fizzy drinks at a little café. But when we ask if we may go into a shaded park to eat our lunch and wait we are told that it will take a little time to get the proper authority. We do not, we think and sincerely hope, have the time. So we draw up by the roadside under an avenue of eucalyptus trees to eat our lunch and, laying out our cots, to fight with the flies for sleeping space. No Arab sleeping by the roadside like a bundle of laundry, his turban pulled across his face, could be more careless of the passer-by than we. We are hot and we are tired and discouraged.

The police have offered us the guest-house for the night and a friendly local resident, whom we met at the café, offered to kill a goat for us and cook us a splendid curry. But we are so sure that the others will appear momentarily, and that we will be able to get on the way, that we have refused all of these pleasant offers.

Now our peace is shattered by a raft of little boys who squat across the road from us chattering and giggling and pointing. It is not that they have never seen such ragged dirty people sleeping by the roadside, but beggars with cars are novel, even here! Eventually Liv says, carefully and clearly in English, 'You are very rude.'

'No,' says the largest boy, also in English, 'I am not very rude, I am very good.'

To this Liv cannot agree. 'No,' he says, 'very bad manners.'

'I will go away,' says the boy haughtily, and gathering his

friends takes off for fifty paces where to our dismay they about-face and return, having had a change of heart, if you could call it that. Or perhaps their native sharpness told them that they were merely doing what we wanted them to do.

'I will not go away now,' says the boy. And they all squat down and continue to insult us. It is getting late and seems a good time to pack up and find the others, for it doesn't look as though they are going to find us this day.

We stop at the café to pick up some 'Verigoud' soda and Kitty-cola' for the 'troops', and while we wait for it to be packed up have a chat with the local resident, who like a character actor in an under-staffed theatre company appears in every scene. He is either shaven or completely bald, with a well-shaped skull and protruding ears. He tells us that he has travelled all over the desert and was even blown up by a mine outside Kufra, but he seems to be all in one piece. Hearing where we have come from he says that he has just returned from a trip which took him over the same route, though he did not call on the French. We wonder if his were the tracks we saw before Ounianga and which the French patrol chased about the Rocher Noir. It is a pity that we cannot spend an evening with our friend, for he is obviously full of good travel information and the curry is tempting.

Going backwards, undoing each hard-won kilometre, is depressing work. We drive for an hour, worriedly peering into the dark, afraid of passing the others without seeing them. Twice we swoop down upon a huddle of lights to find ourselves at a road-gang camp with none of our people in sight. Eventually we come upon Nos. 4 and 5 patching each other up and No. 3 impatiently tapping its toe. Taffy has replaced the sheared bolts and John has mended two tyres. Now there is water in the petrol. John comes up from under the car uniformly coated with dust and looking more than ever like a Greek statue. Someone writes 'Dust' on his back. We make a fire in the middle of the track, praying that no late contracting truck will buzz by to puff a cloud into our supper. We dine on this and that with a little soy sauce and whisky to cut the dust. We have taken a vote and decide to push on tonight to the beginning of the tarmac. We will sleep by the road and, as Francis says imploringly, have a 'long lie-in in the morning till six o'clock'. Catherine tells him that he's lost his sense of proportion if he calls that a long lie-in. But there is really not much choice if we are to make Agedabia anywhere near on time. We still have five hundred and fifty miles to go and there is no telling what kind of a day we have ahead.

Hon is asleep as we shoot through in a haze of weariness. The embryo road is barricaded off from here on and the desert rough. We dare not travel fast what with our temperamental bolts. Every ten miles Taffy and John get under Nos. 4 and 5 to check the state of things, which is a speed deterrent to begin with. Catherine and I doze and wake; Hank's back, he says, needs a splicing job, and so does Liv's temper. The road-builders' camps, sleeping bulldozers and morasses of churned-up sand become more and more frequent. Every now and again we drive up to the road to see what stage it has achieved and wonder if we will ever reach the beautiful stretch of velvet tarmac. At first there is nothing for miles but the ribbed surface that has already wreaked such havoc among our bolts, then miles of big stones, a steam-roller outlined in the starlight, more miles of smaller stones, another roller. At last we come upon the tar-spreading machine, fine gravel, a flock of wheelbarrows and the barricade we have been looking for, and a sign. Thankfully we turn off into the hills to find a camp-site. We cross a two-hundred-acre field generously sown with rocks, and square off behind a dip of hill. Tired as we are we wash out our ochre-coloured shirts and 'smalls', for tomorrow we will be at the coast, and while we can't expect to look clean we will indulge ourselves by feeling it. We won't have more than two nights now under the stars. Catherine says that they already seem smaller to her and the moon colder and more distant. Yet they keep their magic, and in a moment every ache and pain of what has been without question the most trying day of our trip is gone, and we are peacefully asleep.

| 24TH APRIL |

SIX O'CLOCK COMES down like a headsman's axe. Some say we were not in bed before three but there are very few watches still functioning. Whether this dictum comes from a watch-owner or a seer, I believe it. My own built-in rest-control

195

says that I have not slept enough. Francis and Charlie Pollock have had even less than we, for they were up at five to go on ahead to Bou Ndjem where the Army has promised to leave a depot of petrol for us. We expect to rejoin him there before noon, fill up quickly and drive on. Machiavelli might have warned us not to be so trusting, saying, 'Put not thy faith in petrol-dumps,' for the Army, Francis finds, has decamped taking its petrol with it. We will be able to get petrol at the coast road, but at a cost of sixty cents per gallon, unless Liv gives up our diplomatic coupons which will probably mean that for the rest of our stay in Libya we shall have to walk.

The tarmac is all that we could dream of. Our trail-blazing days are over and we spin along, without a worry for soft sand or bumps. No. 5 has to keep close inspection of its bolts, which are in danger of being sheared off again since the wheels are out of alignment. We are in pretty good order aside from that, and always excepting the dozen unexplained rattles in No. 3 and a slipping clutch in No. 2. The road itself is impressive and so it should be, for it has already cost over twelve million dollars. It climbs sombre hills of grey-black sandstone, dips into sandy valleys peppered with scrub grass, thorn-trees and gazelle. In places the sand has already encroached, leaving only a narrow strip of tarmac clear. While the *ghibli* is not as fierce as yesterday's it is whipping the sand on, and at one point miniature dunes have formed in the middle of the road, and even as we come upon them they seem to grow. Pointing to two great crested dunes half a mile to the west Liv says:

'Those are the parents, and these are the dune-children. "Go out and play, dears," the parents say, "and don't be afraid of playing in the middle of the road." The work on these desert roads never ends, for once built, man's struggle with the dune-children begins.

Our thoughts are in Benghazi now and we wonder if the Humfreys and Alan and the children have already left for the rendezvous at Agedabia. Arriving in time for our last night's camp does not particularly worry Francis who is only concerned now to shepherd his lame flock into barracks by twelve-thirty tomorrow. It is Regimental Day, birthday of H.R.H. the Princess Royal, and he is anxious not to keep the senior officers waiting.

The men, apart from wanting to see if there are letters from home, would rather turn back into the desert, and stay there until it is time to go home to Scotland, Wales or Yorkshire. Beads and beards will have to go, sergeant-majors must be suffered; it must be like going back to boarding-school after a long summer's vacation.

We drive hard all day coming at two o'clock to the junction of the coast road. In this civilized spot are a petrol station and a small Italian restaurant. We lunch on spaghetti, salami, loaves of fresh bread and cups of espresso. It is decided that Liv and Catherine and I will make a mad dash for Agedabia, still two hundred miles off. We are in Tripolitania and we warn the others that they may have trouble passing the frontier of the province at Marble Arch, where their carnets will surely be wanted. Our car has a diplomatic licence and we will do what we can to soften the path for them by saying that our servants are following with our luggage.

Marble Arch, built in 1937 by order of Mussolini to commemorate the completion of the east-west coastal highway and to symbolize the rebirth of the Roman Empire, stands on a place already dedicated to one of the oldest tales of patriotism. History and myth battle with the bones of this story. It is a fact that the Greeks of Cyrene, a beautiful and powerful city on the Libyan coast, and the Carthaginians were at war and had been unable to agree upon a boundary. I don't know whose idea it was to have a race to settle this dispute; it sounds very Greek. Envoys were to set out simultaneously from the two cities, race towards each other with all possible speed, and, where they met, there would the new boundary be. The Carthaginian envoys were two brothers, the Philaeni, and they seem to have been blessed of the gods in every manner excepting a long life. They covered so much ground and with such speed that they were well into Greek territory before they met the dawdling Greeks. This caused somewhat of a furore. The Greeks didn't like it and the war looked to be on again with increased impetus, something that nobody wanted. The Greeks offered a further trial, a compromise. If the Philaeni were so sure of their rights let them demonstrate this by allowing themselves to be buried alive on the spot where they wished the boundary to be drawn. If they refused to do so the Greeks would then be permitted to advance to the point where they wished to draw the boundary and there would allow themselves to be buried alive. The Philaeni brothers accepted the challenge and here, where they were sacrificed, two mounds are still faintly visible where some day excavation may find the altars of the Philaeni, if indeed it did not all happen in quite another spot.

It is dark by the time we reach Marble Arch and the keepers of the frontier are sleepy and rather resent the *ghibli* we have brought with us. They promise to look out for our 'luggage train' and we sweep through. We stop once to fill up with petrol. Otherwise we drive without stops. When Liv begins to droop we put in motion an old routine, which we have long since worked out together. He keeps one hand on the wheel, one foot on the accelerator, and I climb round the back of him, gradually edging him out of his place. Soon he is sleeping in the centre and I am at the wheel and we have not lost momentum for a second. As we bowl through the night the dunes on either side and the blowing sand lose their reality and we feel as though we were driving through a snow storm and that a plough has gone ahead building up the high white banks.

It is ten o'clock when we come to Agedabia, having driven eight hours with less than a ten-minute stop. The police have a road-block just outside the town for what reason we are too weary to inquire. But they do have a message for us. Alan and Charles Humfrey with the children have given us up at the beach rendezvous and gone on to the hotel. We find them there already in bed, never having dreamed that we would drive after dark. The children are asleep and with the useful proverb about dogs and trouble in mind we decide to let them lie. But we turn the adults out and make them sit with us while we eat a leather omelette and a dank salad. Haj Morsi could do something for this hotel, but then so could a demolition team. Catherine is toying with her food, after all the only civilized thing to do with this food. I fear she has a gloating expression, chalking up to her own credit the victory of Alan returned from the foreign entanglements (holy or unholy) available in Rome. After a gay if not epicurian supper we send these two semi-civilized men back to their beds. I only say semi- for they have a hooded falcon in their room with which they were entertaining themselves while they waited for us this afternoon. Alan says that he is taking this little pet to New York where he will fly him in Central Park. We go on to meet the other cars and make camp and Alan and Charles promise to bring the children for an early breakfast.

I HARDLY KNEW where I was last night, though this eucalyptus grove is a favourite camp site of ours, for fishing weekends from Benghazi. Nos. 3, 4 and 5 were not long behind us, and even wearier than we for they had not even had a leather omelette.

Come the sun the children are with us, full of glee, demands for presents and trophies and, in Julia's case, evident relief that I have not grown a beard like her father. The lizards make an enormous hit. Julia, snatching up one monster, kisses it on its anything-but-lovely mouth.

And now there is nothing to do but pack ourselves up as neatly as is possible and put on our cleanest shirts for our appointment with the top brass. We do in fact roll into barracks at twelve-thirty, which is a vindication of a sort, or would be if the Brigadier did not dash our pride by saying that he had expected us at twelve. However, he is in a most forgiving mood. It is Regimental Day. All the officers are in tartan with white jackets and full decorations, and all the ladies in floating chiffon and garden-party hats. We are given champagne in silver regimental goblets which date to George III, that connoisseur of beautiful silver and fumbler of party platforms.

The Brigadier, as we have surmised, looks askance at his troops in French bush hats decorated with beads and feathers, and makes some jolly but meaningful remark about a dateline on beards. I feel that every move we make powders our hosts with dust samples from the Tibesti and back, but dirty and ungodly though we look we are most warmly welcomed.

Coming home is like pulling a curtain on everything that we have seen and done. And yet behind the curtain the other scene will always be there, something none of us can ever forget for have we not been through the birth, growth and death of the world itself? Everything in the desert has meaning: a fragment of an ostrich egg lying in the dip of a dune, a pebble worn smooth by tides of an ancient sea, an arrowhead chipped by a man whose own bones now lie petrified beneath the sand. At Jebel Sherif we held in our hands a piece of khaki sweater which a man wore when his life exploded and became as much a part of history as the parched land around him. Nor is the desert only the past; it is alive with small furry creatures which live on nothing more substantial than seeds and dew and are for ever threatened by birds of prey that watch and swoop from the sky. And where there is nothing to see but sky and sand, there is still a delicious anticipation, a knowing that there will be something just over the horizon—a will-o'-the-wisp sensation lacking in normal life.

As for the Tibesti Mountains, I feel that we shall go back there one day if the dune-children let us through, because we haven't seen enough of them or of the Tebu people who live there. Perhaps next time we shall follow the advice of the Lieutenant at Zouar—take a bag of rice, a bundle of dates, a camel and a gun —or perhaps on the other hand we shall slip in a handful of other useful items. I have a list on hand of forty or fifty.

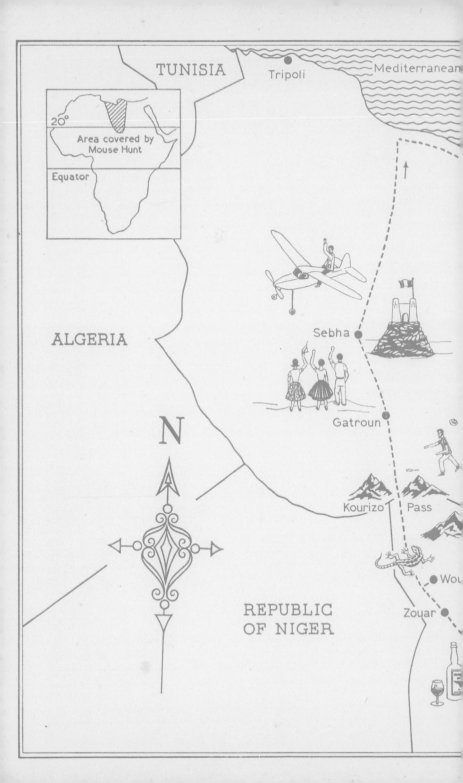